Bible Beginnings
And It Was Good

OLD TESTAMENT LESSONS FOR LITTLE LISTENERS

EXPLORER'S BIBLE STUDY
FOR
THE VERY YOUNG BIBLE SCHOLAR

Remember now your Creator in the days of your youth . . .
Ecclesiastes 12:1

With my whole heart I have sought You;
Oh, let me not wander from Your commandments!
Your word I have hidden in my heart, that I might not sin against You.
Psalms 119: 10 - 11

Published By
Explorer's Bible Study

Dickson, Tennessee

Curriculum Development/Author
Patricia Constance Russell

Editor
Virginia A. Clark

Cover Art & Graphic Design
Troy D. Russell

Project Editor
Tom M. Constance, Jr.

We believe the Bible is God's Word, a divine revelation, in the original language
verbally inspired in its entirety, and that it is the supreme infallible authority
in all matters of faith and conduct.

(II Peter 1:21; II Timothy 3:16)

Printed in the United States of America

Published by

Explorer's Bible Study
2652 Highway 46 South
Post Office Box 425
Dickson, Tennessee 37056-0425
615-446-7316

Contents

About the Author

Pat Russell has been a Christian educator for over 25 years. She began her teaching career by forming a preschool in her home. Later she accepted a position as a teacher in a private Christian School and also served as a curriculum coordinator and consultant. Most recently, she helped to co-found Carden Christian Academy. Through years of writing and development, she has crafted a curriculum that comes from practical "hands on" experience. This curriculum has been "classroom tested" in Christian schools, in homeschool settings, as well as having been used in Explorer's Bible Study classes throughout the U.S.

Pat's goal in developing this curriculum is to provide the young Bible scholar with a chronological and historical method of Bible study. It is through this means that the Bible is seen in its entirety, not in broken pieces. The importance of understanding the true meaning of God's Word and His plan for each of us comes through careful study. Interpretation follows a knowledge of what God says, what God means, and finally how each individual applies this knowledge to his or her personal life experience.

How to Use this Book

The daily lessons in this book will help you as you teach your child about God. The goal is to give you a useful tool to give your child a better understanding of who God is and what His Word, the Bible says.

Each day's lesson has the following elements:

Bible Love Lesson establishes an important foundation every time you open God's Word. God is love. God loves you! This is the central truth for even the youngest child.

Bible Story & Key Points presents a Bible story in easy to understand language along with key discussion points to help explain in detail the lesson to your child.

Word and Phrase Meanings give brief definitions to help explain difficult words or concepts.

Guided Prayer Thoughts presents a short prayer as a model for learning to talk with God.

Questions: Thinking & Remembering gives questions and answers to help the child recall and relate the story concepts in the lesson.

Bible Words to Remember are provided to encourage and develop memorization skills. You may notice that some of the verses are abbreviated or paraphrased to make it easier for a preschool child to understand and remember. We have chosen the New King James version for this book.

Praise Hymns give a variety of songs and hymns for making worship time meaningful for little ones.

> **Note:** You may choose to purchase a copy of *My First Hymnal* to use along with your Bible Beginnings book. It contains 75 favorite Bible songs along with text by Karen Henley explaining the meaning of each song. It is published by Sparrow Music (Item # SKB1034, ISBN 0-917143-35-3) and is available at your local Christian Bookstore. A companion CD or cassette is also available in split tract recording. We highly recommend this valuable resource.

Virtue Lessons help children apply God's Word to their lives.

Curriculum Implementation

These lessons may be used for preschool children beginning at age two. Two year olds will understand the Bible Love Lesson and become confident in God's love. The Key Points will establish a basis for greater meaning and detail in the Bible lessons.

Preschool children at age three are ready for more content and can relate to the story with teacher discussion of word meanings with short and concise explanation. Songs are very important to them and help establish repetition in Bible truths.

Four year olds are expanding their understanding of the content and will be able to answer most, if not all of the questions. Review and discuss how their experiences relate to the Bible story. All elements of the lesson will help the child grow and develop in God's ways.

Five year olds will be enthusiastic and perceptive about what happened in the story. They will want to know the "why" of what occurred and begin to see a pattern of cause and effect in biblical truth. They will ask more questions, which will give opportunity for discussion and application of God's Word.

A preschool child's attention span is usually as follows:

> 2 year olds - two to four minutes, expanding to five
> 3 year olds - three to five minutes, expanding to eight
> 4 year olds - five to eight minutes, expanding to ten
> 5 year olds - eight to twelve minutes, expanding to fifteen

Adjust your time accordingly and pace each segment of the lesson to keep a vigorous flow of content. Choose an appropriate amount (depending on the child or children you are teaching) of questions and keep your own mind sharp on the sequence of the lesson to keep it alive and relevant. Each moment will count!

A Note to Parents and Teachers

During the writing of this curriculum, I have been constantly reminded of the awesome task that is set before us as teachers of God's Word. As with no other written word, we stand as facilitator's in the greatest and most solemn responsibility. In the search for meaningful and thoughtful questions that would plant God's Words firmly in the hearts and minds of these precious ones who are so tender and receptive, it seemed that there was a need for much greater depth for our youngest of students than is often assumed.

The Bible stories do not just cover the familiar "wrapped in cotton" lessons. Rather, there has been a desire to tell the whole story within the child's frame of reference. It has been my prayerful desire to remain true to the biblical text. Some events may seem limited and you may consider expanding on the text. Other events may be more extended than you feel comfortable with teaching. Let God be your ultimate guide in what you present.

The purpose is not only to show God's love for the people He created, but to also reveal God's great truth in His plan and purpose for each of us. The lessons deliberately do not seek to hide or cover the consequences of sin and wrongdoing, because omitting this leaves a child to wonder why there is a need for forgiveness. Sin is dealt with as the Bible deals with it, without a pretense that there is no judgement. But the compassion of God is evident. The child is never left with hopeless despair or the impression of an angry or distant God.

The lessons endeavor to teach the following:
> God's Care: His love is infinite
> God's Concern: His ways of guiding and directing people and events to show His love
> God's Communication: He instructs and expresses His love in many ways
> God's Consequences: There are results from our choices
> God's Compassion: He does not stop loving us. God forgives and continues to
> help us grow and change

It is my prayerful anticipation as you use this Bible curriculum that you will find and be delighted to observe, as I have, a response from those little ones that you teach. As they respond to God's love, may you be given the guidance that we all need as we seek HIM - the perfect one! These are exciting days with the most wondrous opportunities we can imagine.

Pray, seek, and study diligently – then teach with your heart.

Prayerfully,

Patricia Russell

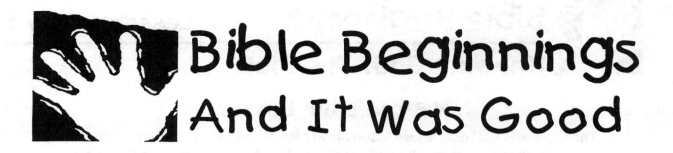

Bible Beginnings
And It Was Good

OLD TESTAMENT LESSONS FOR LITTLE LISTENERS

My Opportunity

Dear Lord, I do not ask
That Thou shouldst give me some high work of Thine,
Some noble calling, or some wondrous task;
Give me a little hand to hold in mine;
Give me a little child to point the way
Over the strange, sweet path that leads to Thee;
Give me a little voice to teach to pray;
Give me two shining eyes Thy face to see.
The only crown I ask, dear Lord, to wear is this:
That I may lead a little child.
I do not ask that I may ever stand
Among the wise, the worthy or the great;
I only ask that softly, hand in hand,
A child and I may enter at the gate.

Author Unknown

Fix these words of mine in your hearts and minds; tie them as symbols on your hands and bind them on your foreheads. Teach them to your children, talking about them when you sit at home and when you walk along the road, when you lie down and when you get up. Write them on the doorframes of your houses and on your gates, so that your days and the days of your children may be many in the land that the LORD swore to give your forefathers, as many as the days that the heavens are above the earth.
Deuteronomy 11:18-21 (NIV)

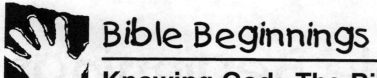

Bible Beginnings

Knowing God: The Bible

❤ Bible Love Lesson ❤

The Bible tells us: "God is love." God always loved you - even before you were born! God gives your mom and dad great bunches of love so they can take care of you and give you what you need.

Bible Story: Learning About God

Key Points

❖ God was before anything else was made--God was first.

❖ God loved you even before you were born.

❖ Without God, you cannot be happy.

❖ God is love. God shows parents how to love their children.

Before we can even **think** about the world God made, we must first think about God.

God was BEFORE anything else. The Bible tells us that God ALWAYS was. There was not a time before God. Knowing that God is the beginning and end of all things is very **important**. Then we know how much we **need** Him.

God loved you when you were only a loving thought by your parents. He loved you before you were born. He loved you before there were any pictures of you!

When you were a very tiny baby, you needed to be loved and cared for. You could not take care of yourself. You needed your mother and father but you needed God most of all. God is **love**. Parents would not know how to love you, except for God. He shows everyone how to love.

Word and Phrase Meanings

love:	a great, warm feeling about someone
learn:	listening carefully so that you can know something new
think:	to quietly remember what you can know from listening
important:	something that matters more
need:	something you *must* have; things you need: water, food, clothing, love; things you want: toys, soda pop, games.

Guided Prayer Thought

Dear Loving God and Heavenly Father, We want to know You and love You more. Thank You for loving us even before we were born. Thank You for giving us parents to take care of us and love us.

Amen

Questions:
Thinking & Remembering

1. What do we need to think about first?
   God

2. Who was before anything else?
   God

3. How do we know that God always was?
   the Bible tells us

4. Was there ever a time before God was?
   No

5. What is God the beginning and ending of?
   all things

6. Why is it important to know that God always was?
   so that we know how much we need God

7. When did God start loving you?
   before I was born

8. What did you need when you were a tiny baby?
   to be loved and cared for

9. Who gives parents the love to care for you in the best way?
   God

10. Will you ever stop needing God's love?
    No

 # Bible Words To Remember

. . God is love.   1 John 4:8

We love Him, because He first loved us.   1 John 4:19

Praise Hymn

Sing or say these words
Resource: My First Hymnal Pg.14

THE B-I-B-L-E

The B-I-B-L-E,
Yes, that's the book for me,
I stand alone on the Word of God,
The B-I-B-L-E

❤ Bible Love Lesson ❤

God is all around you. He loves and cares for you wherever you are. Even though you cannot see God, you can feel His love. Where can you find God? Everywhere!

Bible Story: Looking for God

 Key Points

❖ Know that you *need* God.

❖ No one can love you the way God loves you.

❖ God is very great and powerful.

❖ God made you to love Him.

We **know** that we **need** God. Everyone needs God. Mothers and fathers need God. Children need God. Big people and little people and medium-sized people need God. Tall people and short people need God.

Where can we see God? Can we find Him if we look for Him? Does He live in the same country we live in? Does He live in the city you live in?

God does not live in a **certain** place. The wonderful thing is that God is everywhere! But we will not see Him even though we look for Him. There are people who think that they can see Him when they look at the things God made. "The sun is god; the trees can be god," they say. They even pray to the things God made. But 'things' cannot love us the way God loves us.

God is so great and so powerful. **God is a spirit**. Knowing this wonderful God will make everything you do seem brighter and happier, because God made us to love Him. We are just beginning to learn more so that we can love Him more. We will love others more, too!

Word and Phrase Meanings

certain: something or somewhere that can be seen so you can know for sure

need: something you must have

know: to understand and accept; to be sure of something

God is a Spirit: He cannot be seen but He can see, hear and love. We have this spirit inside of us that feels His love.

Guided Prayer Thought

Dear God, Even though we cannot see You, we know that You are always with us. We can feel Your love for us. We can know that You love us by listening to Your Words in the Bible. Thank You for loving us.

Amen

Questions:
Thinking & Remembering

1. Who needs God?
   everyone --all people everywhere need God

2. Where can we see God?
   We cannot see God with our eyes.

3. Will you see Him if you always look for Him?
   No. God is a spirit. He does not have a body. We cannot see God with our eyes.

4. Where does God live?
   He does not live in a certain place. He is everywhere.

5. Where do *some* people think they can see God?
   in the things He made

6. What are some of the things God made that you can see?
   sun, stars, trees, etc.

7. Who do some people say these things are?
   that these things can be god

8. What else do people do to show that they think these things are God?
   they pray to them

9. Can trees or the sun hear prayers? Can these things love us like God loves us?
   No

10. How can God be everywhere and love everyone all the time?
    God is a spirit

 Bible Words To Remember

. . . God is love.   1 John 4:8

We love Him, because He first loved us.   1 John 4:19

Choosing
God's Way

God's Love

The words in the Bible say that "God is love." You are learning many things about God and you can learn much more!

Where does it tell you that "God is love?"
Do you know everything there is to know about God?

5

❤ Bible Love Lesson ❤

God loves you so much that He gave you a family. Mom and dad make sure that you have food and clothes and rest at night, because they love you. This was God's plan . . . that families would love each other.

Bible Story: God is Everywhere

Key Points

❖ **We cannot see God. God is a *spirit*.**

❖ **God can be in many places all at the same time!**

❖ **God will not leave you. He is always with you.**

❖ **God will take care of you -- He is so wonderful!**

Did you **know** that God can be with your grandma and right here with you at the very same time? We know that even though we cannot see God--because He does not have a body--He is close to you.

When you are at school, you cannot be at home. Your body can only be in one place at a time. But God can be in many places all at once! You are never alone--**God promises** to stay with you and take care of you wherever you are.

It can be very dark and scary sometimes when night comes, but God is there. God is with you when you are playing in the sunshine, too. He will not leave you. You are loved so much!

Whenever you look around, you can know that, even though you cannot see God, He sees you. He loves you. He will take care of you.

We have a wonderful God!

Word and Phrase Meanings

know: to understand and accept; to be sure of something

spirit: what is not physical; the inside of a person that can feel and love

God's promises: doing what He said He will do--ALWAYS!

Guided Prayer Thought

Dear God, I think You are wonderful! You know everything. You will be with me and help me all the time. I want to learn about You and love You more!

Amen

Questions:
Thinking & Remembering

1. Where is God when He is with your grandma or grandpa?

   He is with me too--at the same time.

2. Where is God even though you cannot see Him?

   close to me

3. Why can't you see God?

   He does not have a body.

4. Can you be at your house and at school at the same time?

   No

5. Why can't you be everywhere?

   I have a body.

6. Why are you never alone?

   God is always with me.

7. When does God take care of you?

   All the time--day and night--wherever I am.

8. Can you hide from God?

   No. He can always see me.

9. Why does God stay with you all the time?

   He loves me.

10. What do you think about God?

    He is wonderful!

 # Bible Words To Remember

. . . God is love.   1 John 4:8

We love Him, because He first loved us.   1 John 4:19

Choosing God's Way

Kindness

You will learn in the Bible that love is patient and kind. When you love someone, you will always be kind and think about how they feel.

Where do you learn that love is patient and kind? What will you do if you love someone?

♥ Bible Love Lesson ♥

God knows when you hurt your finger. God knows when you feel sad.
He knows if you are crying. God cares! Pray to Him and He
will make things much better!

Bible Story: God Knows Everything

 Key Points

❖ **You can learn so many things every day!**

❖ **God knows all that there is to know about everything.**

❖ **God planned the world and He knows what will happen tomorrow, too!**

❖ **God wants what is good for you.**

When you listen to your parents or your teachers, you can **learn** many things. There is so much to learn! We can listen and look at things around us to learn about our world. You will also learn to read and will **discover** that there is more and more that you can know about.

God already knows all that there is to know about everything. He planned and created the world and everything in it. He made YOU! He knows all about you. He knows the color of your eyes. He knows how many **freckles** you have. He knows how tall you are. He knows how many hairs you have on your head! And He loves you just the way you are.

God does not need to **learn** because He knows everything. He knows what you are thinking. He knows if you are sad and afraid. He knows when you are happy and feel loved. God already knows what will happen tomorrow.

God wants everything that is good for you. He wants you to learn about Him. He wants you to love Him. He wants you to be happy.

Word and Phrase Meanings

discover: to find; to find out about

freckles: very tiny spots on your skin

learn: listening carefully so that you can know something new

Guided Prayer Thought

Dear God, Your love is so great! Thank You for loving me and caring about me so much. I want to love You more and do the things that will make You happy, too. Help me to love the way You do.
Amen

Questions:
Thinking & Remembering

1. How can you learn right now?
   by listening and looking around me

2. Will you learn more when you can read?
   Yes

3. Does God need to learn to read?
   No. He knows everything.

4. How did the world happen?
   God planned it and created it.

5. What did He make that was so special?
   all people

6. What does God know about you?
   everything

7. Does He know how many hairs are on your head?
   Yes

8. Does God love only the children with blue eyes?
   No. God loves ME just the way I am.

9. What else does God know about you?
   God knows what I am thinking and the way I feel.

10. What does God want for you?
    to be happy, to love Him, and to learn about Him

 # Bible Words To Remember

. . . God is love.   1 John 4:8

We love Him, because He first loved us.   1 John 4:19

Choosing God's Way

Loving Others

God is so happy when you think of others in a loving way. God will help you be kind, even when you don't feel like it!

What will happen when you think of others in a loving way?
Who will help you think of others and be kind?

❤ Bible Love Lesson ❤

God tells us many times in the Bible how much He loves us! God shows us over
and over how much He loves us! And God does everything He says He
will do -- He never forgets!

Bible Story: God Always Keeps His Promise

 Key Points

❖ **A promise is doing what you say you will do.**

❖ **God always does what His word tells us He will do.**

❖ **God promised that He will love you and take care of you.**

❖ **The Bible tells about God's wonderful promises.**

Do you remember what a **promise** is? A promise means doing what you say you will do. If you promise your mother that you will not take another cookie before dinner and you do, you did not keep your promise. God knows it is sometimes hard to keep promises, but He will help us when we ask Him. He is very sad when we do not keep a promise.

God NEVER does what He says He will not do. He ALWAYS does what He says He will do. He keeps His promises. He **remembers** them. He does not **forget** what He promises.

We will learn about the many promises God made in the stories from the Bible. There are many wonderful **lessons** about the way God loves His people and keeps His promises to them. He will keep doing what He said He will do. He will keep loving us. He will keep taking care of us. He will keep giving us what He promised.

Think about your promises. Ask God to help you keep your promises. God wants you to love Him and believe in His promises. God's greatest promise was that He would send Jesus. Jesus was God's **gift** to you to help you love God in the right way--we cannot love God enough all by ourselves! He promised to send the **Holy Spirit** to live inside us to help us know the right way to live. And God has kept all of His promises!

Word and Phrase Meanings

promise:	doing what you say you will do
remembers:	think about again; to not forget
forget:	to not remember
lessons:	things we can learn
gift:	a present or kindness that is given to you
Holy Spirit:	the part of God who lives inside those who love God to help them

Guided Prayer Thought

Dear God, Thank You for hearing our prayers. Help us to ask for Your help when it is hard to keep a promise. We love You and want to learn more about You every day.
Amen

Questions:
Thinking & Remembering

1. What is a promise?
   doing what you say you will do

2. Can you remember a time when you did not keep a promise?

3. Did you tell God you were sorry? Did you tell the person you hurt how sorry you were? God wants to do that and He will forgive us when we ask Him.

4. What does God always remember?
   His promises

5. Does God ever get busy and forget to do what He said He will do?
   No. He never forgets.

6. What will we learn about in the Bible?
   all of God's wonderful promises

7. What are some things that God has promised?
   to love me and take care of me

8. What can we ask God to help us do?
   to help us keep our promises

9. What does God want you to do?
   love Him and believe in His promises

10. What was God's greatest promise?
    to send Jesus

11. Whom did God promise to send to help us do the right things?
    the Holy Spirit

12. Did God keep these promises?
    Yes

Bible Words To Remember

. . . God is love.   1 John 4:8

We love Him, because He first loved us.   1 John 4:19

Choosing God's Way

Endurance

God's love never ends. He wants your love to be like His.

Does God just love you when you are good? What does God want your love to be like?

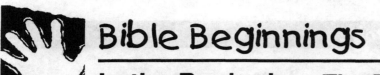

In the Beginning: The Book of Genesis

♥ Bible Love Lesson ♥

We live in such a beautiful world. God made everything good.
God made you. He loves you very much.

Bible Story: God was in the Beginning

 Key Points

❖ **God was before anything else.**

❖ **God made the light so that the world would not be all darkness.**

❖ **God's words made the light happen.**

❖ **Everything God made on the first day of creation was good.**

Before anything was, there was God. The world was very dark. There was no light. There was nothing at all!

But God was in the beginning. God made heaven and earth and everything in it.

God's Spirit was **hovering** over the **surface** of the waters. God did not want everything to be all darkness--So He decided to make some light. God said, "Let there be light" and there was light.

When God saw the light, He saw that it was good. God **divided** the light from the darkness. He called the light Day. He called the darkness Night.

This was the very beginning of God's world. The evening and morning were the first day.

Word and Phrase Meanings

hovering:	remaining in air in one place
surface:	on top of or above the waters
divided:	separated; to bring apart
created:	to make something from nothing
mighty:	powerful
handiwork:	done by God's hand

Guided Prayer Thought

Thank You God, for making our world. The light is so good! We love You for making everything wonderful!
Amen

Questions:
Thinking & Remembering

1. Before anything was, there was _____.
   God

2. What was the world like?
   it was very dark; there was no light-- there was nothing at all.

3. Where was God's Spirit?
   hovering over the face of the waters

4. What words did God say?
   "Let there be light."

5. What happened when God spoke?
   There was light!

6. When God saw the light, He saw that it was _____.
   good

7. What did God do with the light and darkness?
   divided it

8. What did God call the light?
   Day

9. What was the darkness called?
   Night

10. What was this the beginning of?
    God's world

 # Bible Words To Remember

In the beginning God **created** the heavens and the earth.
Genesis 1:1

Let heaven and earth praise Him. . .
Psalm 69:34

Praise Hymn

Sing or say these words
Resource: My First Hymnal Pg. 7

MY GOD IS SO GREAT

My God is so great, so strong and so **mighty**!
There's nothing my God cannot do!
My God is so great, so strong and so mighty!
There's nothing my God cannot do!
The mountains are His,
The rivers are His,
The stars are His **handiwork** too,
My God is so great, so strong and so mighty!
There's nothing my God cannot do!

♥ Bible Love Lesson ♥

Close your eyes and think about what the world was like before God made the light.
God wanted you to see many beautiful things. He made the light.
God loves you!

Bible Story: God Made Day and Night

Key Points

❖ God's word made the water separate into two parts.

❖ Heaven is a wonderful, beautiful place.

❖ God made the waters to stay below the earth.

❖ God planned and made the whole world. The second day was good.

Look all around you. What can you see? You can see many things because it is daytime. If it were dark, you couldn't see many things. God made the daytime for us. God made the nighttime, too, so we could sleep.

God was making a world. He planned it all. God had created light and darkness. He called the light DAY and the darkness NIGHT.

There was water over and in everyplace in the world. So God said, "Let there be a **firmament** in the middle of the waters." The waters started dividing and **separating** into two parts! There was part of the water below and part above with air and space between it. Can you imagine how wonderful it was when this happened? God's words are powerful!

God called the part above the waters, Heaven. This part above was beautiful and peaceful. There was blue sky with clouds floating past.

In the part below, there were waters tumbling and swishing and roaring. There was lots of water moving that was everywhere under the **firmament** in which God had said with His words, 'divide'. The Bible says, "So the evening and the morning were the second day."

Word and Phrase Meanings

firmament:	the air and space between the waters above and the waters below
divide:	to pull apart
separate:	to move and keep apart

Guided Prayer Thought

Thank You God, for eyes to see all of the wonderful things You created in Your world. For the love You give and for the love we can have for each other, Thank You.
Amen

Questions:
Thinking & Remembering

1. What was God making?
   a world

2. What did God do before He started making the world?
   He planned it all

3. What did God make on the first day?
   light and dark ; day and night

4. What did He put in the middle of the waters?
   a firmament

5. What is a firmament?
   the air and space between the waters

6. Into how many parts was the water divided?
   two parts

7. How did God make this happen?
   He said the words

8. What did God call the part above the waters?
   Heaven

9. What was under the firmament?
   the waters

10. What day had just ended?
    the second day of creation

 # Bible Words To Remember

In the beginning God created the heavens and the earth.
Genesis 1:1
Let heaven and earth praise Him. . .
Psalm 69:34

Choosing God's Way

Loving Enemies

God loves you very much. Love others in the way God loves you---even if they hurt your feelings.

Who loves you very much?
How should you love others?

❤ Bible Love Lesson ❤

God had a great **plan**! He could even make the water stay in one place, and the land in another place. He just said the words and it was done! God has great love for you--that is part of His plan.

Bible Story: God Speaks To The Waters

Key Points

❖ The waters gathered together in certain places that God planned.

❖ God made the land in all the right places.

❖ God named all the different waters.

❖ God saw that everything He made on the third day was good.

On the third day of creation, God said, "Let the waters under the heavens be **gathered** together into one place, and let the dry land **appear**." All that swirling, twirling water rushed to one place! And all at once, there was dry land where the water had once been. The water had obeyed God's word. Everything happened as soon as God spoke the words!

It is so good that God put the water in just the right places, and the land in all the right places--only the fish would like water covering everything! God put some of the water in lakes and streams. Some of the water is in rivers that flow into the big oceans. God called the waters Seas. And God saw that it was good.

God knew we would **need** water for many things. **Plants** need water. People need water to drink--so do the animals. Some water comes from the rain. When the sun shines on the water, it becomes warm and turns into little drops of water that go up into the **clouds** in the sky. Then, when the clouds are full of water, it starts to rain and the water comes back to us on the land, just the way God **planned** it!

Word and Phrase Meanings

gathered:	to come together in one place
appear:	something that can be seen
need:	something we must have to stay alive
plants:	growing things
cloud:	a collection of tiny drops of water floating high in the sky. Clouds look fluffy and white sometimes. They become dark when there is a storm and it is going to rain.
plan:	to decide how to do something

Guided Prayer Thought

Thank You God, for putting everything in order in our world. You put the waters in a place, and You put the land in a place. You planned the world so that it would be just right!
Amen

Questions:
Thinking & Remembering

1. On which day did God gather the waters together in one place?
   on the third day

2. What appeared when the waters had gone to their place?
   dry land appeared

3. Where were the waters?
   under the heavens

4. Into which places had God divided the waters before?
   above and below the firmament

5. On which day did God do this?
   on the second day of creation

6. What did the water do?
   obeyed God's Word

7. Into how many places was the water gathered together?
   into one place

8. What did God call the waters?
   Seas

9. What does the Bible say that God saw?
   that everything was good

 # Bible Words To Remember

In the beginning God created the heavens and the earth.
Genesis 1:1

Let heaven and earth praise Him. . .
Psalm 69:34

Choosing God's Way

Choosing to Love

The Bible tells us to do everything in love. That will mean that you will make some hard choices about the things you do.

What does the Bible tell about how you should love? Will choosing the right way always be easy?

❤ Bible Love Lesson ❤

God is so good! He made many kinds of plants. Some of the plants are pretty to look
at, and some plants are good for food. God cares about you and wanted
you to have wonderful foods to eat. God loves you so much!

Bible Story: God Makes a Place for Food to Grow

 Key Points

❖ The earth was a perfect place
  to grow food.

❖ God made many kinds of
  plants and trees.

❖ All the seeds grew the same
  plants each time.

❖ God made these wonderful
  things on the third day of His
  creation.

God made daytime so we can work and play. God made nighttime
so we can rest and sleep. God made water and the land. God
called the dry land Earth.

God looked at the wonderful earth and saw that it was a perfect
place for things to grow.

Everything was just right for plants and trees to grow strong.
There are small plants and little tiny flowers. There are big plants
like trees. God made them all!

God said, "Let the earth bring forth grass, the herb that **yields**
seed **according** to its kind, and the tree that yields fruit, whose
seed is in itself according to its kind."

God knew we would need the land for plants to grow. We get our
food from plants. There are many things we can do on the land.
Animals need land, too! Children love to play on the nice green
grass which grows on the land.

I think God thought of everything! God looked at everything He
had made and said, "It is good." This was the end of the third day.

── Word and Phrase Meanings ──

yield:	to produce (make)
consider:	think about carefully
according:	just the same as the one before it (or what has already been established)

Guided Prayer Thought

*When we **consider** all that You made for us, God, we are so thankful and we know how much You love us!*
Amen

Questions:
Thinking & Remembering

1. What did God create before He made plants?
   day and night; water and land

2. What did God call the dry land?
   Earth

3. Name a plant that is tiny.
   flower (describe different kinds)

4. Name a plant that is small.
   bush (describe different kinds)

5. Name a plant that is big.
   tree (describe different kinds)

6. How did God plan for us to have food?
   He made plants

7. Where does some of the food grow?
   In the ground (potatoes)

8. Where does other food grow?
   on top of the ground (corn)

9. Name some of the foods you like that grow in the ground.

10. Name some of the foods you like that grow on top of the ground.

11. Name some of the food that grows on trees.

 # Bible Words To Remember

In the beginning God created the heavens and the earth.
Genesis 1:1

Let heaven and earth praise Him. . .
Psalm 69:34

Choosing God's Way

Showing Love

If what you say or do cannot be done in a loving way, you need to think about whether God would want you to do it at all.

What should be done in a loving way?
What do you need to decide before you do or say something?

❤ Bible Love Lesson ❤

When we think about all that God made, we know how much He loves us.
We just want to tell Him how much we love Him, too!

Bible Story: God's Wonderful World

Key Points

❖ God planned a very beautiful world for us to live in.

❖ God started at the beginning and everything was planned to be just right.

❖ God made everything by saying the words to make it happen.

❖ God did not make anything bad or *evil* -- everything was good.

Close your eyes very tight so that you cannot see the light. That is how the world was before the world was made by God. God did not want the world to be dark like that, so He planned a very beautiful world for us to live in . . . and I'm so glad He did!

Always **remember** that "In the beginning God created the heavens and the earth." The first day God made day and night. He called the light day and the darkness He called night.

The second day God said that there would be space between the waters above and the waters below. He divided the waters.

The third day God made the waters gather together and He called them Seas. He made the land and called it Earth.

And on the earth He created grass and trees; flowers and vegetables--all kinds of plants. God made everything by just saying the words. And it was good.

When we see the beautiful world, we know that God loves us very much and we want to always thank Him.

Word and Phrase Meanings

evil:	sin, doing wrong
remember:	think about again, to not forget
firmament:	the air and space between the waters above and the waters below

Guided Prayer Thought

*Thank You God, for making our world a beautiful place to live.
Thank You for loving us so much.*
                                    Amen

Questions:
Thinking & Remembering

1. What was the world like a very long time ago?
   dark

2. Did God want the world to be dark?
   No

3. What can we always remember about the beginning of the world?
   God created the heavens and the earth

4. What did God call the light?
   Day

5. Was it light all of the time?
   No

6. What was the world like when there was not light?
   complete darkness

7. What did God call the darkness?
   Night

8. What did God do on the second day?
   He *divided the waters and put space (the firmament) between them.*

9. What did God make on the third day?
   He gathered the waters together and called them Seas. He made land. He made many things grow on the land.

10. How did God create everything?
    He just said the words and it happened

 # Bible Words To Remember

In the beginning God created the heavens and the earth.
Genesis 1:1

Let heaven and earth praise Him. . .
Psalm 69:34

Choosing God's Way

Loving Each Day

Give love to someone each day. There are many special ways to show love.

How often can you give love to someone else? Think of some ways to show love.

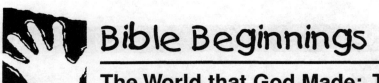

Bible Beginnings

Lesson 3 - DAY 1

The World that God Made: The Book of Genesis

♥ Bible Love Lesson ♥

God is so good! He made the sun to keep us warm and to help the plants grow.
He made the stars and moon for lights in the night sky. God made
everything just right because He loves you so!

Bible Story: God Made the Sun, Moon and Stars

Key Points

❖ The lights God made were different for the day and night.

❖ The sun was the bright light for the day.

❖ God made the twinkling lights with the moon for night.

❖ What a wonderful fourth day of creation!

God looked at everything He had made. He wanted some special lights in the night sky. God said, "Let there be lights in the heavens to divide the day from the night; and let them be for **signs** and **seasons**, and for days and years. Let them give light on the earth." Then God made two great lights: the **greater** light to rule the day, and the **lesser** light to rule the night. He made the stars also. And God saw that it was good. This was the end of the fourth day of creation.

God is so good! He knew we would need the sun to keep us warm. When it is morning the sun comes up in the sky and we know it is daytime! God did not want it to be so totally dark in the nighttime, so He said, "The night needs a little light, too." God made the moon. The moon was all alone in the dark night. Then God made many, many stars. There were big stars and there were little stars up in the sky with the moon. Now the moon was shining and the stars were twinkling. The night is quiet and we can go to sleep. Children need to sleep. Mommies and daddies need to sleep, too. The trees and flowers need a rest time, too. Animals need a time to rest.

Everything was just right!

Word and Phrase Meanings

signs:	a way of telling something
seasons:	a period of time (God made four seasons: spring, summer, autumn/fall, winter)
greater:	big, huge
lesser:	not as much
purpose:	the reason why
praise:	a way of telling God how great He is. Saying words or singing words to tell that you are thankful for how wonderful God is.

Guided Prayer Thought

Thank You God, for loving us so much! Thank You for making the sunshine to keep us warm. Thank You for the nighttime so we can rest . . . for the wonderful moon and stars. Thank You for making everything just right!
Amen

Questions:
Thinking & Remembering

1. What did God want in the sky?
   some special lights

2. What **purpose** did God have for the lights?
   to divide the day and night; to be for signs and seasons; to be for days and years; to give light on the earth

3. How many great lights did God make?
   two

4. How were the lights different?
   one was bright; one was dim or soft

5. What was the purpose of the sun?
   to rule over the day

6. What was the purpose of the moon?
   to rule over the night

7. What other lights did God make?
   the stars

8. Which light keeps us warm?
   the sun

9. Which light makes it best for us to rest?
   the moon

10. What are the four seasons of the year?
    Spring, Summer, Autumn (Fall), Winter

11. How many hours are there in a day?
    twenty-four (24)

12. How many minutes are there in an hour?
    sixty (60)

 # Bible Words To Remember

God has made everything beautiful . . .
Ecclesiastes 3:11

Then God saw everything that He had made, and indeed it was very good.
Genesis 1:31

Praise Hymn

Sing or say these words
Resource: My First Hymnal Pg. 60

ALL CREATURES OF OUR GOD AND KING

All creatures of our God and King,
Lift up your voice and with us sing,
Alleluia! Alleluia!
Thou burning sun with golden beam,
Thou silver moon with softer gleam!
O **Praise** Him, O Praise Him!
Alleluia! Alleluia! Alleluia!

❤ Bible Love Lesson ❤

God planned for water in many places . . . and God planned what He would make to put into the waters. The fish God made loved to swim in the water! God's plan was good!

Bible Story: God Made Fish

 Key Points

❖ **The waters were empty before God made the fish.**

❖ **God made all kinds of fish with many different colors.**

❖ **God put the big fish in the ocean.**

❖ **The smaller fish are in the streams and lakes.**

It was the fifth day that God worked on His creation. He had already made the water. Then He put the water in **streams** and **ponds**; **rivers** and **oceans**. But there were no fish swimming in the water. So God said, "I will make fish to swim in the waters." And He did!

God made so many fish! He put fish in the big ocean. He put fish in little streams--and into the small ponds. Some fish are so very small you might not even see them in the water. Other fish are very BIG--like the whale that lives in the ocean. The fish God made are many different colors, too. I think God knew that the world would be beautiful with many colors.

I'm glad God decided to make the fish. We like to see them swimming in the water--and we like to see their beautiful colors. I like God's plan for everything. God saw that it was good. We can look around us and see that 'It is good!'

── Word and Phrase Meanings ──

streams: a small river or brook (flow of water)

pond: a still body of water, smaller than a lake

river: natural flowing water that runs between banks into a lake, another river, or the sea

ocean: great body of water

Guided Prayer Thought

Dear God, Thank You for making the fish. You made our world so beautiful. Thank You for caring for Your world. Thank You for taking care of us.

Amen

Questions:
Thinking & Remembering

1. Name some of the places where God put the waters.
   streams and ponds; rivers and oceans

2. What did God put in the waters?
   fish

3. Are fish all the same color?
   No--they are many different colors

4. Are all fish the same size?
   No--they are many different sizes

5. Name some fish that are tiny.
   goldfish, guppies, minnows, etc.

6. Name some fish that are in lakes and streams.
   trout, bass, etc.

7. Name some fish that are in the ocean.
   whales, sharks, etc.

8. Are some fish good to eat? Do you like fish?
   Yes

9. What do you think about God's plan?

10. What did God see?
    that everything was good

 # Bible Words To Remember

God has made everything beautiful . . .
Ecclesiastes 3:11

Then God saw everything that He had made, and indeed it was very good.
Genesis 1:31

Choosing God's Way

Cheerfulness

Notice the faces of other people and your friends, look at their expressions. The expression on your face should be cheerful and happy.

What kind of a face gives joy?
What is the expression on your face?

❤ Bible Love Lesson ❤

God planned for birds to fly. He gave each kind of bird the right wings. Eagles could not fly high above the mountains with sparrows wings. Robins could not fly to their nest in the trees with a hawk's wings--they would be much too big! God gave each just what was needed. . . He planned for you in the same way--He knew just what you needed to make you wonderful because He loves you so!

Bible Story: God Made Birds

 Key Points

❖ **The sky was empty before God made the birds.**

❖ **The birds God made are beautiful and many have songs to sing!**

❖ **The mother and father birds take good care of their babies.**

❖ **God planned for all the living things He made on the fifth day.**

God's creation was most **marvelous** now. After God made the fish for the water, He must have looked into the beautiful blue sky. He saw that it was very empty. So God said, "I will make birds to fly in the big sky." And He did!

God made many kinds of birds. Some birds fly in the sky and also take a swim in the water, like the ducks. There are birds that are tiny, like the hummingbird. There are birds that are small, like the sparrow. There are large birds, like the eagle. God made some birds with pretty songs to sing. Other birds have many beautiful colors on their wings. God said to the **creatures** He had made, "Be **fruitful** and **multiply**."

One special kind of bird God made is called a robin. The mother and father work hard to make a nest for their babies out of twigs and branches. Then the father goes to find worms to feed the babies. Soon the robins grow big enough to fly out of their nest and find their own food.

God has a wonderful plan for all of the living things He made! God planned everything so it would be just right. God has a plan for us, too. We know God loves us because He gave us such a beautiful world.

Word and Phrase Meanings

marvelous:	very wonderful; a miracle
creatures:	anything created that breathes and lives
rhyme:	to sound the same
fruitful:	productive; successful
multiply:	to add to and make more of

Guided Prayer Thought

Thank You God, for our wonderful world. We love the birds that sing.
Help us to take good care of all Your creation.
Amen

Questions:
Thinking & Remembering

1. What was God's creation like now?
   marvelous (let children describe)

2. What did God notice when He saw the beautiful blue sky?
   it was empty

3. What did God put in the sky so that it would not be empty?
   many kinds of birds

4. Name a bird that is tiny. Name one that is small. Name one that is large.
   hummingbird-sparrow-eagle

5. Which bird also swims in the water?
   duck

6. What did God tell the birds that they should do?
   multiply

7. Which kind of bird builds a nest out of twigs and branches?
   the robin

8. What kind of food do these birds feed their babies?
   worms

9. Which words are missing? God made birds with pretty songs to _sing_. God made birds with colors on their _wing_.

10. Which words **rhyme**?
    sing, wing

 # Bible Words To Remember

God has made everything beautiful . . .
Ecclesiastes 3:11

Then God saw everything that He had made, and indeed it was very good.
Genesis 1:31

Choosing God's Way

Being Content

Some children have a face that shows something like, "I don't have everything I want, and I'm not happy!" This kind of expression shows that someone has forgotten what they can be thankful for.

What kind of face (expression) makes you feel bad?
What does a sad face tell you?
Have you forgotten something?

❤ Bible Love Lesson ❤

Everywhere you look you can see new things in God's world. There are big things, like the wide ocean and tall mountains. There are little things, like ladybugs and snails. And God takes care of the things He made. That is how we can know how loving God is.

Bible Story: God Made all the Living Creatures

Key Points

❖ **God had created many things, but He wasn't finished yet.**

❖ **God's next creation was the animals.**

❖ **Everything God made was interesting and exciting.**

❖ **God cares so much about the creation He made on the sixth day.**

God created many things: He had made day and night; He had made land and water;　He had made all kinds of plants; He had made the sun, moon and stars; He had made fish and birds . . . and it was good. But God wasn't finished yet!

On the sixth day, God said, "Let the earth be filled with all kinds of living creatures, and each **according to its kind.**" God made each animal in the way that would not **change.** A dog would always be a dog, not a lion! A horse would always be a horse, not a pig! A monkey would always be a monkey, not a squirrel! Because God is so great, He made even more kinds of animals than you can imagine!

God wanted our world to be interesting and **fascinating.** There were tiny creatures that crawled along the earth like caterpillars. There were small creatures like bunnies that hopped and scampered everywhere. He made cats that purred and dogs that barked. He made the giraffe very tall. He put stripes on the zebra and spots on the leopard. God liked all of the animals and creatures He had made. God saw that it was good.

He wanted us to live in a wonderful and exciting world. But there was one MORE very special creation . . . Can you guess what it is?

Word and Phrase Meanings

fascinating:　　to be attracted to something unusual

change:　　to be different

"according to its kind":　each creature would be like its mother and father created in a way that would not change; would always be the same kind

Guided Prayer Thought

Thank You God, for all the wonderful animals and creatures . . . from the smallest to the biggest. You care about all of Your creation. Help us to love and take care of what You made.
Amen

Questions: Thinking & Remembering

1. **Name some of the things that God had made.**
   day and night; water and land; plants, sun, moon, stars, fish and birds

2. **Was God finished yet?**
   No

3. **What did God say on the sixth day?**
   "Let there be many creatures on the earth."

4. **How was each and every creature created by God?**
   each according to its kind

5. **What does 'according to its kind' mean?**
   They would always be the same. A cat is a cat; a dog is a dog, etc.

6. **Why do you think God made so many different kinds of creatures?**
   He wanted His creation to be interesting and fascinating.

7. **Name some creatures that are tiny and some that are small.**
   caterpillar, cat, rabbits, etc.

8. **Name some creatures that are big or tall.**
   lions, giraffes, etc.

9. **What kind of a world did God want us to live in?**
   a wonderful, exciting world

10. **What does the Bible say that God saw when He looked at all the creatures He had created?**
    God saw that it was good.

 # Bible Words To Remember

God has made everything beautiful . . .
Ecclesiastes 3:11

Then God saw everything that He had made, and indeed it was very good.
Genesis 1:31

Choosing God's Way

Joyfulness

You can be happy even if everything isn't 'super' because God can give you joy on the inside!

Who gives you joy that comes from the inside?
How do you look to other people?
How do you look to your parents?

❤ Bible Love Lesson ❤

Have you ever heard the thunder and watched the lightning flash in the sky during a storm? Can you make that powerful noise or a light that bright? No, you cannot and I cannot! Only God can. We know that He is very great to make these things. This great God loves you!

Bible Story: Praising God

Key Points

❖ The world had gone from darkness to light to beauty and life!

❖ God had said the words to make it happen in six days.

❖ God was in the beginning. He always was and always will be.

❖ God saw all that He had made and was pleased.

God's **creation** is so wonderful! Remember what the world was like before God created it? It was very dark and black. God **planned** a very beautiful world for us to live in. There is a beautiful big, blue sky over our heads and wonderful white clouds--all different shapes. There are flowers and trees of many colors.

Of course, the world was not always this beautiful. Before God created all things, there was no sky, no trees, no flowers and no birds singing. But God was there! God has always been!

God made so many things! First, God created daytime and nighttime. God said, "Let there be light," and as soon as He said the words, it was so! Then He made water and land, and put fish in the water and animals on the land. He made the plants to grow on the land so that we could have all kinds of delicious food to eat. He made special lights for the sky--the sunshine for the day and the moon and stars for the nighttime sky. And He made birds--and butterflies to fly in the sky. God was glad for all that He had created. God saw that it was good. But God still wasn't finished . . .

Word and Phrase Meanings

creation: what God made

planned: to decide how to do something

Guided Prayer Thought

We give praise to You, O God, for all Your wonderful works. We thank You for all Your gifts to us. We are thankful for the Bible that tells us how great You are!
Amen

Questions:
Thinking & Remembering

1. What was the world like before God created it?
   black and dark

2. What is over our heads?
   sky and clouds

3. Are all the clouds the same shape? Tell about the clouds you have seen.
   No. There are many different shapes.

4. What did God make in many colors?
   flowers, trees, birds, fish, etc.

5. Was the world always beautiful?
   No. The world was dark with nothing in it.

6. Who was in the very beginning?
   God--He has always been

7. What did God create first by just saying the words?
   light

8. What did God put on the land? What did He put in the water?
   plants and animals; fish

9. What did God put in the sky?
   sun, moon, stars, birds

10. What did God see when He saw what He had made?
    that it was good

 # Bible Words To Remember

God has made everything beautiful . . .
Ecclesiastes 3:11

Then God saw everything that He had made, and indeed it was very good.
Genesis 1:31

Choosing God's Way

Thankfulness

When you think of what you can be thankful for, it is not so difficult to smile! God made all the wonderful things around you, and people to love you, and most important of all----God loves you!

What can you be thankful for?
Who made all the wonderful things around you?
What is most important of all?

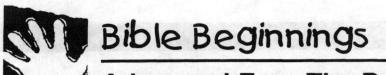

Adam and Eve: The Book of Genesis

❤ Bible Love Lesson ❤

God made you! God wanted people to enjoy the world He made. He looked at all of the things He had made and He said, "It is good." God loved the people He made. He loves you!

Bible Story: God Made People

Key Points

❖ God's world was beautiful but God had one more important piece of work.

❖ God made people to enjoy all that He had made.

❖ People could love God in a very special way.

❖ God was finished with His work -- it was perfect!

The world God **created** was so beautiful! But there were no people to enjoy the wonderful things God had made. So God made a man. His name was Adam. God made him to be like Himself. Someone who could think and love. Then He gave him a body like a man. Adam took care of the garden and the many animals God had made.

Adam cared for the animals, but he didn't have another special person to talk with. He was lonely all by himself. God said, "It is not good for man to be alone." God made a woman for Adam. Adam named the woman Eve. The people God made were very different from the animals. He made them so that they had a mind to think and a heart to love. People could love God in a very special way.

God Himself breathed into Adam the breath of life to make him a living being. Now God was finished---and everything was **perfect.**

And ALL that God made was VERY GOOD!

Word and Phrase Meanings

created:	to make something from nothing
complete:	finished
describe:	tell about
perfect:	the very best that can be; with nothing missing or spoiled

Guided Prayer Thought

*Dear God, Your creation was **complete** when You created people.*
Thank You for creating us! We love You so much!
Amen

Questions:
Thinking & Remembering

1. Which word or words **describe** God's world?
   beautiful, wonderful, marvelous, perfect, "very good"

2. What was missing in this world after God created the garden?
   people

3. Why was this creation important?
   There were no people to enjoy the wonderful things God had made.

4. Whom did God make and what name did He give him?
   A man. His name was Adam.

5. What work did God give Adam to do?
   caring for the garden and all the animals

6. Whom did God make for Adam because he was lonely?
   a woman

7. What name did Adam give the woman?
   Eve

8. How were people different from the animals?
   They had a mind to think and a heart that could love.

9. How did Adam become a living being?
   God breathed into him the breath of life.

10. What do we know about God's world and all that He made?
    It was very good.

 # Bible Words To Remember

Know that the Lord, He is God; it is He who has made us . . .
Psalm 100:3

He rested from all His work which God had created and made.
Genesis 2:3

Praise Hymn

Sing or say these words
Resource: My First Hymnal Pg. 34

GOD IS SO GOOD

God is so good, God is so good,
God is so good, He's so good to me.
God loves me so, God loves me so,
God loves me so, He's so good to me.
God answers prayer, God answers prayer
God answers prayer, He's so good to me.

❤ Bible Love Lesson ❤

After you have played and played, your body needs rest. You need a quiet day to think about God's love and care for you. God worked for six days, and then He rested. He wants us to remember to rest on the special day that He planned. He wants you to remember how much He loves you!

Bible Story: A Special and Holy Day

Key Points

❖ When God had finished His creation work, He rested.

❖ God said that this day should be different from all of the other days.

❖ This is a day to remember all that God did and how wonderful He is.

❖ What a special time to rest and think about God!

The **Heavens** and the Earth and everything in them were **finished!** On the seventh day, God ended His work which He had done. God rested from all His work. God said, "This is a special and **holy** day."

It is important for us to remember this day of rest. It is different from all the other days when we work and play. We can be with others who love God and sing praises to God. We can listen as God's Word is read. We can pray with our families and ask God to help us live in the right way and love others. We can think of God's love for us and tell Him how much we love Him.

We want to think about God every day, too, as we go to school and work and while we play. God is very **pleased** when we take time to remember Him in this way. What a special day! I'm glad God rested!

— Word and Phrase Meanings —

heavens: all that is above the earth

holy: blessed, sacred, pure

finished: to be done with something; complete----nothing missing

pleased: happy, satisfied

Guided Prayer Thought

What a wonderful plan You had, God, when You made a special day of rest and worship. When another week starts, we can feel almost like new because we have taken time to be with You and think about You! Thank You for making this special day.   *Amen*

Questions:
Thinking & Remembering

1. What did God finish making?
   the heavens and the earth and everything in them

2. Name some things that God created.
   answers will vary

3. What happened on the seventh day?
   God ended His work

4. What did God do when He ended His work?
   He rested

5. What did God say about this day?
   "This is a special and holy day."

6. Why is it important to remember this day of rest?
   it is different from all the other days

7. How is this day different from the other days of the week?
   we can rest from our regular work and play

8. What can we do to make this day different from other days?
   going to church, singing praises to God, listening to God's word, praying

9. Will God be pleased if we remember this day in a special way?
   Yes

10. Why do you like this special day?
    answers will vary

Bible Words To Remember

Know that the Lord, He is God; it is He who has made us . . .
Psalm 100:3

He rested from all His work which God had created and made.
Genesis 2:3

Choosing God's Way

Obeying God

To obey means that you do what God wants you to do. God gave you parents who want to help you grow in the right way.

What does it mean to obey?
Whom did God give you to help you grow in the right way?

❤ Bible Love Lesson ❤

God wanted the people He made to enjoy the garden. God wanted the people He made to love Him. God wanted the people He made to love each other. He planned everything this way because He loves you and wants you to be happy.

Bible Story: Adam and Eve in the Garden

 Key Points

❖ The garden was a wonderful place for Adam and Eve to live.

❖ There was no sadness in the garden. There was a lot of love!

❖ Adam took care of the animals and named each one.

❖ There were two special trees in the middle of the garden.

❖ God gave Adam and Eve special instructions about the tree called "The knowledge of good and evil."

God made our beautiful world. He made people to enjoy all the wonderful things He had made. Adam and Eve were very happy in God's world. It was so **perfect**! All of God's creation was in **harmony**. Their home was a beautiful garden, called Eden. Adam took good care of the animals, birds, and fish. He gave each one a name. The animals did not hurt each other. It was very peaceful.

God had made every tree grow that is **pleasant to the sight** and good for food. The **tree of life** was in the **middle** of the garden. There was also **the tree of the knowledge of good and evil**. God gave Adam and Eve special **instructions** about this tree. God watered the garden with a **mist** that went up from the earth. No wonder Adam and Eve were happy in this garden!

Word and Phrase Meanings

perfect:	the very best that can be
harmony:	peaceful agreement
middle:	center
instructions:	to tell how to do something
mist:	a soft spray of water
tree of life:	eating the fruit of this tree would make it possible to live forever
pleasant to the sight:	good to look at

the tree of the knowledge of good and evil: the fruit from this tree made Adam and Eve know sin and its results

Guided Prayer Thought

Dear God, When I think about the perfect world You made, I know that You had a wonderful plan and that You cared about the people You made most of all!
Amen

Questions:
Thinking & Remembering

1. Who made our beautiful world?
   God

2. Whom did God make to enjoy this world?
   people

3. What were the names of the first two people God made?
   Adam and Eve

4. What was the name of the garden where they lived?
   Eden

5. Were Adam and Eve happy or sad in the garden?
   they were happy

6. What work had God given Adam to do?
   taking care of the animals and the garden

7. What two things does the Bible tell us about the trees in the garden?
   they were pleasant to look at and they were good for food

8. Which tree was in the middle of the garden?
   the tree of life

9. What other tree does the Bible tell us about?
   the tree of the knowledge of good and evil

10. How did God water the garden?
    with a mist that went up from the earth

 # Bible Words To Remember

Know that the Lord, He is God; it is He who has made us . . .
Psalm 100:3

He rested from all His work which God had created and made.
Genesis 2:3

Choosing God's Way

Obeying Parents

God's Word says to children, "Obey your parents." Other people will also care for you----your teachers and people with jobs that help keep you safe.

What does God's word tell children to do?
Who else will care for you that you need to obey?

♥ Bible Love Lesson ♥

God made you to love Him! He knows that you can only be happy when you think about how much He loves you. Then you will want to do the right things. God loves you so much and wants you to be happy!

Bible Story: A Sad Day in the Garden

 Key Points

❖ Could anything go wrong in the perfect garden? One day, something did go wrong.

❖ God gave Adam and Eve only one rule. They could not eat from *one* tree.

❖ Eve broke God's rule by eating the fruit from that tree.

❖ Adam listened to Eve and broke God's rule, too. They were not happy any longer.

❖ Adam and Eve had to leave the garden.

The garden God made for Adam and Eve was beautiful. Everything was perfect! But one of the best things that happened was that God would come to the garden to be with the people He made. These were wonderful visits with God every evening.

There was only one rule that God gave Adam and Eve. "You may not eat the fruit from the tree that is in the middle of the garden." This was the tree of the knowledge of good and **evil**. God said to them, "If you eat from that tree, you shall surely die."

Then a very sad thing happened. **Satan** (who hates God) told Eve that it would *not* hurt her if she ate from the tree. He said eating the fruit would make her **wise**. So Eve did what God had said not to do. She ate the fruit and then gave the fruit to Adam. He ate it too. Everything changed that day. Adam and Eve were not happy anymore. They had to leave the garden. They had disobeyed God.

Adam and Eve had children. Their boys were named Cain and Abel. Life was very hard outside the garden that God had made. Because Adam and Eve sinned, their children were born into a world that was not perfect.

── Word and Phrase Meanings ──

Satan(devil):	God's enemy and our enemy. He hates God. Satan wants people to sin.
wise:	knowing and understanding what is right
evil:	sin; disobeying God and doing wrong continually over a period of time

Guided Prayer Thought

Dear God, Help us to listen to Your Word. We know how much You love us and we want to obey You. Help us choose to obey You.
Amen

Questions:
Thinking & Remembering

1. What word in our story tells how wonderful the garden was?
   perfect

2. What was the best part of being in the garden for Adam and Eve?
   God walked with them there.

3. What was the one rule God gave?
   *Not to eat from one tree in the middle of the garden. The tree of knowledge of good and **evil**.*

4. What would happen to them if they ate from that tree?
   they would die

5. Who told Eve that it would not hurt if she ate the fruit from that tree?
   Satan

6. What did Satan tell Eve would happen?
   she would be wise

7. Did Eve choose to obey God or Satan?
   Satan

8. Did Adam also disobey?
   Yes

9. How did things change for Adam and Eve that sad day?
   They were not happy anymore. They had to leave the garden.

10. When Cain and Able were born, was the world perfect?
    No. The world had been spoiled by sin.

 # Bible Words To Remember

Know that the Lord, He is God; it is He who has made us . . .
Psalm 100:3

He rested from all His work which God had created and made.
Genesis 2:3

Choosing God's Way

Doing the Right Thing

When you disobey those who care about you and love you, you will feel bad. You may try to act like it doesn't matter but it will hurt you.

How will you feel if you disobey?
Will you be able to act like it doesn't matter without hurting?

❤ Bible Love Lesson ❤

God wants families to love each other. God planned for families to care for each other.
Even when things don't go our own way, we can know that we have each other.
We can talk to each other about what we don't understand.

Bible Story: Cain and Abel

Key Points

❖ Sin spoiled God's perfect
world.

❖ Adam and Eve's children
each had to make a choice to
obey God.

❖ Abel chose to obey God. Cain
chose not to love and obey
God.

❖ God was sad that His world
was a place where there was
hate instead of love.

After sin spoiled God's wonderful and beautiful world, things were very different for Adam and Eve and the children that were born to them. Because sin had changed the way people loved each other, the brothers did not always agree. Both of them wanted to be right. Cain and Abel soon went separate ways. Cain had a garden and grew vegetables. Abel took care of the sheep.

Adam and Eve taught Cain and Abel how to please God. Abel wanted to please his God and his parents. Cain wanted to do things his own way. Abel took the **offering** that God **required**. Cain decided that he would only give God the offering that *he* wanted to give, and that God should **accept** it.

God was **pleased** with Abel's offering. God could not accept Cain's offering. Cain became very angry and killed his brother Abel. When God asked Cain where his brother was, Cain said to God, "I don't know. Am I supposed to take care of my brother?" God was very sad that the perfect world had become a place where there was hate. He sent Cain away, but God kept on loving His people. Some day He would send a **Savior** to show them how much He loved them-a way to bring them back to Him.

Word and Phrase Meanings

offering:	to present for acceptance or refusal; something given to God
required:	something that *must* be done
accept:	to receive with satisfaction
pleased:	happy; satisfied
Savior:	One who saves. God sent Jesus to show His love and save people from their sins.

Guided Prayer Thought

Dear God, You made us to love each other in a very special way. You made families to love and not hate. When we forget to love our brothers and sisters, help us to remember Your love and ask You to help us love the way You want us to.   Amen

Questions:
Thinking & Remembering

1. Was everything almost the same after Adam and Eve left the garden?
   No. Things were different.

2. What did Cain do?
   he was a gardener

3. What did his brother Abel do?
   he took care of sheep

4. What had changed from the way God had planned?
   the way people would love each other

5. Who taught Cain and Abel the offering that God **required**?
   Adam and Eve

6. What did Cain decide to do?
   *take the offering that **he** wanted to give*

7. Which brother took the offering that God accepted?
   Abel

8. What did Cain do because he was angry?
   killed Abel, his brother

9. What did God ask Cain?
   "Where is your brother?"

10. Was Cain sorry for what he had done? What did he tell God?
   No. "Am I supposed to take care of my brother?"

11. Why was God sad?
   that people could hate each other instead of love each other

12. What would God do?
   Cain was sent away. God would keep loving people and find a way to bring them back to Him.

Bible Words To Remember

Know that the Lord, He is God; it is He who has made us . . .
Psalm 100:3

He rested from all His work which God had created and made.
Genesis 2:3

Choosing God's Way

God's Best

Because your mom and dad love you they want what is best for you----God knew that you could not grow up and learn many things without loving parents to guide you.

What does God want for you?
What do your parents want for you?

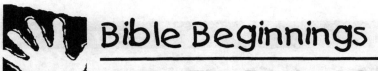

❤ Bible Love Lesson ❤

God loved you so much that He made a plan for you even before you were born. God loves you even when you do wrong. He hates the wrong things, but keeps on loving YOU! God made a way for you to live in heaven with Him forever. He sent Jesus to show you His love.

Bible Story: A World that had Forgotten God

Key Points

❖ God loved His people, even though they had done wrong.

❖ God promised to send a Savior who would save people from sin.

❖ The people did not obey and love God.

❖ Only one man listened to God's word and believed in Him. His name was Noah.

❖ God kept Noah and his family safe when the earth had a big flood.

Even though Adam and Eve had disobeyed God, God did not stop loving them. God gave them a **promise** that He would send a **Savior** who would make everything wonderful again. This **Savior** is Jesus who takes away sin and makes a way for people to come back to God. God does not want us to be afraid.

It would be wonderful if we could read in God's Book, the Bible, that the people obeyed and loved God. But the Bible tells us what really happened.

The people became very **wicked**. They did not love God. There was only one man who believed God's words and loved Him. The man's name was Noah.

God told Noah what He was going to do. He said, "I will send rain and **floods** for many days." The earth would be destroyed by the waters. God saved Noah and his family because Noah loved God.

Word and Phrase Meanings

promise:	doing what you say you will do; an agreement
Savior:	One who saves someone else
wicked:	to keep doing many bad things and not being sorry
flood:	waters that cover everything
unfold:	open up
immortal:	constant---continues forever

"I will establish My covenant with you": "I will keep my agreement/promise to you."

Guided Prayer Thought

Dear God, We know that some of our friends do not love You. Help us to believe and obey the words in Your book, the Bible, and share Your love with them so they will believe in You, too.

Amen

Questions:
Thinking & Remembering

1. Did God stop loving Adam and Eve?
   No

2. What promise did God give to them?
   that He would someday send a Savior

3. What would the Savior do?
   take away sin and make a way for people to come back to God

4. Did Adam and Eve's children love God?
   No. The people became very wicked.

5. Was there anyone who believed and obeyed God?
   Yes. One man.

6. What was the name of the man who loved God?
   Noah

7. What did God tell Noah would happen?
   that he would send rain and floods for many days

8. How would the earth be destroyed?
   by waters

9. Who would be saved from the flood of waters?
   Noah and his family

10. Why would God keep them safe?
    because Noah loved God

Bible Words To Remember

Noah did all that the Lord commanded him.
Genesis 7:5

God said to Noah, 'I will **establish My covenant with you**.'
Genesis 6:18

Praise Hymn

Sing or say these words
Resource: My First Hymnal Pg. 62

JOYFUL, JOYFUL, WE ADORE THEE

Joyful, Joyful, we adore Thee,
God of Glory, Lord of love;
Hearts **unfold** like flowers before Thee,
Opening to the sun above.
Melt the clouds of sin and sadness;
Drive the dark of doubt away;
Giver of **immortal** gladness,
Fill us with the light of day!

❤ Bible Love Lesson ❤

God gave you His Words in the Bible. The words tell that He loves you. The words tell you what you can do to make God happy. God cares about you and will keep you safe.

Bible Story: A Big Boat

Key Points

❖ **God told Noah to build a big boat, called an ark.**

❖ **God gave Noah all the instructions so that Noah and his family would be safe.**

❖ **Noah obeyed God and did exactly what God said to do.**

❖ **Even though people laughed at Noah, Noah listened to God.**

God gave Noah **instructions** to build a very big boat, called an **ark**. He told him exactly how to build it: how big to make it; what kind of wood to use; and how to make room inside for many animals.

Noah talked to his sons and told them what God said. They **obeyed** God and built the boat in just the right way, as God had told them to do.

It took Noah and his family many years to finish the ark. The people asked him: "Noah, what are you building?" "Why are you building a boat?" The people laughed at Noah for building a boat. But Noah obeyed God.

Word and Phrase Meanings

instructions:	to tell how to do something
ark:	a very large (huge) boat
obey:	to do what God says to do

Guided Prayer Thought

Dear God, Maybe it was hard when people laughed at Noah for obeying You. Help us to obey You, even when it is hard.
Amen

Questions:
Thinking & Remembering

1. **What did God tell Noah to build?**
   an ark; a very big boat

2. **How did Noah know how to build the ark?**
   God gave him instructions

3. **What exact instructions did God give him?**
   how big (size) and kind of wood (materials)

4. **What else would go into the ark?**
   animals

5. **Who helped Noah build the ark?**
   his sons and his family

6. **Did they follow God's plans?**
   Yes

7. **How long did it take to finish the ark?**
   many years

8. **Did people ask why Noah was building a boat?**
   Yes

9. **What did they do when Noah told them.**
   they laughed

10. **What did Noah do?**
    obeyed God

 # Bible Words To Remember

Noah did all that the Lord commanded him.
Genesis 7:5

God said to Noah, 'I will establish My covenant with you.'
Genesis 6:18

Choosing
God's Way

God's Promises

God ALWAYS keeps His promises! He NEVER forgets what He says He will do!

Who always keeps promises?
Does God ever forget what He says He will do?

❤ Bible Love Lesson ❤

God did not forget how much He cared for all the creatures He had made in the beginning.
He told Noah to take two of each kind into the ark to keep them safe from the water
that would cover all the earth. God will never forget how much He loves YOU!
He will always do what He says. He will take care of you.

Bible Story: The Ark is Finished

Key Points

❖ **Noah and his family worked together to make the ark ready before the rain started.**

❖ **They needed to take a lot of food onto the ark.**

❖ **Noah took two of each kind of animal into the ark.**

❖ **Noah and his family were the only ones who believed and obeyed God.**

All the work was done. Noah and his family all worked together to get ready for the rain. The ark was complete. The rain had not started yet. God told Noah, "Take two of each kind of animal onto the ark. Take plenty of food for your family and all the animals."

It was a big job to get all of the animals, a mother and a father of each kind, into the ark, but God helped Noah. The animals came to Noah. Soon all of the animals, the horses, cows, sheep, pigs, lions, bears, giraffes, zebras, dogs, cats, and many more -- birds, too, were on the ark.

God said to Noah, "Come into the ark, you and your family, because I have seen that you are the only one who **obeys** and believes in Me."

Word and Phrase Meanings

covenant: an agreement; promise

obey: to do what you are told---doing what God says to do

Guided Prayer Thought

Dear God, Thank You for taking care of Noah and his family. Help us to obey and believe in You. We know You will keep us safe.
Amen

Questions:
Thinking & Remembering

1. What was finished?
   the ark

2. Who worked together to get ready?
   Noah and his family

3. Had the rain started?
   No

4. What work did Noah have left to do?
   to get two of every animal and bring them to the ark; to get enough food ready for his family and all the animals

5. Who helped Noah and his family?
   God

6. Name some animals that went into the ark.

7. What did God tell Noah to do?
   "Come into the ark, you and your family."

8. Why did God want them to be safe?
   because Noah obeyed and believed in Him

 # Bible Words To Remember

Noah did all that the Lord commanded him.
Genesis 7:5

God said to Noah, 'I will establish My **covenant** with you.'
Genesis 6:18

Choosing God's Way

People Promises

Because we all came from Adam and Eve who sinned in the garden, we do forget promises sometimes. You must be careful not to use the words 'always' and 'never' unless you really mean them.

Why can't people always keep a promise?
Which words should you be careful not to use unless you mean them?

❤ Bible Love Lesson ❤

When Noah and his family were safe in the big boat, they remembered to thank God for taking care of them and loving them so much! You can say "Thank You" to God right now for loving you and giving you parents to help God take care of you.

Bible Story: All on Board!

Key Points

❖ God closed the door of the ark when Noah, his family, and the animals were safely inside.

❖ It rained very hard for forty days and forty nights.

❖ The earth was covered with water.

❖ When the rain stopped, water still covered the earth.

When Noah and his family and all of the animals were **safe** on the ark, God closed the door. Noah and his family waited. The animals were noisy. Could they hear raindrops on the boat? Not yet.

But soon it began to rain. The drops came down faster and faster. Soon it roared with the rain pouring down on the boat. It rained for many days, forty days and forty nights without stopping!

The whole earth was covered with water. The only safe place was inside the ark that God kept for Noah and his family. Finally the rain stopped. It was quiet again. But water still covered the earth.

Word and Phrase Meanings

safe: a place where you will not get hurt

covenant: agreement; promise

Guided Prayer Thought

Dear God, When the water covered the earth, You kept Noah and his family safe in the ark. Thank You for keeping me safe, too.
Amen

Questions:
Thinking & Remembering

1. Who was inside the ark?
   Noah and his family and the animals

2. Who closed the door of the ark?
   God did

3. Was it raining when they entered the ark?
   No

4. Did it start raining when God closed the door?
   No. They had to wait.

5. How long did the rain last after it had begun?
   forty days and forty nights

6. What covered the whole earth?
   water

7. Where was there a safe place?
   only inside the ark

8. What still covered the earth?
   water

 # Bible Words To Remember

Noah did all that the Lord commanded him.
Genesis 7:5

God said to Noah, 'I will establish My **covenant** with you.'
Genesis 6:18

Choosing God's Way

Making Promises

Even though you want to keep every **promise** you make, sometimes you cannot. Being careful of the promises you make is important.

Think of some other ways to tell someone that you will do something.
Can you tell someone that you will do your best to do what you say you will do?

♥ Bible Love Lesson ♥

Sometimes waiting is hard to do. Noah, his family and all of the animals waited on the big boat for the rain to start. After the rain came, they waited again and listened to the rain for many days. When the rain stopped, they had to wait for the earth to dry. God always has a reason when you have to wait. But don't wait to tell God how much you love Him--because He loves you a lot!

Bible Story: God's Wonderful Promise

 Key Points

❖ **Everyone inside the ark had to be patient while the earth dried out.**

❖ **Noah waited until a bird had found something to eat before they left the ark.**

❖ **Noah thanked God for saving them from the flood that destroyed the earth.**

❖ **God sent a rainbow as a promise that He would not flood the earth again.**

Noah and his family had to be **patient** a little longer. The animals had to be patient, too! They waited for the waters to go down so that there would be dry land for them to stand on. God sent a wind to help dry the land.

Then Noah sent a raven out of the boat first to see if it could find a resting spot. Then he sent out a dove. When the dove did not return, Noah knew that they could leave the ark.

How wonderful it must have been to see the beautiful sky and the land again! Noah and his family thanked God for keeping them safe and helping them. Then God said, "I am making a promise to you. I will never again cover the whole earth with water to destroy the earth." As a **reminder** of God's **promise**, He put a rainbow in the sky. Whenever we see a rainbow, we can think of God's promise. We can know that God always keeps His promises.

Word and Phrase Meanings

patient:	to wait without complaining
reminder:	something that helps us remember
promise:	doing what you say you will do; an agreement

Guided Prayer Thought

Dear God, Thank You for always keeping Your promises! Help us to remember to thank You for keeping us safe and taking care of us.
Amen

Questions:
Thinking & Remembering

1. What word in the story tells us that Noah and his family had to wait a period of time?
   patient

2. Why did they have to be patient and wait?
   so there would be dry land for them

3. What did God send to help dry the land?
   wind

4. Which birds did Noah send out of the ark?
   a raven and a dove

5. How did Noah know that it was time to leave the ark?
   the dove did not return

6. What do you think it was like when they came outside the ark?
   sky, trees, sunshine, etc.

7. What did Noah and his family do when they were outside?
   they thanked God for keeping them safe and for helping them

8. What promise did God make to Noah?
   that He would never send a flood to destroy the earth again

9. What did God show Noah as a **reminder** of that promise?
   a rainbow

10. What can we think of when we see a rainbow?
    that God always keeps His promises

 # Bible Words To Remember

Noah did all that the Lord commanded him.
Genesis 7:5

God said to Noah, 'I will establish My covenant with you.'
Genesis 6:18

Choosing God's Way

Keeping Promises

When you truly love others and care about them, you will not tell them that you will do something that maybe won't or can't happen. Use the word "promise" carefully.

What will you do if you are showing love when you say something?
Which word should you use very carefully?

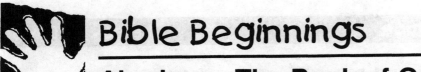

Bible Beginnings

Abraham: The Book of Genesis

♥ Bible Love Lesson ♥

Does God know where you live? If you move to another house or another state, will He know where you are? YES! God is everywhere and He knows everything. He **especially** loves you and cares about you no matter where you are.

Bible Story: Abram Moves to a New Land

 Key Points

❖ Abram loved God.

❖ God told Abram to move to a new country.

❖ Abram listened to God and trusted Him to show him the way to the new land.

❖ Abram obeyed what God said.

There is a story in the Bible about a man named Abram. His wife's name was Sarai. Many people did not worship the one true God where Abram lived. But Abram loved God.

Abram was seventy-five years old. He had many **possessions**. He and Sarai had a nice home. They had many servants. It was a **comfortable** life.

One day God said to Abram, "I want you to move to a new country. I will show you where it is."

Abram believed and **trusted** God. He obeyed God. So Abram took Sarai and his **nephew**, Lot. He also took his servants. They packed all of the things that belonged to them. They then left to go to a new land and home.

Word and Phrase Meanings

especially:	you are very special
possessions:	things that belong to you
comfortable:	to be able to have the things you need and want
trusted:	to know and believe that God will do what He said
nephew:	a brother's son
spheres:	earth; planets in the universe
wrought:	made

Guided Prayer Thought

Thank You God, for taking care of us, just as You took care of Abram. Help us to believe and trust in You.
Amen

Questions: Thinking & Remembering

1. What was the name of the man who loved God?
   Abram

2. How old was Abram?
   seventy-five years old

3. What was his wife's name?
   Sarai

4. Did all of the people worship God in Abram's country?
   No.

5. Were Sarai and Abram comfortable where they lived?
   Yes. They had a nice home and servants.

6. What did God ask Abram to do?
   move to a new country

7. What did God say He would do?
   show him where it was

8. Did Abram ask God many questions about the new land?
   No. He believed and trusted God. (this is an inference question, so help the children if needed.)

9. Whom did Abram take with him?
   his wife Sarai, Lot, and his servants

10. What else did he take?
   the things that belonged to them (possessions)

 ## Bible Words To Remember

Is anything too hard for the Lord? Genesis 18:14

...God is with you in all that you do. Genesis 21:22

O Lord God, please give me success this day. Genesis 24:12

Praise Hymn

Sing or say these words
Resource: My First Hymnal Pg. 65

THIS IS MY FATHER'S WORLD

This is my Father's world,
And to my listening ears
All nature sings,
and round me rings
The music of the **spheres.**
This is my Father's world;
I rest me in the thought
Of rocks and trees,
of skies and seas
His hand the wonders **wrought.**

♥ Bible Love Lesson ♥

Abram and Sarai left their family and friends to go where God told them to go.
They would miss the people they loved, but they knew that they did not
need to be afraid or lonely--God loved them! He would be
with them wherever they were. God loves you, too!

Bible Story: A Long Journey

Key Points

❖ Abram knew God would show him the way to his new home.

❖ It was a long journey to the land where God wanted them to live in.

❖ God said that this land would belong to Abram's family.

❖ Abram thanked God for taking him to a new land.

Abram didn't have a map, but he believed God. He knew that God would show him the way. They started on a long **journey**.

They walked and walked. It took them many days, but they just kept going until God would tell them where the new home would be. Finally, they came to the new country. God said, "This is the land I will give to you and your children."

The first thing Abram did was to take stones and put them in a big pile to make an **altar**. He prayed to God by the altar. He said, "Thank You, God, for showing me this new land."

Word and Phrase Meanings

journey: a long trip

altar: a place to worship and thank God

Guided Prayer Thought

Thank You God, for our homes. We know that wherever our home is, You will be there with us.
Amen

Questions:
Thinking & Remembering

1. Did Abram have a map to show him the way?
   No. He knew that God would show him.

2. Were they taking a short journey?
   No. It would be a long journey.

3. How were they going to get to where they were going?
   walking

4. Who was leading them to this new land?
   God

5. Who spoke to Abram when they came to the new country?
   God spoke to him

6. To whom did God say this land would be given?
   to Abram and his children

7. What was the first thing Abram did?
   He made an altar.

8. What did Abram say to God?
   "Thank You."

 # Bible Words To Remember

Is anything too hard for the Lord? Genesis 18:14

. . .God is with you in all that you do. Genesis 21:22

O Lord God, please give me success this day. Genesis 24:12

Choosing God's Way

Believing God

There are some days when you wake up and things don't go 'just right'. A little thing might be that your mom makes hot cereal and you wanted pancakes. A big thing might be that your dog is very sick and has to go to the veterinarian. You need faith--believing God that He will be with you is important.

Does everything go 'just right' every day?
What will help you that is important to remember?

♦ Bible Love Lesson ♥

Do your parents sometimes make a promise and it seems like a long time before it comes true? Sometimes it can feel like you have waited and waited for hours or days. But you know that your parents love you and will do what they said they would do. Abram and Sarai had to wait a long time when God promised them that they would have a baby. But they knew God loved them and that He would keep His promise. God loves you and He will never stop loving you. He keeps His promises!

Bible Story: A New Land, A New Home

 Key Points

❖ Abram and Sarai obeyed God.

❖ God gave Abram and Sarai many things.

❖ Abram and Sarai were sad because they did not have any children.

❖ God kept His promise to make them a great family. They had a son.

Abram and Sarai loved and obeyed God. They were in a new land and worked to build their home. God was pleased and God **blessed** them with **plenty** of land and animals.

But Abram and Sarai were sad. They did not have any children. God promised that they would have a baby boy. God told Abram that someday there would be as many people in his family as there were stars in the sky!

God also gave Abram and Sarai new names. Their new names were Abraham and Sarah.

Abraham and Sarah waited a long time. God did not forget His promise. Abraham and Sarah had a baby boy and named him Isaac. Now they were very glad.

── Word and Phrase Meanings ──

blessed: giving of good things

plenty: many or a lot of something

Guided Prayer Thought

Dear God, Sometimes it is hard to wait. Help us to remember that You will always keep Your promises.
Amen

Questions:
Thinking & Remembering

1. Abram and Sarai _loved_ and _obeyed_ God.

2. What work did they do in the new land they lived in?
   they built a home

3. Was God pleased with Abram and Sarai?
   Yes

4. With what things did God bless them?
   land and animals

5. Why were Abram and Sarai sad?
   they did not have any children

6. What had God promised?
   that they would have as many in their family as there were stars in the sky

7. What new names did God give Abram and Sarai?
   Abraham, Sarah

8. Why do you think they might have wondered if God forgot His promise?
   they had to wait a long time before they had a baby

9. Did God forget His promise?
   No. They had a baby boy.

10. What did they name the boy baby?
    Isaac

 # Bible Words To Remember

Is anything too hard for the Lord? Genesis 18:14

...God is with you in all that you do. Genesis 21:22

O Lord God, please give me success this day. Genesis 24:12

Choosing God's Way

God's Plans are the Best

Thinking about what you will do and when you will do it happens a lot! There are so many things to do! There are things we must do. There are things we want to do. There are things God says to do---this is the most important. God plans the very best for you!

What are your plans?
Are there many things that you can choose to do?
Who knows what is the very best for us?

❤ Bible Love Lesson ❤

Isn't it wonderful to be inside your house and feel **safe** with your parents who love you so much? God gave you moms and dads to make peanut butter sandwiches and read you stories and love you! It was all in God's plan--tell God that you love Him for making a plan for your happy home.

Bible Story: A Happy Family

Key Points

❖ Abraham, Sarah and Isaac were a happy family.

❖ They lived in a tent house that could move to where the grass was green for the animals.

❖ They had a happy home because they loved God.

❖ Abraham, Sarah, and Isaac loved each other.

Abraham and Sarah were very happy. God had given them a son and now they were a **family**. They lived in a tent house. It was a special tent made from strong cloth from the wool of sheep. It was large enough for Abraham, Sarah, and Isaac.

When Abraham's sheep ate all the grass where their tent was, they would move their tent to a new place to give the animals more green grass to eat.

Isaac loved his tent home. He knew that they had a happy home because they loved God. They were a happy family because they loved each other.

⸺ Word and Phrase Meanings ⸺

safe: a place where you will not get hurt

success: to turn out well

family: parents, children, grandchildren, etc.

Guided Prayer Thought

Thank You God, for happy homes. Help us to love You and love each other in a special way.
Amen

Questions:
Thinking & Remembering

1. What do we know about Abraham and Sarah from the story?
   They were very happy.

2. What had God given them?
   a son

3. Where did Abraham, Sarah and Isaac live?
   in a tent house

4. What was the tent made from?
   strong cloth from the wool of sheep

5. Was the tent large or small?
   it was large

6. When did they move their tent?
   when the animals needed new grass to eat

7. Was Isaac happy in his home?
   Yes

8. Why were they happy?
   because they loved God

9. How did they feel about each other?
   they loved each other

10. How can you make your home happy?
    by loving each other

 # Bible Words To Remember

Is anything too hard for the Lord? Genesis 18:14

. . .God is with you in all that you do. Genesis 21:22

O Lord God, please give me **success** this day. Genesis 24:12

Choosing God's Way

Careful Plans

God wants you to enjoy every day He gives to you. God cares about your plans, too!

What does God want for you?
Does God care about your plans

❤ Bible Love Lesson ❤

Do you ever have a hard job to do? Maybe your mom asks you to pick up all your toys or says, "Please color inside the lines." Just because it might be difficult to do, doesn't mean that she dosen't love you. Some things are important to do, even if it seems hard. God knows that you will learn from doing things that you have never done before. If everything you tried to do were easy, it would stop being fun.
God loves you and wants you to learn and grow!

Bible Story: Finding a Wife for Isaac

Key Points

❖ Abraham's servant traveled far away to find the right girl for Isaac to marry.

❖ God's angel helped the servant know which girl to choose.

❖ God answered the servant's prayer to help him choose.

❖ Rebekah went with the servant to marry Isaac.

Abraham's **trusted servant** was given a hard job to do! Abraham asked him to **journey** back to the land where Abraham's family lived. He wanted him to find a wife for Isaac his son. Isaac would be the beginning of a great family with many, many people. It was important that the woman Isaac married loved and believed in God.

The servant said, "Maybe the woman will not come back with me to **marry** Isaac." Abraham said, "God will send His angel with you to find this special woman for my son Isaac."

The servant came to the place Abraham told him. He prayed, "Lord, help me find the right wife for my master. Let the young woman who gives me a drink and offers to give water to my camels be the right one."

God answered the servant's prayer. It happened just as he prayed! The young woman's name was Rebekah. She returned with the servant to be Isaac's wife.

Word and Phrase Meanings

trusted:	someone you know you can depend on
journey:	long trip
marry:	join as husband and wife
servant:	one who serves another

Guided Prayer Thought

Thank You God, for answering our prayers. Help us to remember that You will be with us, even when we have a hard job to do!
Amen

Questions:
Thinking & Remembering

1. What hard job did Abraham's servant have to do?
   find the right wife for Isaac

2. Why was Isaac and the girl he married so important?
   Isaac was the son of God's promise to Abraham

3. Why did the servant need to go to another country to find this wife for Isaac?
   the woman must love God

4. Did the servant think the young woman might not come back with him?
   Yes. He thought she might refuse. (She might say "no".)

5. Did Abraham believe that God would show his servant the right young woman?
   Yes. He believed in God's promise.

6. What did Abraham say to the servant?
   God's angel will go with you to help you

7. When the servant came to the land, what did he do?
   he prayed and asked God to show him the right young woman

8. What was the test for the right young woman?
   she would give him a drink and offer water to his camels

9. Did God answer the servant's prayer?
   Yes

10. What was the young woman's name?
    Rebekah

 ## Bible Words To Remember

Is anything too hard for the Lord? Genesis 18:14

...God is with you in all that you do. Genesis 21:22

O Lord God, please give me success this day. Genesis 24:12

Choosing God's Way

Knowing God Cares

When you have faith in God it means that you believe that He has the best plan ever for you. It is not just a plan for today or tomorrow, but for your whole life! WOW! That's a pretty big plan. It's wonderful to know that God cares that much.

What does God have planned for you?
Who cares the most about your life and what you do?

Isaac, Jacob & Esau: The Book of Genesis

♥ Bible Love Lesson ♥

God always has a perfect plan. He planned for a wonderful world and He has a plan for you in this world! Families are part of God's plan. Love in families is like a picture of God's love. When families love God, loving each other happens in a way that is so special others can see God's love.

Bible Story: Twin Boys

Key Points

❖ God promised that Abraham's family would be great.

❖ Abraham's family would someday be a great nation.

❖ Isaac and Rebekah had twin sons.

❖ The twins were very different from each other.

Rebekah and Isaac loved each other very much. They wanted to have a **family**. God had promised that there would be many people in their family. They would become a great **nation**.

They waited a long time, praying that God would send them a child. Then there was excitement . . . Rebekah was not going to have only one baby, but two! And God told Rebekah that His promise would come true from the baby born second.

The **twins** were born--Esau first, and Jacob second. Esau was born with lots of hair all over. Jacob had very smooth skin. As they grew older, their parents could see that they were very different in other ways. Esau loved to hunt with his father and Jacob liked to stay at home and work in the garden.

Isaac and Rebekah loved their twin boys and **taught** them about God. God said, "Your sons will be the **leaders** of two great nations someday."

Word and Phrase Meanings

family: parents, children, grandchildren that makes a group of people

nation: group of people living together in the same land or country

twins: two babies born on the same day

taught: to teach and instruct

leader: someone who guides others

Guided Prayer Thought

Thank You God, for my family. Help us to always love each other and be kind to one another.
Amen

Questions:
Thinking & Remembering

1. Who were the two people who loved each other?
   Isaac and Rebekah

2. What did they want to have?
   a family (children)

3. What was special about this family that came from Abraham?
   God promised that they would have many people in their family and be a great nation some day.

4. Why was there excitement?
   Rebekah was going to have two babies (twins)

5. Who was born first?
   Esau

6. Who was born second?
   Jacob

7. From which boy would God's promise come true?
   Jacob, the second son

8. How were the twin boys different from each other?
   Esau was hairy and liked to hunt. Jacob had smooth skin and liked to be at home.

9. What did Isaac and Rebekah teach their boys?
   They taught them about God.

10. What did God tell Isaac and Rebekah?
    that the boys would each be leaders of two great nations

Bible Words To Remember

The Lord said, "I am with you and will keep you wherever you go."
Genesis 28:15

I will trust and not be afraid.   Isaiah 12:2

Praise Hymn

Sing or say these words
Resource: My First Hymnal Pg. 42

FOR HEALTH AND STRENGTH

For health and strength
and daily food,
We praise Thy name,
O Lord.

❤ Bible Love Lesson ❤

God did not make anyone else **exactly** like you. He made you to be very special.
In the Bible there is a story about two brothers that were very different. They
had the same parents and they were even born on the same day. But they
looked different and they liked different things. And that was okay!
God loves everyone the same.

Bible Story: The Inheritance

Key Points

❖ Esau was the first baby born and had first place in the family.

❖ Jacob was the second baby born and he wanted to have the first place.

❖ Jacob got Esau to agree to let him have his right to that place.

❖ Esau thought that eating was more important than being first in the family.

Since Esau was born first into the family of Isaac and Rebekah, he would someday receive all that his father had. Jacob wanted that place in the family. One day he thought of a way to get Esau's place.

When Esau arrived home hungry from hunting all day, Jacob offered to cook a meal for him. But only if Esau would give him the first son's place. Because Esau was so hungry, he **agreed** that he would give him the right to be first place in the family.

Being head, or first, in the family was an important **honor**. Esau did not think of how important it was. Esau would be sorry later that he gave away his right to being first place in the family. He showed that he didn't **value** or care about God's promise.

Word and Phrase Meanings

inheritance:	receiving possessions and being the leader of the family when the father dies; the birthright (inheritance) was given to the oldest son
exactly:	the very same
agreed:	to say "yes" to someone when they ask you something
honor:	having respect
value:	to know that something is very important; to be treasured

Guided Prayer Thought

Dear God, Help us remember what is most important. We want to love You more than anything else.
Amen

Questions:
Thinking & Remembering

1. Who was born first into the family of Isaac and Rebekah?
   Esau

2. What was important about being born first?
   the one born first would receive all that his father had

3. Who wanted the highest place in the family?
   Jacob

4. What kind of work did Esau do?
   he was a hunter

5. What happened one day after Esau had been hunting?
   he came home and was hungry

6. What did Jacob offer to do when Esau came home hungry?
   cook a meal for him

7. What did Jacob want from Esau?
   the first son's place in the family

8. What was most important to Esau--being hungry or his first place in the family?
   being hungry

 Bible Words To Remember

The Lord said, "I am with you and will keep you wherever you go."

Genesis 28:15

I will trust and not be afraid.   Isaiah 12:2

Choosing God's Way

Telling the Truth

Does not *telling the whole truth* seem like the right thing to do sometimes? The evil one, Satan tries to get us to believe that it is. But that is never what God wants us to do. He will help you say what is true.

Who tries to make you believe that telling a lie is right?
Who will help you say only what is true?

❤ Bible Love Lesson ❤

Do you ever like to pretend that you are someone else? Maybe you pretend to be all grown-up and dressup in different or funny clothes. In our story about Jacob and Esau, one of these boys pretends, but this time it really hurt someone because it was a trick to make the father believe something that was not true. Remember that God loves YOU just the way you are. You do not have to pretend, because He knows everything about you already!

Bible Story: Something Not True

 Key Points

❖ When Isaac was old, it was time to give the blessing to his oldest son, Esau.

❖ Rebekah and Jacob tricked Isaac into believing that Jacob was Esau.

❖ Isaac gave his blessing to the youngest instead of the oldest.

❖ When Esau found out what Jacob did, he was angry and the brothers were enemies.

Isaac was very old and was ready to give Esau, his oldest son, the blessing that came with being born first.

Rebekah wanted Jacob to receive the blessing, so she thought of a plan to **trick** Isaac. She told Jacob what they would do, and he agreed. Jacob put skins of animals on his hands so that he would feel hairy like Esau. Then they made a stew like Esau would make to give the father, Isaac. Jacob **pretended** to be Esau!

Isaac was very old and could not see clearly. He gave the **blessing** to Jacob, the younger son instead of Esau, the oldest. He gave the special promise to Jacob to be the head of the family.

When Esau came back from hunting to bring his father food, he found out that Jacob had **tricked** his father Isaac. The blessing had already been given. It could not be taken back.

Esau was angry and hated his brother. He said, "I will kill Jacob for doing this!"

The brothers were now enemies. The family that once had happy times together was afraid and sad.

— Word and Phrase Meanings —

pretend:	to make believe that something is true that is not
tricked:	to not tell the truth
blessing:	giving special favor (kindness) to someone
value:	to know that something is very important; to be treasured

Guided Prayer Thought

Dear God, We know that You love us very much . . . even when we do the wrong thing. Jacob did want the right thing--the blessing--but he got it in the wrong way. Help us to always ask You to know what is right.
Amen

Questions:
Thinking & Remembering

1. Had Jacob already tricked his brother into giving him the first son's place?
   Yes

2. How did Jacob and his mother, Rebekah, plan for Jacob to get the father's blessing?
   Jacob put skins of animals on his arms so he would feel like Esau, and Rebekah made a stew that would be like Esau's

3. What word do you use when you are trying to be like someone else?
   pretend

4. Why did this plan work?
   Isaac was old and could not see clearly

5. What did he give to Jacob that should have been Esau's?
   the blessing for the oldest son

6. What happened when Esau returned from hunting?
   he was angry that the blessing had been given to Jacob

7. What did he say he would do?
   kill Jacob

8. Do you remember what Esau had done in our first story to cause all of this to happen?
   *he did not **value** (care about) the right to be first in the family*

9. What had Jacob done wrong?
   he had lied and cheated

10. Did the brother's love each other?
    No, they were enemies

 # Bible Words To Remember

The Lord said, "I am with you and will keep you wherever you go."
Genesis 28:15

I will trust and not be afraid.   Isaiah 12:2

Choosing God's Way

Honesty

There may be a time when you will think, "if I do or say this, it will turn out to be the best or the right thing in the end." That will not be God telling you to do that! He will never want you to lie. That will never be God's way.

Is there ever a time that doing the wrong thing will make the right thing happen?
What will God always want you to do?

❤ Bible Love Lesson ❤

Have you ever packed your pajamas and toothbrush in a bag to go and stay overnight with a grandma or a friend? It may seem like a fun adventure--until it gets dark and you miss your mom and dad. Jacob was all alone when it got dark after he had left his home. He was very **afraid**. But God was there. God loved him and was with him. God loves you and will always be with you, too.

Bible Story: Jacob Leaves His Home

 Key Points

❖ Jacob left to go to another country where he would be *safe* from Esau.

❖ Jacob was lonely as he traveled away from his family.

❖ Jacob thought about God and remembered that God would be with him.

❖ God loved Jacob, even though he had done the wrong thing to get the blessing.

When Rebekah heard Esau say that he would kill Jacob, she knew that Jacob would have to go to another place where Esau could not find him. Isaac agreed to this plan. The **journey** took Jacob back to his mother's country.

Jacob packed and left to go far away from his home. He walked and walked all day. He was very tired when it was nighttime. Jacob didn't have any friends far away from home and there were no beds or places to stay where he was in the **wilderness**. But Jacob remembered that God would take care of him. Jacob loved God.

Word and Phrase Meanings

journey: a long trip

wilderness: desert land that is empty and where food does not grow

safe: a place where you will not get hurt

afraid: a fear (feeling) that you will be hurt

Guided Prayer Thought

Dear God, Sometimes we are afraid at night and feel like we are all alone. We know that You will be there with us.

Amen

Questions:
Thinking & Remembering

1. Why was Jacob leaving his home?
   because Esau was angry and wanted to hurt him

2. Where did Jacob's parents send him?
   to the country where Rebekah's family lived

3. How was he going to get to this place?
   he was going to walk

4. When it was night and Jacob was tired, was there a place to stay?
   No. There were no beds or places to stay in the wilderness.

5. Was Jacob all by himself in the wilderness?
   Yes. There were no other people.

6. What did Jacob remember?
   that God would take care of him

7. Whom did Jacob love?
   God

8. Who will take care of us when we are afraid?
   God

 # Bible Words To Remember

The Lord said, "I am with you and will keep you wherever you go."
Genesis 28:15

I will trust and not be afraid.   Isaiah 12:2

Choosing God's Way

Obeying God

In the Bible story, Jacob and Rebekah thought that it was right to tell a lie to make the right thing happen to get a blessing. God always has a best way. He will always make the best happen without disobedience to His Word.

Who tried to get the right thing to happen in the wrong way?

Will you ever need to disobey God to make the right thing happen?

❤ Bible Love Lesson ❤

When it is quiet at night, it is a good time to just think about God's love for you. You can know that God cares about you and will love you in the darkness of night and He will love you in the daytime sunshine while you are playing. He is a very great God to love you so much!

Bible Story: Jacob's Dream

Key Points

❖ Jacob had an unusual dream when he was sleeping.

❖ God told Jacob that He would take care of him.

❖ God said that Jacob would be able to go back to his home someday.

❖ Jacob wasn't afraid any longer.

Jacob found a nice place to rest on the ground. Then he looked for a flat, smooth rock to use for a pillow. Soon he was fast asleep.

While he was sleeping, Jacob had an **unusual** dream. He dreamed of a ladder that went to heaven. God talked to Jacob. He said, "I will take care of you. I will be with you wherever you go. I will take you back home safely."

Then Jacob woke up from his dream. He felt very **safe**. He thought, "God talked to me! Even though I am far from home, I don't need to be **afraid**. God will be with me."

Word and Phrase Meanings

unusual:	different or uncommon--not the same as always
trust:	to know and believe that God will do what He said
safe:	a place where you will not get hurt
afraid:	a fear (feeling) that you will get hurt

Guided Prayer Thought

*Thank You God, for being with us always. Help us not to be afraid and to **trust** in You.*
Amen

Questions:
Thinking & Remembering

1. Where did Jacob find a place to rest?
   on the ground

2. What did he use for a pillow?
   a flat, smooth rock

3. What happened after Jacob was asleep?
   he had a dream

4. What did he see in his dream?
   a ladder going to heaven

5. Who talked to Jacob?
   God

6. What did God say to him?
   "I will take care of you. I will be with you wherever you go."

7. How did Jacob feel when he woke up from his dream?
   very safe

8. What did he think about and know?
   that he didn't need to be afraid because God was with him

 # Bible Words To Remember

The Lord said, "I am with you and will keep you wherever you go."
Genesis 28:15

I will trust and not be afraid.   Isaiah 12:2

Choosing God's Way

Truthfulness

Remember to believe what God says and believe that He will make it happen. He won't ask you to be untruthful. He wants you to be honest and tell what is true.

What should you remember?
What does God want you to do?

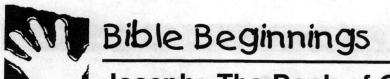
❤ Bible Love Lesson ❤

It is wonderful to feel special . . . to know that you are loved in an **extraordinary** way.
God loves you that way, too! He does not just decide to love you if He feels like it,
or just when you are good, or just if you are pretty or handsome. God loves
you all the time. God *is* love! God is perfect!

Bible Story: Jacob Returns to His Home

 Key Points

❖ Jacob lived far from home for many years. Now he was going back!

❖ Jacob and Esau met each other. Esau was no longer angry.

❖ Jacob had many sons, but one was very special to him. His name was Joseph.

❖ God was keeping His promise to make this family a great nation.

Jacob and his family were **returning** to his home. He had been away so long! Many things had happened to help Jacob know how much God loved him. He had married and had many sons and daughters.

But before Jacob went home he knew he would see his brother Esau. Did Esau still want to kill him? Was he still angry? Jacob was afraid, but an angel of God told Jacob that God would **protect** him. When Esau and Jacob saw each other, they only remembered that they were brothers. They hugged each other and Jacob gave Esau gifts.

One of Jacob's sons was very special to him. His name was Joseph. The Bible tells how God cared for him and kept him safe to do a very important job.

God had a special plan for this family to make His people, the Israelites strong. He wanted them to understand that He had **chosen** them and that He loved them. From this family there would be a great **nation.**

Word and Phrase Meanings

extraordinary:	more than usual; very special
returning:	to come back to
protect:	to keep safe from harm
chosen:	to decide between more than one group or more than one thing
nation:	group of people living together in the same land or country
wondrous:	wonderful and amazing
rejoices:	celebrate with joy and happiness
countless:	a great many, too many to count

Guided Prayer Thought

Thank You God, for our homes and the love of our mom's and dad's.
Help us to be good workers in our homes and help our parents.
Amen

Questions:
Thinking & Remembering

1. Where were Jacob and his family returning?
   to the home where Jacob had lived when he was a boy

2. What had happened to Jacob since he had left his home?
   he had married and had children

3. Whom was Jacob afraid to see and why?
   Esau had wanted to kill him because Jacob had taken the birthright and blessing from him. (see lesson 7, day 4)

4. Who told Jacob that God would protect him?
   an angel of the Lord

5. What happened when the brothers met?
   they hugged each other

6. Which son was very special to Jacob?
   Joseph

7. Whom had God chosen to be his special people?
   the Israelites

8. What important plan did God have for this family?
   they would become a great nation

 # Bible Words To Remember

May the Lord watch between you and me when we are
absent one from another. Genesis 31:49

Praise Hymn

Sing or say these words
Resource: My First Hymnal Pg. 40

NOW THANK THEE WE ALL OUR GOD
Now thank we all our God,
with heart and hands and voices.
Who **wondrous** things hath done,
In whom His world **rejoices**;
Who, from our mother's arms,
Hath blessed us on our way,
With **countless** gifts of love,
And still is ours today.

❤ Bible Love Lesson ❤

Do you like getting a special gift? When someone gives you a gift, it means that they thought about you and care for you. It makes you feel loved. God gives us many good gifts, but the greatest and most wonderful gift is Jesus. Jesus came to show us God's love. It is a gift of love that is yours always! It will never break or get old.

Bible Story: A Special Coat

 Key Points

❖ Joseph was a good son. He helped his father and obeyed.

❖ Jacob gave Joseph a very beautiful coat.

❖ Joseph's brothers were jealous because he received such a special gift.

❖ The brothers wanted Jacob to love them in the same way.

The family in which Joseph lived was very busy. There was so much work to do! They were shepherds and had many animals to take care of and feed each day. They took the animals to a stream of water each day to get a drink. Joseph and his little brother, Benjamin, stayed at home with their father, Jacob, while the older brothers took care of the animals out in the field.

Joseph was a good helper at home. He **obeyed** his father and took food to his brothers.

One day Joseph's father said, "You are a good boy and I want to give you something special." Jacob gave Joseph a beautiful coat with many colors. Joseph was very happy. He said, "Thank you, Father!" Joseph was surprised that his older brothers did not seem happy when he showed them his new coat. They were **jealous** and angry. They wanted their father to love them as much as he loved Joseph.

Word and Phrase Meanings

jealous: wanting what someone else has

obeyed: to do what is asked of you

Guided Prayer Thought

Dear God, Sometimes someone gets something that we want for ourselves. Help us to know that Your love is more important than anything we can have given to us. Help us to be happy when others receive gifts.
Amen

Questions:
Thinking & Remembering

1. What work did Jacob's family do?
   cared for animals (they were called shepherds)

2. What did Joseph and Benjamin do?
   stayed at home with their father

3. How did Joseph please his father?
   He was a good helper and obeyed him.

4. What did he take to his brothers?
   food

5. What did Joseph's father tell him he was going to do?
   give him something special

6. What special gift did Jacob give Joseph?
   a beautiful coat with many colors

7. Was Joseph happy with the new coat?
   Yes

8. Who was not happy about the coat?
   Joseph's older brothers

9. How did they feel?
   angry

10. Why did they feel this way?
    They wanted their father to love them as much as he loved Joseph.

 # Bible Words To Remember

May the Lord watch between you and me when we are

absent one from another.   Genesis 31:49

Choosing God's Way

Being Sorry

There are three important words to say when you have hurt someone or have done something wrong. The words are, "I am sorry." It is also important that you include "I" ---- just saying "sorry" does not really show that you feel responsible. Being sorry also means that you will not do it again.

What are the three important words you can say when you have hurt someone or done something wrong?
How hard is it for you to say those words?
When you are sorry, what does that mean?

❤ Bible Love Lesson ❤

Wanting what someone else has can get you into trouble. Enjoy the things you already have and be glad for what you have. God always knows what is best for you and He wants you to be **content**. Most of all, remember how much you are loved!

Bible Story: Dreams

Key Points

❖ Joseph had strange dreams that he shared with his family.

❖ The dreams made the brothers angry because they told of Joseph being great.

❖ Joseph took food to his brothers while they were taking care of the sheep.

❖ The brothers thought that this was their chance to get rid of their 'dreamer' brother because the father was not there to protect him.

Joseph often had **dreams** that he did not understand. He told these dreams to his brothers and father. In one of his dreams, he dreamed that the sun, moon and eleven stars bowed down to him. The brothers were very angry. They said, "Does this mean that you will **rule over** us?"

One day Joseph was sent by his father to take food to his brothers who were out tending the sheep. When his brothers saw him coming, they said to each other, "This is our chance to get rid of this dreamer!"

They took off Joseph's coat with the many colors and threw Joseph into a deep hole in the ground. They planned to leave him there to die.

— Word and Phrase Meanings —

content: happy and satisfied

dream: what happens in your mind while you are sleeping

rule over: to be a leader having power over others making important decisions

absent: to be away from someone; you cannot see them or be with them

Guided Prayer Thought

Dear God, We know that sometimes bad things happen. Joseph must have been scared when he was in the bottom of that hole. He must have been sad, too, because his brothers did not love him. But we know that You will take care of us because You love us.

Amen

Questions:
Thinking & Remembering

1. What did Joseph not understand?
   his dreams

2. Whom did he tell these dreams to?
   his brothers and father

3. What was one of his dreams?
   that the sun, moon and eleven stars bowed down to him (the mother, father and brothers)

4. How did the brothers feel about this dream?
   they were angry

5. What did they think the dream meant?
   that Joseph would rule over them

6. What did the brothers say when they saw Joseph coming to them in the fields?
   "We will get rid of this dreamer."

7. What did they take from Joseph?
   his coat of many colors

8. What did they do with Joseph?
   They threw him into a deep hole in the ground and left him to die.

 # Bible Words To Remember

May the Lord watch between you and me when we are

absent one from another. **Genesis 31:49**

Choosing God's Way

Caring

Think about hearing the words "I am sorry" when someone has hurt you. Because you have done wrong things and know that it is sometimes hard to say those words will help you love and understand others.

Do the words "I am sorry" help start to make everything right?
What makes it easier to understand others?

❤ Bible Love Lesson ❤

There may be a time when you think your brother or sister does not love you. They may
be mean and unkind. Sometime you may even think your friend does not like you.
But even when people are unkind, you can still know that God loves you. He
will know when you feel sad and lonely and He will help you think of Him
and remember that He loves you more than anybody!

Bible Story: God Cares

Key Points

❖ Joseph's brothers put
him in a deep black hole.
He could not escape.

❖ God would not let Joseph
die. He had a special
plan for him.

❖ Joseph's brothers
decided to sell him to be
a slave in Egypt.

❖ The brothers told their
father that Joseph had
been killed.

Joseph is in an awfully difficult **situation**! He's in a deep, black
hole while his brothers are eating their lunch! But God had a plan
for Joseph. God would take care of him.

The brothers paid no attention to Joseph's cries for help. But they
did notice some travelers coming toward them. They had an idea.
The men were traveling toward Egypt---far away from Joseph's
father and his home. They could sell Joseph as a **slave** and get
some money!

So they sold Joseph to the men for twenty pieces of **silver**. They
took the colorful coat and put the blood of an animal on it. When
they took the coat back to their father, he thought that Joseph had
been killed by a wild animal. Jacob was very sad.

Word and Phrase Meanings

situation:	place
slave:	someone who works hard and is not free to do what he or she wants to do
silver:	an amount of money; payment

Guided Prayer Thought

Dear God, Thank You for taking care of us when it is dark and scary and we think that no one cares about us. We thank You for loving us.
Amen

Questions:
Thinking & Remembering

1. What happened to Joseph?
   his brothers put him in a deep, black hole

2. What did his brothers do after they put him there?
   they ate their lunch

3. Did God know Joseph was in trouble?
   Yes

4. Did God care that Joseph was scared?
   Yes

5. Did the brothers feel sorry for Joseph when he cried for help?
   No

6. Who did they see coming?
   men who were traveling

7. Where were the travelers going?
   to Egypt

8. What did the brothers decide to do?
   to sell Joseph as a slave to these men

9. How much money did they sell Joseph for?
   twenty pieces of silver

10. What did they do with Joseph's coat?
    they put blood on it and took it to their father

11. What did the father think had happened to Joseph?
    that he had been killed by a wild animal

12. How did Jacob feel?
    very sad

 # Bible Words To Remember

May the Lord watch between you and me when we are

absent one from another. Genesis 31:49

Choosing God's Way

Forgiveness

God wants you to forgive--- that means saying, "That's okay, you are still my friend." You can always ask God to help you forgive.

What can you say when someone tells you "I am sorry?" Who will help you forgive someone who has hurt you?

❤ Bible Love Lesson ❤

There are so many things to understand! Grown-up people tell you what to do and you wonder why some things are so important---like eating all your vegetables, and going to bed before everyone else. But because your parents love you, they know what is best for you. It's hard to understand, but someday you will. Right now just know that they love you and God loves you, too!

Bible Story: Joseph Becomes a Ruler in Egypt

 Key Points

❖ The king in Egypt had a dream he did not understand.

❖ God helped Joseph tell the king what his dream meant.

❖ The dreams meant that no rain would come for a long time.

❖ Joseph helped the king save food for this time and save his family.

❖ Joseph forgave his brothers for selling him as a slave.

The **Pharaoh** in Egypt had a **dream**. He asked all of his **wise men** to tell him what it meant, but they could not **understand** or find the **meaning** of the king's dream. Finally, Joseph was asked to tell him the meaning of this strange dream.

God gave Joseph the meaning of Pharaoh's **dream**. Soon the time would come when no food would grow in the land. There would be time in the next seven years to gather and store enough food to take care of the people before this happened. Pharaoh was pleased with Joseph and gave him gifts. He made him **ruler** over many things. And this is how Joseph's dream when he was a boy came true. His brothers came and bowed before him when there was no food in the land. They had to buy from the ruler in Egypt. The ruler was their own brother, Joseph!

Joseph forgave his brothers and sent for his father to come and live in Egypt.

Word and Phrase Meanings

Pharaoh:	a king; ruler of a country
meaning:	to explain something so it can be understood
dream:	what happens in your mind while sleeping
understand:	to know the reason why
wise men:	those who study and know many things
ruler:	to be in charge of other people and tell them what to do

Guided Prayer Thought

Dear God, We know that You will make everything work out, just as You planned. Even when bad things happen, You will turn it into good!
Help us to trust in You.
Amen

Questions:
Thinking & Remembering

1. What happened to the Pharaoh in Egypt while he was sleeping?
   he had a dream

2. Whom did he ask first to tell him what his dream meant?
   wise men

3. Could the wise men tell Pharaoh what the dream meant?
   No

4. Who was asked to come and tell the king about this strange dream?
   Joseph

5. What did Joseph tell Pharaoh the dream meant?
   that there would be a time when no food would grow in the land

6. How many years did they have to get ready before this happened?
   seven years

7. Did the dream Joseph told his brothers about when he was a boy come true?
   Yes

8. Did Joseph forgive his brothers for the wrong they did to him?
   Yes

 Bible Words To Remember

May the Lord watch between you and me when we are

absent one from another.   Genesis 31:49

Choosing God's Way

Working Things Out

Forgiving is sometimes even harder than saying "I'm sorry". God wants us to care about each other in a way that we will try to work things out instead of being angry.

What can be harder sometimes than saying "I'm sorry"? What does God want us to do?

Moses: The Book of Exodus

♥ Bible Love Lesson ♥

Even though you are still a child, sometimes your mother says, "You're so **strong**!"
God made your body wonderful to do many things. He wants you to be strong
so you can run and jump and help your parents. God loves you and will
give you strength to do what He wants you to do.

Bible Story: Living In Egypt

Key Points

❖ Jacob's family lived in Egypt for a long time. Soon there were many people!

❖ God gave these people a special name. They were called the children of Israel, or Israelites.

❖ The new king in Egypt did not like Joseph and the children of Israel. He made them slaves.

❖ God helped His people stay strong.

For a very long time, the people from Jacob's family lived in Egypt. There were many people from that family and they were called the children of Israel (Israelites). God gave them that special name.

The Pharaoh who had known Joseph died and there were other kings that ruled. These kings did not remember all the good things Joseph had done in saving their people from **starving** when there was no food in the land.

The king who was ruling in Egypt said, "There are too many of these people. I will make them my slaves and **force** them to work hard so they will not be strong." But the children of Israel did not become weak. They just became stronger. God was with them.

Word and Phrase Meanings

strong: to have power or energy

starving: to be very hungry

preserves: to keep safe from danger

force: to make someone do something they don't want to do

Holy: blessed, sacred, pure

Almighty: our God who has the power to do anything

Mighty: having great power or strength; very great

Trinity: the unity of God the Father, God the Son, and God the holy Spirit in one.

"I AM WHO I AM": The name God gives Himself. This means that God always was and
always will be--forever and ever!

Guided Prayer Thought

Thank You God, for being with Your people and making them strong.
No one--not even a king on earth can be greater than You!
Amen

Questions:
Thinking & Remembering

1. Who lived in Egypt?
   the people from Jacob's family

2. What were these people called?
   the children of Israel

3. Who gave them this special name?
   God

4. What did the king not remember?
   the good things Joseph had done

5. What had Joseph done in Egypt?
   he helped save the people from starving when there was no food

6. What did the king say about the children of Israel?
   "There are too many."

7. What plan did he have for keeping them from being strong?
   he made them slaves and work very hard

8. Did his plan work?
   No. They became stronger.

9. Who was with them?
   God

Bible Words To Remember

The Lord **preserves** all who love Him.　Psalm 145:20

God said, "**I AM WHO I AM.**"　Exodus 3:14

"I will certainly be with you."　Exodus 3:12

Praise Hymn

Sing or say these words
Resource: My First Hymnal Pg. 64

HOLY, HOLY, HOLY

Holy, Holy, Holy,
Lord, God **Almighty**!
Early in the morning
our song shall rise to Thee.
Holy, Holy, Holy!
Merciful and **Mighty**!
God in three Persons,
blessed **Trinity**!

❤ Bible Love Lesson ❤

When you were just a tiny baby, your mother held you in her arms and wanted to always keep you safe. God planned for your mother and father to love with this special love. He wanted you to be protected in the very best way. God will love you and **protect** you--even when your parents are not with you. God is your wonderful Heavenly Father!

Bible Story: A Baby Boy

Key Points

❖ Because God's people were so strong, the king was angry.

❖ The king wanted to kill all the baby boys.

❖ A family thought of a plan to save their baby boy.

❖ God protected the baby who was named Moses by the princess who found him.

The wicked king in Egypt was angry. He had tried to make the Israelites weak by making them work hard. But there were more and more of them. And they were strong! The king **ordered** that all of the baby boys who were Israelites be killed.

There was a family who loved their baby boy very much. The mother thought of a plan. First, she hid the baby for as long as she could. She loved him and took good care of him very quietly. Then, she made a special basket bed that would float on the water. Carefully she laid her precious baby into the basket and took it to the river. The baby's sister stayed close by in the bushes to watch and see what would happen.

Soon, the princess who was the wicked king's daughter, came down to the river with her maids. She listened--yes, she did think that she heard a baby crying. The princess and her maidens **discovered** the beautiful baby boy inside the basket. The princess wanted to keep this baby as her own! This baby's name was Moses. God was taking care of this baby.

Word and Phrase Meanings

ordered:	to tell what to do
discovered:	to find
protect:	to keep safe from harm
I AM WHO I AM:	the name God gives Himself

Guided Prayer Thought

Dear God, Thank You for mothers and fathers who care for us.
You are a wonderful God to give us families who love us.
Amen

Questions:
Thinking & Remembering

1. Why was the king in Egypt angry?
   the people of Israel were strong

2. What was the king's order?
   that all of the baby boys be killed

3. How did one mother plan to save her baby?
   she hid him for as long as she could

4. What did she do after hiding him?
   she made a basket bed that would float on the water

5. Who stayed close by in the bushes to watch?
   the baby's sister

6. Who came to the river?
   the princess and her maids

7. What sound did she hear?
   a baby crying

8. What did the princess want to do?
   keep the baby as her own

9. What was the baby's name?
   Moses

10. Who was taking care of Moses?
    God

 # Bible Words To Remember

The Lord preserves all who love Him. Psalm 145:20

God said, "**I AM WHO I AM.**" Exodus 3:14

"**I will certainly be with you.**" Exodus 3:12

Choosing God's Way

Being Sensitive

Being sensitive is trying to understand how someone else feels. There are many times when we all feel like we need a little extra love. You want someone to notice that you are sad.

What does it mean to be sensitive?
Do you ever feel like you need an extra hug?
How can you show someone some extra love when they are sad?

❤ Bible Love Lesson ❤

God always wants you to work hard and do your very best. Saying "I can't" is like saying "I won't"! God can help you because He loves you and His promise is that He will be with you. He is with you when you choose to obey your parents when your friend is telling you not to. Don't give up, know that you can do it if you try!

Bible Story: God's Leader

Key Points

❖ God had a special plan for Moses.

❖ God talked to Moses from a burning bush.

❖ God told Moses to take His people away from Egypt to their own land.

❖ God promised Moses that He would be with him.

God had a special job for Moses to do. It would be very hard but God would be with him. God told Moses what He wanted him to do in a **strange** way. God's voice came from out of a bush that was full of fire! Moses listened. Could it really be true? Was he hearing a voice from this bush that was on fire, but was not burning up?

The voice said to Moses, "God is talking to you!" Moses was afraid, but he kept listening to the voice of God. God said, "My people are **suffering** in Egypt. I am sending you to the king to tell him to let My people go from that land to a new land to be free to worship Me."

Moses said to God, "The people will not listen to me. I don't think they will believe that You sent me. I don't speak very well. Please send someone else to do this hard thing!" God said, "Moses, I will help you."

Word and Phrase Meanings

strange: very unusual or different from the ordinary

suffering: to experience pain and difficulty

preserves: to keep safe from danger

Guided Prayer Thought

Dear God, Help us to obey You and do what You want us to do, even if it is hard. We know that You will be with us to help us.

Amen

Questions:
Thinking & Remembering

1. God had a special job for Moses to do. Was it easy or hard?
   it was a hard job

2. Who would be with Moses?
   God

3. In what strange way did God talk to Moses?
   in a burning bush

4. What was so unusual about the bush that was on fire?
   it did not burn up

5. What did the voice say to Moses?
   "God is talking to you!"

6. How did Moses feel?
   he was afraid

7. Why did God want Moses to do this job?
   His people were suffering in Egypt

8. What did God want Moses to do?
   tell the king to let the people go to a new land

9. Why did Moses think that God should send someone else?
   He thought that the people wouldn't listen to him. He didn't think the people would believe him. He told God that he didn't speak very well.

10. What did God tell Moses?
    "I will be with you."

 Bible Words To Remember

The Lord **preserves** all who love Him. Psalm 145:20

God said, "I AM WHO I AM." Exodus 3:14

"I will certainly be with you." Exodus 3:12

Choosing God's Way

Feeling Special

There are many people who care when you are feeling sad. Maybe your dad will say, "How about a game of ball outside?" Your mom might notice and say, "Do you want to call Grandma and talk to her?" Grandma and Grandpa can always make you feel special.

Who notices you when you are feeling unhappy?
Does it help to know that there are people who care?

❤ Bible Love Lesson ❤

Isn't it wonderful that you can know who God is? In God's Book, the Bible, God tells you of His power. He tells you that He loves you. He tells you that He will be with you ---and much, much more! I'm glad we can know about God and that we can love Him!

Bible Story: The King Who Said 'No' to God

 Key Points

❖ The king did not want to let the Children of Israel leave Egypt.

❖ He made them work even harder.

❖ God said, "I will keep My promise. My people will leave Egypt."

❖ Many times, the king said "No!" But God showed His power, and the king finally let them go.

The king said, "I don't know who your God is!" Pharaoh was angry that Moses had **disturbed** him with this order that he must let the people of Israel go. He made the slaves work harder.

God said to Moses, "I will keep My promise. Pharaoh and his people will know that I am the God of Israel. When I show My power, the king will obey and let the people out of the land of Egypt."

These are the ten terrible things that happened in Egypt:
One: the water in the rivers turned to blood.
Two: the land was covered with frogs.
Three: the dust all over the land became **lice**.
Four: flies covered all the people and bit them.
Five: the cattle of the Egyptians died.
Six: The Egyptians had terrible sores all over their bodies.
Seven: Thunderstorms **ruined** everything that was outside.
Eight: **Locusts** came and ate all the growing things.
Nine: Egypt was full of darkness for three days.
Ten: the oldest child from each family died.

Ten times the king was given a chance to believe God. Nine times Pharaoh said "No" again and would not let the people go. Finally, when his son died, he knew how powerful God was. He said "Go!"

— Word and Phrase Meanings —

disturbed: bothered; irritated

lice: very small insects

ruined: destroyed

locusts: large grasshoppers

Guided Prayer Thought

Dear God, Help us to believe in Your power and Your love. We know that You will always keep Your promises.
Amen

Questions:
Thinking & Remembering

1. What did the king tell Moses?
   "I do not know who your God is."

2. What did Moses tell the king God wanted him to do?
   to let the people of Israel go out from Egypt

3. What did Pharaoh make the people of Israel do?
   work harder

4. What did God tell Moses about His promise?
   that He would keep His promise

5. What would God show king Pharaoh?
   His power

6. How many terrible things happened in Egypt?
   ten

7. How many times did Pharaoh have a chance to listen and obey God?
   ten

8. How many times did he say "No"?
   nine

9. When did he finally say that the people could go?
   when his son died

10. What did Pharaoh know?
    that God was very powerful

Bible Words To Remember

The Lord preserves all who love Him. Psalm 145:20

God said, "I AM WHO I AM." Exodus 3:14

"I will certainly be with you." Exodus 3:12

Choosing God's Way

God Cares

You can always tell God when you are feeling sad. He will always be with you... and He always loves you.

Who can you tell when you are sad?
Who always loves you and is always with you?

❤ Bible Love Lesson ❤

It is sometimes hard to listen. You want to do things your own way and not have anyone tell you not to do what you want to do. But God wants you to listen. He does not want you to do wrong things or do anything that will hurt you.
God loves you so much!

Bible Story: Leaving Egypt

 Key Points

❖ **Moses led the people out of Egypt. They were going to their own land!**

❖ **When the king came after the people, God showed His power again.**

❖ **God made a dry path across the sea for them to escape.**

❖ **The people thanked God for taking care of them.**

God's people, the Israelites, were ready! They were going to a new land! God would show them the way. They soon came to the Red Sea. But what was the noise they heard? It was Pharaoh and his **army** coming after them! How could God keep His **promise** now, they thought? They were **trapped!**

God told Moses to lift up his **rod** over the sea. Moses obeyed. Immediately the sea opened up and there was dry land to walk across. The people walked to the other side and when they were safe, the waters closed again over Pharaoh and his army.

Moses and the people of Israel sang a song to God. They thanked Him for taking them out of Egypt and saving them from Pharaoh. God always keeps His promises!

Word and Phrase Meanings

army: large group of soldiers

trapped: to be in a place where one cannot get out of

rod: a long straight thick stick or pole made of wood

promise   God always doing what He says He will do

Guided Prayer Thought

Dear God, Thank You for always keeping Your promises. Help us not to worry. We want to believe You and trust You. Help us to listen and obey because we know that You love us and are taking care of us.

Amen

Questions:
Thinking & Remembering

1. Where were God's people ready to go?
   to a new land

2. Who would show them the way?
   God

3. What was the name of the sea they came to?
   the Red Sea

4. What did they hear?
   the noise from Pharaoh and his army coming after them

5. Did they wonder how God could keep His promise?
   Yes. They thought they were trapped.

6. What did God tell Moses to do?
   to lift his rod over the sea

7. When Moses obeyed God's command, what happened?
   the sea opened up and there was dry land to walk on

8. What happened when they were safe on the other side?
   the sea closed up

9. What did the people do to show that they were thankful to God?
   they sang a song to Him

10. Does God always keep His promises?
    Yes

 # Bible Words To Remember

The Lord preserves all who love Him. Psalm 145:20

God said, "I AM WHO I AM." Exodus 3:14

"I will certainly be with you." Exodus 3:12

Choosing God's Way

Concern for Others

Try to notice when a friend or someone you know needs extra love. If your friend is feeling bad, tell them you care. Ask how you can help. Share a smile and a hug.

How can you know if someone needs extra love? What can you do to make a friend feel better?

God's Commandments: The Book of Exodus

❤ Bible Love Lesson ❤

Mom and Dad talk to you in a soft, quiet, loving voice---most of the time. But if you don't hear them or if you choose not to listen, they may have to use a loud voice. God wanted to speak to His people in the Bible in the quiet, loving way, but they would not listen. To get their **attention** he spoke with a lot of noise! Try to listen to your parents--and God when they speak in a still, small, voice. They love you very much and what they say is important.

Bible Story: The Mountain of God

Key Points

❖ **God wanted to speak to His people from a mountain.**

❖ **The people were afraid, because God was so powerful.**

❖ **God told Moses ten important rules for people to follow.**

❖ **God helped the people follow His commandments.**

Soon the people of Israel were **camping** at the foot of a great mountain. This was a very special mountain where God would speak to His people. God told Moses to tell the people to be ready to listen to His word. He was going to tell them some very **important** words.

When the time came for the Lord to speak to His people, there was thunder and lightning and a thick cloud came over the mountain. There was the sound of a trumpet and it was so loud that all the people were frightened! The mountain was covered in smoke and fire and it was shaking. The trumpet sound was longer and louder.

The people begged Moses, "Do not make us stay in this place! We are afraid! We will listen to you tell us what God says." Moses said, "Do not **fear** God, only do what He tells you." God gave Moses ten important **rules** (called commandments) for the people to follow.

Word and Phrase Meanings

attention:	to notice in a special way
important:	something that has value and to think about seriously
camping:	to stay in a place for a short time, usually in tents
fear:	to be afraid of something or somebody
rules:	firm directions (not suggestions) which mean that you must obey
honor:	to show respect and consideration (being thoughtful)
joy:	a feeling of happiness, delight or gladness
full:	completely filled---up to the top!
commandment:	a rule that must be followed

Guided Prayer Thought

Help us to listen to You, God. You love us so much and You know what is right for us to do. We love You through Jesus our Savior.
Amen

Questions:
Thinking & Remembering

1. **Where were the people of Israel camping?**
   at the foot of a great mountain

2. **What happened at this place?**
   God spoke to His people

3. **What were the people supposed to be ready to do?**
   to listen to God's Word

4. **What happened when it was time for the Lord to speak?**
   there was thunder and lightning

5. **What sound did they hear?**
   the sound of a trumpet

6. **What covered the mountain?**
   smoke and fire

7. **What else happened?**
   the mountain was shaking

8. **Why did the people beg Moses to listen for them and tell them what God said?**
   they were afraid

9. **What did Moses tell the people they should do?**
   Obey God. (Do what God tells you to do)

10. **What did God give Moses for the people to follow?**
    ten important rules

 ## Bible Words To Remember

Honor your father and your mother. . . Exodus 20:12

Love God with all your heart and love others as much as you love yourself.
Matthew 22:37; 39

Praise Hymn

Sing or say these words
Resource: My First Hymnal Pg. 71

THIS IS MY COMMANDMENT

This is my **commandment**
that you love one another,
that your **joy** may be **full**.
This is my commandment
that you love one another,
that your joy may be full;
That your joy may be full,
That your joy may be full.

❤ Bible Love Lesson ❤

Because God made us, He knows what will make us happy. We cannot be happy if
we are not loving God, for He made us to love Him. He knows what is best
for us. God tells us in the rules He gave in the Bible how to love Him.

Bible Story: Loving God--God's Rules I

Key Points

❖ **God did many wonderful things for His people.**

❖ **God wants people to love Him and to love each other.**

❖ **Making God most important will help people know how to live.**

❖ **By loving God first, we will be happy.**

God's people had seen Him do many wonderful things. He had saved them from the Egyptians. He had opened up the sea for them to cross over safely to the other side. But God knew that they would need **instructions** to help them love Him and love each other. These are the **rules** God gave on the mountain.

One: You must not worship other gods. That is the first important rule. When we see other people that are great, we can **appreciate** what they do, but remember that they can never be GOD! We only have ONE God.

Two: Do not make **objects** (things) to worship. There are many things that we think about. Sometimes we forget about God and take care of only what will make us happy for a moment . . . like a special toy or something we like to do all the time. It is wrong to make other things more important than God.

Word and Phrase Meanings

instructions:	to tell how to do something
rules:	firm directions
appreciate:	to notice and be thankful for what someone does or for what you have
objects:	things that can be seen and touched

Guided Prayer Thought

Dear God, We know that You only want what is best for us. Help us learn how to love You and teach us to love You and keep You important to us.
Amen

Questions:
Thinking & Remembering

1. **How does God know what will make us happy?**
   He made us

2. **Can we be happy if we are not loving God?**
   No. He made us to love Him.

3. **What does God know?**
   what is best for us

4. **What do God's rules tell us?**
   how to love Him

5. **What is the first important rule?**
   You must not worship other gods.

6. **What will help us remember what this rule means?**
   We only have ONE GOD.

7. **What is the next rule?**
   Do not make objects to worship.

8. **What is important to remember?**
   not to make other things more important than God

 # Bible Words To Remember

Honor your father and your mother. . . Exodus 20:12

Love God with all your heart and love others as much as you love yourself.
Matthew 22:37; 39

Choosing God's Way

Expressing Joy

How do you feel when someone says, "You are dumb." "You can't have that. It's mine!" "I don't like your dress or shirt!" Those are not words that give us joy, are they? Think of words to say that will give others happiness.

What words of joy can you give to someone?
What words do you like to hear?
What words make you feel sad?

♥ Bible Love Lesson ♥

Loving God with all your heart is a special kind of love that you can know and feel inside.
This kind of love does not happen just so you can have what you want. It is a love
that does not stop---it doesn't even matter how you 'feel' because a 'feeling' can go
away, but knowing God and how wonderful He is keeps that love real always!

Bible Story: How to Love God -- God's Rules II

Key Points

❖ God wants us to say His name in love.

❖ God wants us to keep one day special for Him.

❖ God wants us to think about Him and be close to Him.

❖ God wants us to treat our parents with respect.

Three: When you speak God's name, do it with **awe** and **respect**. Do not say God's name unless you do it in love, not in anger. God's name is **holy** and when we truly love Him, we will only want to use His name in a way that shows how much we love Him.

Four: Keep the **Sabbath** day holy. There is one special day every week that we keep different from all the other days. It is a day to rest, as God rested after He completed His creation. It is also to worship God and be close to Him. You can think about how much He loves you and be with others who love Him, too.

Five: **Honor(respect)** your mother and father. God gave you a mother and father to love you and teach you what God wants you to do. They take care of you and show you in a special way part of what God's love is like. When you respect your parents, you are also showing love to God.

Word and Phrase Meanings

awe: wonder and amazement

Sabbath: the day of worship; the seventh day; the day God rested and wants all His creation to rest

holy: blessed, sacred, pure

respect: to think highly of and treat with honor

honor: to show respect and consideration (being thoughtful)

Guided Prayer Thought

Dear God, It is not always easy to follow the rules you gave us.
It is wonderful to know that we don't have to do it by ourselves.
You are always there to help us.
Amen

Questions:
Thinking & Remembering

1. **How should you speak God's name?**
   with awe and respect and in love

2. **When should you not speak God's name?**
   in anger

3. **Why is God's name different from any other name?**
   It is holy. (separated from what is not perfect)

4. **Which day are we to keep holy?**
   the Sabbath day

5. **How is this day different from the other days in the week?**
   it is for rest and worship

6. **What should you remember on this day?**
   how much God loves you and be with others who love Him, too

7. **How should you treat your mother and father?**
   with honor(respect)

8. **When you respect your parents, to whom are you showing love?**
   to God

 # Bible Words To Remember

Honor your father and your mother... Exodus 20:12

Love God with all your heart and love others as much as you love yourself.
Matthew 22:37; 39

Choosing God's Way

Giving Joy

When someone says, "I love you!", "you are my friend", your day is better and brighter. Make someone else's day happy and bright by saying those words.

How do you feel when someone says "I love you!"?
How do you feel when you make someone else happy with these words?

❤ Bible Love Lesson ❤

God wants you to love others. He says in the Bible that you already love yourself. You think that what you want is most important---and you want it now! God says to think about others and care about them more.

Bible Story: Loving Others -- God's Rules III

Key Points

❖ God wants us to care about others and not hurt anyone.

❖ God wants us to think about others more than ourselves.

❖ God wrote the rules on stones and Moses took them to the people.

❖ God gave rules so that people would be happy.

God gave these rules to help us know how to get along with other people and to love one another.

Six: Do not murder. Murder is taking the life of someone for a selfish reason or because you are angry.

Seven: Do not commit adultery. God planned that when a man and woman marry each other, they belong only to each other---always.

Eight: Do not steal. Never take anything that does not belong to you.

Nine: Do not tell lies about others. Telling something that is not true hurts others and is wrong to do.

Ten: Do not **covet**. This means wanting anything that belongs to someone else. When you are not **content** or happy with what God has given you, you become **jealous** of what others have. When you are jealous, you think about 'things' rather than God. Remember what is important.

After God gave Moses these rules (called **commandments**), He put them on two **stone tablets** so the people would know that God had given these laws Himself to show His people how they should live.

Word and Phrase Meanings

covet: to want something in the wrong way

content: to be happy with what you have

jealous: wanting what someone else has

stone tablets: flat pieces of rock on which God wrote the commandments

commandments: rules you must follow

Guided Prayer Thought

We know that You gave us rules, God, so that we would be happy. You made us and love us so much that You want what is best for us.

Amen

Questions:
Thinking & Remembering

1. Why is murder wrong?
   It is taking the life of someone else on purpose.

2. Why does God want a man and woman to belong only to each other?
   Because it is God's perfect plan. When people follow God's plan, they can be happy.

3. When you take something that does not belong to you, what is that called?
   stealing

4. Why is it wrong to tell lies about others?
   It hurts others to tell something that is not true.

5. What does the word 'covet' mean?
   wanting something that belongs to someone else

6. Does God want you to be happy with what you already have?
   Yes

7. When you are feeling jealous, can you be thinking about God?
   No

8. What were these rules written on?
   two stone tablets

 # Bible Words To Remember

Honor your father and your mother. . . Exodus 20:12

Love God with all your heart and love others as much as you love yourself.
Matthew 22:37; 39

Choosing God's Way

Kind Words

Show someone that you care about them. Tell them that God cares about them. Say "I love you" to someone who needs to hear it today. Then tell them that God loves them, too!

When did you say loving and kind words to someone else?
What other words will make someone happy?

❤ Bible Love Lesson ❤

Even though God is sad when you do not follow the rules, He loves you! He keeps loving you and keeps helping you grow and learn each day. Can anyone else love you as much as God? He loves you in a wonderful way!

Bible Story: God Loves His People

Key Points

❖ God did not forget His promise to Abraham that there would be many people from his family.

❖ God did not forget His promise to send a Savior who would take the sadness of sin away.

❖ God promised that His people would be special and He would take care of them.

❖ God always keeps His promises!

God had made a promise many years before the time of Moses. This promise was made to Abraham. God said that He would make this family a great nation. God said that, because of sin in the world, He would send a Savior who would come from this same family. This Savior, or 'Promised One' would take away the sins of the world! What a wonderful **promise**!

God told Moses that He would make a **covenant** (promise) with the people of Israel. He would take care of them and bring them to a new land. They would always be His special people. Moses told the people what God said. Then he told the people what they must do. They must promise to obey God's laws. They said, "We promise to do what God says."

Moses built an **altar** as a reminder of this day and the promises— the promise God made and what they had promised God. We know that God always keeps His promises. Will the people keep their promise to God?

Word and Phrase Meanings

covenant: an agreement; promise

promise: doing what is said will be done

altar: a special place where people prayed to God and remembered Him

---

Guided Prayer Thought

Dear God, Thank You for always keeping Your promises. Help us to love and obey You. You love us so much, You sent our Savior Jesus to take away the sins of the world.
Amen

Questions:
Thinking & Remembering

1. **To whom had God made a promise before the time of Moses?**
   to Abraham

2. **What had God promised?**
   that He would make his family a great nation

3. **Who would take away the sins of the world?**
   a Savior, or Promised One ---Jesus

4. **What did God promise to the people of Israel?**
   that He would take care of them and bring them to a new land

5. **What was their part to do?**
   to obey God's laws

6. **Did the people agree to do this?**
   Yes

7. **What did Moses build as a reminder of this promise?**
   an altar

8. **Does God always keep His promises? Do we always keep promises?**
   God always keeps His promises. People sometimes forget.

 # Bible Words To Remember

Honor your father and your mother. . . Exodus 20:12

Love God with all your heart and love others as much as you love yourself.
Matthew 22:37; 39

Choosing God's Way

Caring for Others

God wants you to care about others. He wants you to show that you care about your parents. Don't forget to treat others in the way you like to be treated.

Is it more important for you to think of yourself...or is it more important for you to make someone else smile? When you make others happy, do you think it will make you happy, too?

Joshua: The Book of Numbers and The Book of Joshua

♥ Bible Love Lesson ♥

God loves you! Does it make you feel special when your mom or dad; sister or brother; teacher or friend chooses YOU to do something important? The Bible tells us that God has made you and has a special plan just for you--- you don't have to wait for Him to say, "I will choose you." He has already chosen you!

Bible Story: Men On a Mission

Key Points

❖ Twelve men went to look at the land God wanted them to live in.

❖ Two men believed God would help them live in the land He gave them.

❖ Ten men were afraid. They said the city was strong and the people were giants.

❖ The people worried and complained. They did not trust God.

Moses chose twelve men to go to the land of Canaan. This was the land God had promised to give to the people of Israel. Moses told the men to **explore** the land and come back with a **report**.

When the men returned, only two of the men were excited. These men were Joshua and Caleb. They said, "The land is beautiful! There are wonderful plants and fruits growing everywhere! Let's go in and take this land God has promised. We are strong and ready. God will help us do this. He has always taken care of us and kept His promises."

The other ten men said, "There are great **giants** in the land! The city has a high wall around it!" These men made the people frightened and all the people started **worrying** and complaining about being in this wilderness and not being able to go into the land. Why wouldn't they believe that the God who brought them out of Egypt would also help them take the land He had promised?

Word and Phrase Meanings

mission:	those sent to do something for a special purpose
explore:	to find out more about something
report:	to tell what has happened
giants:	immense (extremely large) mighty and powerful
worry:	to think about until you are upset (God does not want us to worry, He wants us to trust him with our problems)
courage:	brave, without fear
dismayed:	discouraged or sad
complain:	to talk about unhappiness; whine

Guided Prayer Thought

*Dear God, You help us so many times! Help us to remember and not be afraid or **complain**. When we worry, it is because we do not believe that You will do what You have said You will do.*
Amen

Questions:
Thinking & Remembering

1. How many men were chosen to explore the new land?
   twelve

2. What did Moses tell them to do when they returned?
   give a report (tell what it was like)

3. Which men were excited and wanted to go back right away?
   Joshua and Caleb

4. What description did they give of the land?
   that it was beautiful and wonderful

5. Why did they think they were strong and ready?
   because God was with them

6. What did the other ten men say that frightened the people?
   that the people in this land were like giants; the city had a high wall around it

7. What did the people do when they heard this report?
   worried and complained

8. What should the people have remembered that God had done before?
   brought them out of Egypt

Bible Words To Remember

Be strong and of good **courage**; do not be afraid, nor be **dismayed**, for the Lord your God is with you wherever you go.
Joshua 1:9

Praise Hymn

Sing or say these words
Resource: My First Hymnal Pg. 25

PRAISE HIM, PRAISE HIM

Praise Him, praise Him,
   all ye little children
God is love, God is love,

Praise Him, praise Him,
   all ye little children,
God is love, God is love.

❤ Bible Love Lesson ❤

God keeps ALL of His promises! The Bible tells us that He loves each one of us----that means YOU. Every word that God says is true. We can always believe what God says. We do not need to be afraid. God says He will take care of you, and He will!

Bible Story: In The Wilderness

  Key Points

❖ God keeps all of His promises. People forget to do what they say they will do.

❖ The people who did not believe God stayed in the desert wilderness.

❖ The people who believed God went to the beautiful land.

❖ God was with the people to show them the way.

Many of the Israelites did not **believe** and **trust** in God. He had promised always to take care of them. He had kept every promise, every word He had said. Still, they were afraid. They believed the men who said there were giants in the land.

God told Moses that these people would never see the **Promised Land**. They would stay in the **wilderness** until they died. How sad that they did not trust God!

Joshua and Caleb did trust God. God said that they would take the children and young people into the wonderful land. God would go with them.

Word and Phrase Meanings

believe: to think that something is true

trust: to know and believe that God will do what He said

wilderness: desert land that is empty and where food does not grow

dismayed: discouraged or sad

Promised Land: the land that God promised to the Israelites when Abraham was alive

Guided Prayer Thought

Dear God, You have kept every word that You have said! Thank You for loving us and always keeping Your promises. We want to trust You always and not listen to those who do not believe Your word.
Amen

Questions:
— Thinking & Remembering —

1. What did the people do that was wrong?
   they did not believe and trust God

2. What had God promised?
   that He would take care of them

3. Had God ever broken His promise to them?
   No, He kept every word He had said

4. Why were they afraid?
   some of the men said there were giants in the land

5. What did God tell Moses would happen because they did not trust Him?
   they had to stay in the wilderness until they died

6. Do you think God is sad when people do not trust Him?
   Yes

7. Which two men did God say could go into the land He had promised?
   Joshua and Caleb

8. Who did Joshua and Caleb take with them?
   the children and young people

 # Bible Words To Remember

Be strong and of good courage; do not be afraid, nor be **dismayed**, for the Lord your God is with you wherever you go.
Joshua 1:9

Choosing God's Way

Trusting God

When God tells us something in His Word, we can be sure it is true. sometimes people who do not love God try to make us believe that God's Word is not true, and we start thinking that they are right. Then we begin to worry and complain. Never doubt what God says! Trust Him completely!

What can we be sure of?
Who sometimes makes us worry and complain?
Who can we trust completely?

❤ Bible Love Lesson ❤

God will not ask you to do something too hard. Some things are hard to do all by yourself, but God will help you be strong and brave. You are never alone because God is with you.

Bible Story: Joshua Leads the People

Key Points

❖ Joshua knew that God would help him be strong and brave.

❖ Joshua listened and did exactly what God told him to do.

❖ Joshua told the people that they must follow God's rules.

❖ Joshua was a good leader.

God told Joshua, "Get ready to take the people into the **Promised Land!**" Joshua did not think he could do this great thing. But he knew that he would not be alone. God would help him be strong and brave.

Joshua listened to God. It was important to have **confidence**. It was important to have **courage**. It was important to **obey** all of God's laws and teach the people to obey them too. God promised to be with him and help him.

"Get ready!" Joshua told the people. "We are going to go into the Promised Land. Believe that God is with us!" Everyone was excited. They had waited a long time. They knew that God had chosen a strong **leader** for them to follow.

— Word and Phrase Meanings —

Promised Land: the land God gave the Israelites

confidence: to know and believe

courage: bravery

obey: to follow

leader: someone who will guide or direct others

Guided Prayer Thought

Knowing that You will help us is wonderful, God. We don't need to be afraid.
We can be strong and brave because You are with us!
Amen

Questions:
Thinking & Remembering

1. What did God tell Joshua?
   to get ready to go into the Promised Land!

2. Did Joshua think that he could be a great leader by himself?
   No, he knew that he needed God to help him

3. What did Joshua know for sure?
   that he would not be alone, God would help him be strong and brave

4. Can we ever be strong and brave by ourselves?
   No, but God will help us

5. What did God tell Joshua was important?
   to have confidence and courage; to obey all of God's laws

6. What did Joshua teach the people?
   to obey God's laws

7. What did Joshua tell the people?
   "Get ready!"

8. Why did the people follow Joshua?
   they knew that God had chosen a strong leader

 # Bible Words To Remember

Be strong and of good **courage**; do not be afraid, nor be dismayed, for
the Lord your God is with you wherever you go.
Joshua 1:9

Choosing God's Way

Obeying

When your mom says, "make your bed" or "clean up your room", it might look like a hard thing to do, but remember that Jesus loves you and He will help you do hard work! It is important to obey your parents, because that is what God wants you to do. Then you are obeying God, too.

Is there something hard you have been asked to do?
Who will help you?
Who are you also obeying when you obey your parents?

♥ Bible Love Lesson ♥

There are times when your parents ask you to be very quiet. It is important that you know that there are times to laugh and play and "be noisy". Being quiet is important sometimes, too! Think of how much God loves you during a quiet time.

Bible Story: A High Wall

Key Points

❖ The city where God's people were going to live had a high wall around it.

❖ God told Joshua that He would tell him exactly what to do to win the battle.

❖ Everyone marched around the high wall for six days without making noise.

❖ The seventh day they marched and shouted. God made the wall fall down!

The people stood with Joshua looking at the city of Jericho. It was a large city with a very **high wall** all around it. How would they break down this wall and take this land? Joshua knew that God would give him **orders**. God would not let them fight this **battle** alone.

God's special messenger told Joshua what to do. He said the priests must march with the special ark of the Lord in front of all the people around the city. God said to march around the city once a day for six days. On the seventh day, God told Joshua to march around seven times! No one could say one word. It must be **silent** as they marched. Except on the seventh day, the seventh time around the city, the priests would blow their trumpets, and all the people of Israel would SHOUT.

On the seventh day, the seventh time around the city, it happened just as God said. The people did not know what God was going to do. They just **obeyed**. When they shouted, the walls of the city fell down! God gave the people of Israel the great city.

Word and Phrase Meanings

imagine:	to put a picture in your mind; think about
obeyed:	to follow and do what one is asked to do
orders:	to tell what to do and how to do it
high wall:	a wall that is much taller than people to keep them safe inside
battle:	a war or fight between two groups of people
silent:	to not make any noise at all

Guided Prayer Thought

Dear God, when we obey You, the work that can be done will be done----all in the right time----all in the right place! Help us to ask You for directions in everything we do.
Amen

Questions:
Thinking & Remembering

1. **What did Joshua and the people see as they came into the land?**
   a city with a high wall around it

2. **Did Joshua think they could break down this wall?**
   No

3. **Whose help did they need?**
   God's help

4. **Who told Joshua what to do?**
   God

5. **How many times were they told to march around the city for six days?**
   one time each day

6. **How many times were they told to march around on the seventh day?**
   seven times

7. **What did God say to do after that?**
   everyone should shout

8. **What happened when Joshua and the people obeyed God?**
   the high walls fell down

 # Bible Words To Remember

Be strong and of good courage; do not be afraid, nor be dismayed, for the Lord your God is with you wherever you go.
Joshua 1:9

Choosing God's Way

Calmness

Can you **imagine** what it would be like to be absolutely silent---that means not talking to your friends---not asking mom or dad a question---not laughing because something is funny? God helped the children be quiet as they marched around Jericho. Being quiet was part of God's plan to help them live in the land that He promised.

When was there a time when you needed to be silent?
Was it easy or hard to do?
Who helped the Israelite children be very quiet?

❤ Bible Love Lesson ❤

God loves you and wants to keep you safe. He gave you a special mom and dad to take care of you. It is very important to listen so you will not do things that will hurt you.

Bible Story: The Promised Land

Key Points

❖ Joshua was a good leader. He reminded the people of how great God was.

❖ Joshua reminded the people that they had promised to follow God's laws.

❖ When they forgot to listen to God, they could not win.

❖ God helped the people when they asked Him to. They lived in the land just like God had promised!

The battle at Jericho was not the last battle the people would have to win to take the Promised Land. There were other nations in the land. Joshua was a good leader. He kept **reminding** the people that they must obey God's laws. They must remember that it was God who made them strong against their **enemies**.

Soon, they had war with other people who were in the land. There was a time when they thought that they did not need to listen to God. They forgot to ask God for **directions**. Some people from one nation tried to **trick** God's people. They wanted to win all by themselves, without asking for God's help.

God was sorry that Joshua had not waited to ask for His help, but He knew that Joshua was ready to listen. God helped them and soon the Promised Land was theirs. The land was **divided** in the way God told them. Everyone was given a **part** as God planned.

Word and Phrase Meanings

reminding: to tell again

enemies: those against you

directions: the way to go

divided: to give each one a part of something

trick: to try to cheat someone

part: to have a piece of something that has been divided

Guided Prayer Thought

Dear God and Lord of all, we thank You that we can trust in You.
For all Your love and Your promises, we thank You.
Amen

Questions:
Thinking & Remembering

1. Was Jericho the only city the people of Israel needed?
   No, there were other nations in the land

2. What did Joshua keep reminding the people of Israel?
   that they must obey God

3. What must the people remember?
   that God made them strong against their enemies

4. Did they forget to ask God's direction?
   Yes, they wanted to win by themselves

5. Did Joshua know that it was wrong not to ask God for help?
   Yes, he was ready to listen

6. What happened when they listened to God and trusted Him?
   God gave them the Promised Land

7. How did each family get a part of the land?
   God told Joshua how it must be divided each got their part

8. Who had planned and promised this land to the people of Israel?
   God

 # Bible Words To Remember

Be strong and of good courage; do not be afraid, nor be dismayed, for the Lord your God is with you wherever you go.
Joshua 1:9

Choosing God's Way

Following Directions

Sometimes you may think that something you want to do is not dangerous, even when those who love and care about you have said "no". Then you get hurt and feel very bad. Remember that your parents tell you what to do because they love you.

Do you ever think you know more than your parents? Why do parents sometimes say "no"?

Bible Beginnings

Deborah: The Book of Judges

♥ Bible Love Lesson ♥

God knows that you will be happy when you do the right things. By learning to obey your parents, you will also learn to obey God---and He loves you even more than your mom and dad do. That's a lot of love!

Bible Story: Keep Doing the Right Things!

 Key Points

❖ Joshua wanted the people to listen to God.

❖ After Joshua died, they didn't remember how important God was to them.

❖ The people saw other nations worshiping gods made of wood and stone.

❖ When the Israelites started doing wrong things like those who did not love God, they were in trouble and were not happy.

Joshua never stopped telling the people of Israel, "Keep God's law, do the right things." After Joshua died, the Israelites didn't think about God's laws. They obeyed God sometimes but they didn't **remember** God's greatness and kindness. Because they did not have a strong **leader,** they started doing just the things they wanted to do.

The Israelites were living close to people who worshiped other gods, and they wanted to be like them. God told His people to "Move those who did not love Him out of the land". God **promised** this land to Israel. God said, "If these people stay they will make My people do wrong things."

Whenever God's people, the Israelites, got into **trouble,** they remembered God again. They prayed and asked Him to help them. Because He **loved** them so much, He heard their prayers and sent another leader who loved God.

Word and Phrase Meanings

remember:	think about again; to not forget
leader:	someone who will guide or direct others
promised:	to do what has been said
loved:	cared about very much
trouble:	something that goes wrong
failed:	to not do something right (God has done *everything* right)

Guided Prayer Thought

Dear God, It is easy to just do the things we want to do, and not listen to Your word. Then we get into trouble and need to ask for Your help. Help us listen to You always.
Amen

Questions:
Thinking & Remembering

1. What did Joshua tell the people?
   "Keep God's law, do the right things."

2. What happened after Joshua died?
   they didn't think about what God said, they disobeyed God's laws

3. What did they forget?
   God's greatness and kindness

4. What did they do?
   just the things they wanted to do

5. What did the people who were living around them do?
   worshiped other gods

6. Did the Israelites follow God's command to get them out of the land?
   No, they wanted to live like them

7. What happened when the Israelites had problems?
   they asked God to help them

8. Why did He listen to their prayers?
   because He loved them so much

9. Whom did He send to help them?
   leaders who loved God

 # Bible Words To Remember

Let those who love Him be like the sun.   Judges 5:31

Not a word failed of any good thing which the Lord had spoken to the house of Israel. All came to pass.   Joshua 21:45

Praise Hymn

Sing or say these words
Resource: My First Hymnal Pg. 18

COME BLESS THE LORD

Come bless the Lord,
all ye servants of the Lord,
Who stand by night,
in the house of the Lord,
Lift up your hands,
in the holy place,
And bless the Lord,
And bless the Lord.

♥ Bible Love Lesson ♥

Your parents will always love you and want you to be the best that you can be.
Listening to what they say will keep you happy and safe. God knows that
they will care for you while you are growing up.

Bible Story: Deborah Leads the Israelites

 Key Points

❖ Deborah loved God and listened to His words.

❖ There were many people who hated the Children of Israel. They tried to hurt them.

❖ Deborah told the Israelites what God wanted them to do.

❖ God gave Deborah a special message.

Deborah loved God and kept His **commandments**. God chose her to help His people and tell them His **will** and **law**.

There were many enemies of God's people. They killed many Israelites and would not let them live in the land in **peace**. One of these enemies was a **commander** named Sisera.

One day Deborah was sitting under a palm tree. She was there so that the Israelites could come and ask her what God wanted them to do. She asked Barak, an important **captain** of the Israelites, to come to hear God's command. God had given her a special message for him. Will the captain **believe** the message?

Word and Phrase Meanings

commandments: rules you must follow

will: that which God wants us to do

law: rules that we must follow

peace: quiet time with no fighting

commander: leader of many groups of men in an army

captain: leader who gives orders to one group of men in an army

believe: to think that something is true

advice: telling what someone should do

Guided Prayer Thought

Dear God, There are special people that will help us know what Your word says. Help us to listen to the right words.
Amen

Questions:
Thinking & Remembering

1. **Who loved God and kept His commandments?**
   Deborah

2. **What was God's special reason for choosing her?**
   to tell the people His will and law

3. **Were there still enemies in the land?**
   Yes

4. **Did they cause problems for the Israelites?**
   Yes, they would not let them live in peace

5. **Who was a commander of the enemy army?**
   Sisera

6. **Where did Deborah sit to give advice?**
   under a palm tree

7. **Whom did Deborah ask to come so that she could speak with him?**
   Barak, an important captain

8. **What did God want Deborah to do?**
   to give Barak a special message

 # Bible Words To Remember

Let those who love Him be like the sun. Judges 5:31

Not a word failed of any good thing which the Lord had spoken to the house of Israel. All came to pass. Joshua 21:45

Choosing God's Way

To Obey is Best

Obeying also means doing what you are asked immediately (right now!). If you tell your mother, "I will do it later," that is disobedience. If you try to pretend that you didn't hear what she said, you are not obeying---and God knows! He knows that you will do your best and be happy when you obey.

Are you obeying if you wait until another time to do what you are asked to do?
How can you be most happy and do you best?

♥ Bible Love Lesson ♥

Do you ever feel afraid when mom or dad ask you to do something? It may be that you think that you will not do it 'good enough'. You are just learning and if you keep trying, it will soon be 'good enough'! God is there loving and helping you each step of the way.

Bible Story: Barak Listens

 Key Points

❖ God's special message was for a man named Barak.

❖ The message was that God would help him win a battle.

❖ Barak was afraid. He did not believe God.

❖ Deborah went with Barak because he was afraid to go alone.

Deborah gave Barak the special **message** from God. God had commanded, "**Gather** your army and get ready for **battle**. God will help you win! Fight against Sisera, your enemy. God will **deliver** him into your hand."

Barak listened as Deborah spoke. He knew that Deborah would tell only what God had said. But Barak was afraid. In fact, he was terrified! Then Barak said, "I will only go if you go with me."

Deborah knew that Barak should believe that God was the only one who could help him win this battle. God had already made a promise to be with him. She said, "I will go with you. But because you are afraid and did not believe God, it will be a woman who will take **action** and bring the Israelites to **victory**. A woman named Jael will kill Sisera, God's enemy and ours."

Word and Phrase Meanings

message:	to tell something to someone
gather:	to come together in one place
battle:	a fight between two groups of people
deliver:	to give something to another
action:	to do something to bring a result or make something happen
victory:	to win and be successful
all came to pass:	everything happened that was said

Guided Prayer Thought

Dear God, When You say You will do something, You will!
Help us to believe You completely.
Amen

Questions:
Thinking & Remembering

1. **What was God's special message for Barak?**
   to get ready for battle and fight against Israel's enemy

2. **Who would be with him to help him win?**
   God

3. **Who was the enemy?**
   Sisera

4. **What did God say He would do?**
   deliver him into his hand

5. **Why didn't Barak just go and do as he was commanded?**
   he was afraid

6. **What did Barak tell Deborah?**
   I will only go if you go with me

7. **Did Barak show that he did not believe in God to help him?**
   Yes

8. **What happened because of this and because he was afraid?**
   women (Deborah and Jael) helped bring victory to God's people

 # Bible Words To Remember

Let those who love Him be like the sun. Judges 5:31

Not a word failed of any good thing which the Lord had spoken to the house of Israel. **All came to pass.** Joshua 21:45

Choosing God's Way

Winning

Pretend that you are running in a race. Your legs are running as fast as they can go. You got there first! "I win!", you will say. It feels so good to be the winner. God wants His children to be winners! But God also knows what is really important for you to win at. He will help you. Pray and ask Him every day.

Tell of a time when you were running to get there 'first'.
How do you feel when you win at a game or a race?
Who will help you know how important it really is for you to win?

❤ Bible Love Lesson ❤

Thinking about God's love will always make you feel warm and happy. It makes you feel cheerful and everyone around you will know that God loves you!

Bible Story: A Song of Victory

Key Points

❖ **God helped Israel win the battle.**

❖ **God always keeps His promises.**

❖ **Deborah sang a song remembering all that God did for them.**

❖ **Those who love God should be like the sun!**

There was victory in the battle. . .Israel won. But a woman named Jael, took the life of the great enemy of God, Sisera. Barak had been afraid to fight this battle without taking Deborah with him, even though God had promised to go with him.

When the battle was over, Deborah and Barak sang on that day. It was a song of victory over their enemy. (from Judges 5)

"I will sing to the Lord;
I will sing praise to the Lord God
    of Israel."
Recount the righteous acts of the Lord,
The righteous acts for His
    villagers in Israel.
The Lord came down for me
    against the mighty.
Let those who love Him be
    like the sun
When it comes out in full
    strength."

Word and Phrase Meanings

villagers: all the people belonging to a certain group or from one place

recount: to remember how many times the Lord was with them

not a word failed: to happen just as was told

Guided Prayer Thought

Help us to be like the sun, dear God! We want to be bright and shine with Your light so others will know how much we love You.
Amen

Questions: Thinking & Remembering

1. **Who won the battle against Sisera?**
   Israel won with God's strength

2. **Who took the life of the enemy Sisera?**
   a woman named Jael

3. **Whom did Barak ask to go with him instead of believing in God?**
   Deborah

4. **What did Deborah and Barak do on the day of victory?**
   they sang a song of victory

5. **Whom did they sing praises to?**
   the Lord God of Israel

6. **What did they remember in this song?**
   the righteous acts of the Lord for Israel

7. **Who helped them win against the mighty?**
   the Lord God

8. **What does the song say about those who love Him?**
   that they be like the sun in its full strength

 # Bible Words To Remember

Let those who love Him be like the sun. Judges 5:31

Not a word failed of any good thing which the Lord had spoken to the house of Israel. All came to pass. Joshua 21:45

Choosing God's Way

Cheerfulness

The words in the Bible say that if you love God, "you will be like the sun." The sun is very bright and wonderful. It makes us warm and makes us feel happy. Even on a cloudy day, YOU can be like the sun and be cheerful about all of the things God gives you every day. Count all of the ways that God shows His love. There are probably too many to count!

What are the words in the Bible about the sun?
How can you be like the sun?

♥ Bible Love Lesson ♥

Rest is so wonderful! God planned for our bodies to have enough rest. Think of God and how much He loves you. You will feel peaceful and happy when you have had a rest time from all your work and play.

Bible Story: Rest and Peace

Key Points

❖ God's people remembered God for many years and had rest.

❖ After a while, they forgot again what they had promised God.

❖ The Israelites hid in caves because they were being hurt by people who did not love God.

❖ When they remembered God and prayed for forgiveness, He helped them again.

For forty years after the wars with other nations, God's people were like the song Deborah sang. They loved God and were like the sun that came out in full strength. For forty years, **the land of Israel had rest.**

Then the children of Israel did **evil** again in the sight of the Lord and their enemy. The Midianites made them afraid again. They chased them away from their food and hurt them. Finally the Israelites made **caves** to hide in and moved to the mountains where they could be safe.

When the children of Israel planted **crops** for their food, the Midianites would come and destroy it. They took all their animals. . . the sheep and ox and donkeys. The children and people were hungry and sad. Every day they would watch from their caves as the enemy came to take all that they had.

The Israelites cried to the Lord. The Lord **reminded** them that He had brought them out of slavery in Egypt. He had given them **victory** over all their enemies and given them the land He had promised. He said, "I am the Lord your God; do not fear." The bad things happened to them because they did not obey God. But He heard them crying and He helped them again.

— Word and Phrase Meanings —

reminded: to tell again what has been told

victory: to win and be successful

evil: great wrongdoing

caves: a carved out place in a rock or mountain

crops: food growing on the land

the land had rest: there was peace with no fighting

Guided Prayer Thought

Dear God, You are very patient with Your people! Even when we do not listen and obey, You still love us. We want to be like the light of the sun and not do things that will bring darkness. Help us to believe You every day!

Amen

Questions:
Thinking & Remembering

1. **What were God's people like after the wars with other nations?**
   they were like the sun that came out in full strength

2. **How many years did the land of Israel have rest?**
   forty years

3. **What happened that changed this peaceful time?**
   the children of Israel did evil in the sight of the Lord

4. **Who was the Israelites enemy?**
   the Midianites

5. **What did the Israelites do because they were afraid?**
   they made caves in the mountains

6. **What did the Midianites do when the Israelites planted food?**
   destroyed it

7. **What did they take that belonged to the Israelites?**
   the animals--sheep, oxen and donkeys

8. **How did the Israelites feel?**
   hungry and sad

9. **Whom did they cry to for help?**
   God

10. **What three things did God remind them of?**
    that He had made them free from the Egyptians; that He had given them a new land; that He loved them and would be with them. "I am the Lord Your God. Do not fear."

Bible Words To Remember

Let those who love Him be like the sun.   Judges 5:31

Not a word failed of any good thing which the Lord had spoken to the house of Israel. All came to pass.   Joshua 21:45

Choosing God's Way

Quiet

When you are young, you need times of rest so that your body can grow. You are always moving when you are awake and you need rest between all the running and playing. Your mom or your teacher know that if you do not take a rest when your body needs it, you will cry over things that are not important and you will not eat enough to be healthy. Be glad for rest time!

Why is rest important?
What will happen if you don't get enough rest?

Gideon: The Book of Judges

❤ Bible Love Lesson ❤

God loves His children so much. He helps them when they get into trouble.
He wants us to remember all the good things He does for them, even
when everything is going 'just right'. He always loves you!

Bible Story: God is Forgotten Again

Key Points

❖ God was so good to the Israelites.

❖ When the Israelites were safe, they thought they didn't need God.

❖ God wanted them to remember Him all the time, not just when they were in trouble!

❖ We should always show love to God.

It seems that the people of Israel would always remember how good God had been to them. So many times, He kept them safe from their enemies. They would obey God for awhile until they didn't think they needed His help any longer.

But as soon as they were in trouble----and they would most **certainly** have problems----they wanted God to help them. Sometimes they even tried to **blame** God because they were in trouble!

It is a good time right now to think about the ways in which we sometimes **treat** God. Do we do the same thing as the Israelites did? Do we just think of God when we have a problem? Do we think it is God's **fault** when we are sad or when someone does something to hurt us? God is with us ALL the time. He wants to be your very best friend. He wants you to show your love to Him during happy times as well as sad times. Let's remember!

___ Word and Phrase Meanings ___

certainly:	something that is thought to be sure to happen
blame:	to say that it is another person's fault for what happens
treat:	the way you act and care for someone
fault:	mistake; wrong

Guided Prayer Thought

Dear God, We know that You are with us all of the time. Because of sin, we know that there will be sadness and sickness on earth. That is why You sent Jesus! For those who Love You and accept Jesus as their Savior, there will be a day that we will be in heaven with You where there will be no tears or sadness.   *Amen*

Questions:
Thinking & Remembering

1. Should the people of Israel have remembered how good God was?
   Yes

2. What had He done for them?
   He had kept them safe from their enemies

3. What would they do for awhile?
   obey Him until they thought they didn't need Him

4. What happened when they were in trouble?
   they asked God to help them

5. What wrong thing did they sometimes do?
   they blamed God for their problems

6. Do we do the same thing as the Israelites did?
   Often, we do. We pray only when we are in trouble.

7. Do we sometimes think it is God's fault when we are sad?
   Even though we might not think we are blaming God, people sometimes get angry at God because they are feeling hurt. They think God should stop bad things from happening.

8. Even when bad things happen, who is with us ALL the time?
   God. Because of sin in the world, there will be sadness until we go to heaven.

 # Bible Words To Remember

Peace be with you; do not fear.   Judges 6:23

If God is for us, who can be against us?   Romans 8:31

Praise Hymn

Sing or say these words
Resource: My First Hymnal Pg. 26

PRAISE THE LORD TOGETHER

Praise the Lord together singing,
   "Alleluia, alleluia, alleluia."

❤ Bible Love Lesson ❤

When people love each other they care about each other. If your friend is hurt you can help by giving him a hug or by getting a band-aid for his cut. Because God loves you, you can love others!

Bible Story: Have I Not Sent You?

Key Points

❖ The Israelites had their food taken away by tribes of people.

❖ Gideon planned how he could get some of the food back.

❖ An angel told Gideon that the Lord was with him.

❖ Gideon did not think he was strong enough. The Lord said, "I am sending you. I will be with you."

Every year, for seven years, there were **tribes** who would come to the Israelite's land and take all of their food and crops. If anyone tried to stop them or protect their lands, they would kill them.

Gideon was a young man who worked on his father's **farm**. Gideon thought of a way to save his family's food. He hid in a **cave** and when the enemy was gone, he hurried and picked up the **wheat** that was left behind.

One night Gideon was visited by an angel. He was so surprised! The angel said to Gideon, "The Lord is with you. You are brave and strong!" The Lord wanted to save Israel from the tribes who were their enemies. Gideon said, "How can I save Israel?" The Lord said, "Have I not sent you? I will be with you."

— Word and Phrase Meanings —

tribes: groups of people belonging to one family or race

farm: a place where food is grown and animals are taken care of

cave: a carved out place in a rock or mountain

wheat: grain that is used to make bread

Guided Prayer Thought

When You ask us to do something Lord, even if it seems hard, we know that
You will be with us. It is because You are the One who sent us to do a job.
Sometimes the hardest thing to do is telling people we love Jesus.
Help us to be brave and strong.   Amen

Questions:
Thinking & Remembering

1. **What happened every year?**
   tribes came to take the Israelites
   food and crops

2. **How many years had this been happening?**
   for seven years

3. **What would happen if someone tried to stop them?**
   they would be killed

4. **Where did Gideon work?**
   on his father's farm

5. **What did Gideon do to save some of the wheat the enemy left?**
   he hid in a cave until they were gone

6. **What did an angel say to Gideon?**
   "The Lord is with you. You are brave and strong."

7. **What did the Lord want Gideon to do?**
   save Israel

8. **When Gideon asked how he could do this, what did the Lord tell him?**
   "I have sent you. I will be with you."

 # Bible Words To Remember

Peace be with you; do not fear.   Judges 6:23

If God is for us, who can be against us? Romans 8:31

Choosing God's Way

Remember God's Love

There are many ways that you can begin to show love and help each other. How can you love someone else? By remembering how much God loves YOU.

What makes it possible to love others?
Have you thought of someone to whom you can show love to today?
In what ways can you show that love?

♥ Bible Love Lesson ♥

You cannot see God, but you can see the wonderful things He made and the wonderful things He does. You can feel His love. Isn't God awesome?

Bible Story: Show Me A Sign

Key Points

❖ **Gideon wanted to know for sure that God was with him.**

❖ **When Gideon gave an offering to God, fire burned it up.**

❖ **The Lord told Gideon not to be afraid.**

Gideon did not feel very strong and brave. God told him that he would be the one to save Israel from the enemy! So Gideon asked God to show him a special **sign**. He said, "Show me a sign that it is You who is talking to me."

Gideon **presented** his **offering** to the Lord under a tree. The angel told him to put the meat and bread on a rock. He said to pour **broth** over it. When he had done this, the Angel of the Lord touched the offering with his **staff** and fire burned up the offering.

Now Gideon knew that the Angel was from God! Then the Lord said to Gideon, "Peace be with you; do not fear." Gideon built an **altar** there to the Lord, and called it "The-Lord-Is-Peace".

Word and Phrase Meanings

sign:	a signal to give direction
presented:	to give something in a special way
offering:	to give something
broth:	thin, meat soup
staff:	a long stick
altar:	a place where an offering is given

Guided Prayer Thought

Dear God, Sometimes we think we are not strong or brave enough to do work for you. Help us never to fear. Help us to have Your peace.
Amen

Questions:
Thinking & Remembering

1. Did Gideon feel strong and brave?
   No

2. Why did Gideon want a special sign?
   to show that it was God who talked to him

3. What did Gideon present to the Lord?
   an offering of meat and bread

4. What did the angel tell Gideon to do?
   to put it on a rock and pour broth over it

5. What did the Angel of the Lord do?
   touched it with his staff

6. What happened to the offering?
   fire burned up the offering

7. What did the Lord say to Gideon?
   "Peace be with you; do not fear."

8. What did Gideon call the altar he built to the Lord?
   "The-Lord-Is-Peace".

 # Bible Words To Remember

Peace be with you; do not fear. Judges 6:23

If God is for us, who can be against us? Romans 8:31

Choosing God's Way

Confidence

When you are afraid at night or lonely when mom and dad are away, you can talk to God and He will surround you with His love to make you feel protected. Gideon asked God to help him know for sure that He was with him. God answered his prayer. God sent an angel to tell him not to be afraid and to be at peace. God will do the same for you!

What can you do when you are afraid?
What will God do when you ask Him?
Who did God help in the Bible to know for sure that He was with him?

❤ Bible Love Lesson ❤

There are so many things to learn!   Asking questions is one way to find out how to do things. God will help you, but you must listen first and then follow instructions.

Bible Story: With God's Help

 Key Points

❖ Gideon listened to all of God's directions.

❖ Gideon knew that God would be with him.

❖ God kept showing Gideon that He was helping him.

Gideon was not sure how he would be a **general** and lead God's people into a battle that would save their **nation**. He kept asking for God's help, and God gave him **directions** for everything he did. Soon, it was time to fight and win. God was on their side.

Gideon prayed to God. He asked God for another **sign** to show him that God was with him. He put a sheepskin outside. In the morning, if it was wet and the ground was dry, he would know that God would let them win.

The next day, the sheepskin was very wet! But Gideon asked for one more sign. He asked that God let the sheepskin be dry the next day, and that the ground around it be wet. The Lord gave Gideon his sign, the sheepskin was dry the next day.

Word and Phrase Meanings

general:	an important leader or chief in an army
directions:	to tell which way to go or what to do and how to do it
nation:	a group of people living together in the same land or country
sign:	a signal to give direction
fear:	to be afraid or scared something bad will happen

Guided Prayer Thought

Dear God, If You are with us, we can do anything You ask us to do, even if we have never done it before. We can always ask You for help and You will show us the way.
Amen

Questions:
Thinking & Remembering

1. Did Gideon know how to be a general in an army?
   No

2. What did he do so he could save the nation of Israel?
   He asked God for help and followed God's direction.

3. Who would be on Israel's side when they went to fight?
   God was on their side

4. Why did Gideon pray to God?
   to ask Him for another sign to show him that God was with him

5. What did he put outside and ask God that it be wet in the morning?
   sheepskin

6. What would the ground be like?
   dry

7. After God showed Gideon this sign, what did Gideon ask Him?
   to make the sheepskin dry and the ground wet

8. Did God give Gideon the answer to his question?
   Yes

 # Bible Words To Remember

Peace be with you; do not **fear**.   Judges 6:23

If God is for us, who can be against us?   Romans 8:31

Choosing God's Way

Following Directions

Grownups sometimes wonder how children can think of so many questions to ask. But asking questions is important. Gideon didn't know how to do everything. He kept asking God to help him. Guess what? God told him all the things he needed to know. He gave him all the right instructions. What Gideon had to do was *follow* God's instruction for things to turn out right!

Why is it important to find out how to do things?
Who will help you find out the answers?
What do you need to do so that things will turn out right?

❤ Bible Love Lesson ❤

When you are a child, it seems like there sure are a lot of bigger people. But God said that BIG doesn't count for what really matters to Him. What matters most is that you ask God to help you. And He will.

Bible Story: God's Victory

Key Points

❖ Many men went with Gideon to fight the Israelite's enemy.

❖ God told Gideon to choose only a few good men.

❖ It is more important to believe God than to try to be strong by yourself.

❖ God helped the Israelites win.

Gideon gathered together his large army of men. They camped beside a cool, mountain stream. In the **distance**, they could see the enemy army of Midian. The Midianite army was huge! Even though Gideon had every man who was able to fight from the Israelites, they seemed to be very few **compared** to the Midianites.

Then God said, "Gideon, your army is too big." God wanted to show Israel that the battle would not be won by a big army. It would not **matter** how many men were fighting. It only mattered that God was with them.

Gideon did what God told him to do. He called the men to him and said, "If any of you are afraid, you may leave and go back home now. It is best that you go." Many men went home---more than half of the men left. God said, "Your army is still too big! Watch as the men drink from the stream. Choose only those men who scoop the water with their hands and stand ready to fight. The men who drink down on their knees, send home." Only three-hundred men were left. God said, "I will give Israel the victory with only three-hundred men." He then **instructed** Gideon to surprise the enemy in the darkness with torches and trumpets. The enemy army was so frightened and **confused** that they were fighting and killing each other! God gave Israel the victory!

── Word and Phrase Meanings ──

distance:	space between two things	
compared:	to see what is alike and what is different	
matter:	what to give attention to; to mean something	
instructed:	to teach and tell how to do something	
confused:	to be mixed up with thinking something	

Guided Prayer Thought

Dear God, It is not how great we are, but how great You are, that counts. Help us to remember that it is You who helps us win.
Amen

Questions:
Thinking & Remembering

1. What was frightening for the army of Israel as they camped?
   the huge Midianite army

2. What did God tell Gideon about his army?
   that it was too big

3. What did God want to show the Israelites?
   that they only needed God to help them win

4. Why did the first group of men leave?
   because they were afraid

5. Which men did God want Gideon to send away next?
   the men who drank the water down on their knees

6. How many men were left for Gideon?
   three-hundred

7. What did this small army use to frighten and confuse the enemy?
   torches and trumpets

8. Who gave Israel the victory?
   God

 Bible Words To Remember

Peace be with you; do not fear.   Judges 6:23

If God is for us, who can be against us?   Romans 8:31

Choosing God's Way

Faith

You can show God and others that you believe that God has plans for you. Pray every day that He will show you the way.

How can you show that you believe in God's plan? What can you do every day so you will discover what God's plan is?

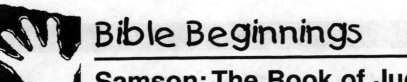

Samson: The Book of Judges

❤ Bible Love Lesson ❤

God will give you strength every day. Some people try to do things 'by themselves'. They soon find out that it is God who makes them strong. Remember to say thank you to God for being able to do so many things 'all by yourself' ---with God's help!

Bible Story: A Baby Dedicated to God

 Key Points

❖ The Philistines hated God and His people.

❖ Israel had not followed God for a long time.

❖ God sent a special baby to fight the Philistines.

The Philistines were people who hated God---and they hated God's people. They kept coming into the Israelite lands and **attacking** them.

Israel was in trouble again! They had stopped following God and chosen to go their own way for a very long time. The people prayed and asked God to send them another leader to help them fight against this strong enemy.

One day God's messenger came to a husband and wife who had no children. "You will have a special baby boy," he told them. God will make your son very strong so that he can **rescue** the Israelites from the Philistines.

Word and Phrase Meanings

might:	strength
dedicated:	to set apart for a special purpose
attacking:	to strike or charge someone
rescue:	to make free
miserable:	very unhappy

Guided Prayer Thought

Help us dear God, to choose to follow You. Help us to obey You every day and not wait until we are in terrible trouble to talk to You.
Amen

Questions:
Thinking & Remembering

1. Which people hated God and God's people?
   the Philistines

2. What did they do to make the Israelites **miserable**?
   they came into their lands and attacked them

3. Why was Israel having trouble again?
   they had stopped following God

4. Did they choose to go their own way?
   Yes

5. What did the people do when they were in trouble?
   they prayed that God would send them a leader to help them fight the enemy

6. What message did God's messenger give to a husband and wife?
   "You will have a special baby boy"

7. What would be different about this child?
   he would be very strong

8. What would he be able to do because of his strength?
   rescue the Israelites from the Philistines

 # Bible Words To Remember

Be strong in the Lord and in the power of His **might**. Ephesians 6:10
O Lord God, remember me, I pray! Judges 16:28

Praise Hymn

Sing or say these words
Resource: My First Hymnal Pg. 23

WHISPER A PRAYER

Whisper a prayer in the morning,
Whisper a prayer at noon,
Whisper a prayer in the evening,
To keep your heart in tune.

❤ Bible Love Lesson ❤

Your parents and teachers will help you learn about God's love. They will tell you the words of the Bible so that you will know that God sent His Son Jesus, to be born on earth just like you! Jesus showed everyone what God's love is like. His love is perfect!

Bible Story: The Very Different Boy

Key Points

❖ God told the parents of the special baby to teach him about God.

❖ The special baby boy was very strong.

❖ Samson was different than other boys. God was with him.

After God's **messenger** came, Manoah, who would be the father of this special baby, prayed to God. He asked, "O my Lord, please teach us what we shall do for the child who will be born."

God listened to Manoah's prayer. God's messenger said that they would need to teach him carefully all that God commanded. He would be **different** from others by the strength and power he would have. This son would serve God in a special way. But his hair must never be cut. If his hair were to be cut, the **vow** would be over. He would no longer be strong.

When the baby was born, they named him Samson. As he grew, everyone **realized** that he was different. He was stronger than any other boy. His hair grew very long. But his parents never cut it. They remembered God's command.

Word and Phrase Meanings

different:	not the same
messenger:	someone who delivers a message
vow:	a special promise
realized:	to come to understand
energy:	power; feeling strong

Guided Prayer Thought

Dear God, Help us to love and serve You more. Help us not be afraid to be different and follow Your commandments.
Amen

Questions:
Thinking & Remembering

1. Who spoke to Manoah and his wife?
   God's messenger

2. What did Manoah pray and ask God?
   to teach them what they should do for this child

3. What did God's messenger tell them they must do?
   teach him carefully all that God commanded

4. How was this child different?
   he had strength and power

5. What must they never do?
   cut his hair

6. What would happen if his hair were cut?
   the vow would be over and he would not be strong

7. What was the name of this special baby?
   Samson

8. How did Samson compare with other boys? (How was he different?)
   he was stronger than any of the other boys

Bible Words To Remember

Be strong in the Lord and in the power of His might. Ephesians 6:10

O Lord God, remember me, I pray! Judges 16:28

Choosing God's Way

Being Energetic

You are getting stronger every day! Maybe you can help carry things for your mom and dad. Sometimes you will say "I can do it by myself!" Your parents might say, "Not yet, but soon you will be able to." It is wonderful to have the **energy** to do the things you enjoy every day. But you will not grow strong without eating the food God provided. You will not grow strong without the rest God planned.

What do we need to be able to do the things we enjoy?
What makes you strong?
Who gives these things?

❤ Bible Love Lesson ❤

Children are born wanting their own way. Sometimes you want things 'right now'
that are not best for you to have. God wants you to wait and trust your parents
for what is best for you. God will always give you good things
when it is the right time!

Bible Story: Samson Wants His Own Way

 Key Points

❖ God chose Samson to be a strong and powerful leader.

❖ Samson decided not to listen to his parents or to God.

❖ Samson did not use his strength to serve God in the right way.

❖ Samson got into trouble because he did not believe that it was God who had made him strong.

Samson was chosen by God to **deliver** Israel from the Philistines. But as he grew bigger and stronger, he also **decided** that because of his strength, he could do whatever he wanted. He did not listen to his parents and did not listen to God.

He went into the Philistine city and saw a woman there that he wanted to be his wife. "Get her for me. She pleases me," he said to his father. As they were on their way to the Philistine city to **arrange** the wedding feast, Samson heard a growling in the bushes. He saw that a lion was there ready to attack him. He tore the lion apart without any **effort** at all!

Samson became an angry man, not using his strength in the right way. He was more **interested** in getting even and showing off his strength than in helping God's people. He did fight the Philistines and because he was so strong, they were very much afraid of him. They tried to think of a way to find out why he was so strong.

Word and Phrase Meanings

deliver: to save from an enemy

decided: to think about and choose

arrange: to get ready

effort: to use energy trying to do something

interested: to want to give attention to

Guided Prayer Thought

Dear God, Help us to listen to our parents. They love us and want to help us do the right thing and to love You, too. Help us remember that our strength comes from You.

Amen

Questions:
Thinking & Remembering

1. Whom had God chosen to deliver Israel from the Philistines?
   Samson

2. Why did Samson think he could do whatever he wanted?
   because he was very strong

3. Whom did he not listen to?
   his parents or God

4. Who did Samson see that he wanted in the Philistine city?
   a girl that he thought should be his wife

5. What did he demand that his parents do?
   "Get her for me. She pleases me."

6. What happened on the way to the wedding?
   he killed a lion by tearing it apart

7. Why didn't Samson use his strength wisely?
   he was more interested in getting even than in helping God's people

8. What did the Philistines try to do because they were afraid of him?
   to find out why he was so strong

 # Bible Words To Remember

Be strong in the Lord and in the power of His might. Ephesians 6:10
O Lord God, remember me, I pray! Judges 16:28

Choosing God's Way

Making Mistakes

We do not always do things 'just right'. We make mistakes, some are little and some are big. People in the Bible made mistakes, too. Jesus came and lived on earth and was perfect! He never did anything wrong. He had power and was very strong. Because of Jesus, we can be strong and He will help us do the right things.

Do people ever make mistakes?
Whom did God send to earth who did nothing wrong?
Who will help us do the right things?

♥ Bible Love Lesson ♥

Many years before Jesus was sent to earth, God tried to show His love through special people who loved Him and obeyed His commandments. Even though these people did not always remember to ask God for directions when they had troubles, God never stopped loving them and showing them the right way. He will show us too, when we ask Him!

Bible Story: The Secret is Found Out

 Key Points

❖ The Philistines wanted to find out why Samson was strong.

❖ Samson did not tell his secret at first.

❖ Samson's long hair was the reason he was strong.

❖ When Samson told the secret, the Philistines cut his hair off.

The Philistines asked the woman that Samson loved to find out what the **secret** of his strength was. At different times, she begged Samson to tell her why he was so strong. She said, "If you really do love me, you will tell me your secret."

At first, Samson would just **tease** her, saying that if he were tied with strong ropes, he would not be strong. Delilah, the woman Samson loved, **pouted** and **begged** until he became tired of her asking him day after day.

Delilah finally **persuaded** Samson to tell her the truth. Samson said, "If my hair is cut, my strength will leave me. I will become weak, and be like any other man." That night, while Samson was sleeping, men came and cut Samson's hair. Samson's strength was gone. Now he became the Philistine's prisoner!

Word and Phrase Meanings

secret:	something not everyone knows about
pouted:	to whine and cry
begged:	to ask over and over again
tease:	to joke with
persuaded:	to talk someone into doing something they didn't want to do at first

Guided Prayer Thought

Dear God, help us to trust only You. We know that You will help us trust those who love You and want what is best for us.
Amen

Questions:
Thinking & Remembering

1. **Whom did the Philistines ask to find out the secret of Samson's strength?**
   the woman whom Samson loved

2. **What did the woman do?**
   she begged Samson to tell her why he was so strong

3. **What words did she use to get him to tell them his secret?**
   "If you really love me!"

4. **Did Samson tell Delilah the truth at first?**
   No. He told her that if he were tied with strong ropes, he would not be strong.

5. **What did Delilah keep doing?**
   pouting and begging

6. **When Samson was tired of her asking him, what did he do?**
   he told her it was because his hair was not cut

7. **What would happen when his hair was cut?**
   he would be weak, like any other man

8. **What happened to Samson when the secret was told?**
   The Philistines cut his hair. His strength was gone and he was their prisoner.

 ## Bible Words To Remember

Be strong in the Lord and in the power of His might.   Ephesians 6:10
O Lord God, remember me, I pray!   Judges 16:28

Choosing God's Way

Being Strong

God wants you to use your strength for good things. He did not make you strong so that you could hurt others. Hitting and pushing someone who is not as strong as you will make God very sad. Helping others because you are strong will please God and make you feel happy, too!

What does God want you to use your strength for?
What will make God sad?

♥ Bible Love Lesson ♥

God gives us strong minds and bodies to help us live for Him. There are many wonderful things we can do if we let God show us what He has planned for us! He loves you so much!

Bible Story: Samson is Strong One More Time

Key Points

❖ The Philistines made Samson their prisoner.

❖ When Samson's hair grew long, he was strong again.

❖ Samson prayed that God would give him power.

❖ Samson helped the Israelites one more time.

The Philistines were very happy that they had Samson as their prisoner! They **celebrated** and had parties and praised their own gods for getting Samson as their **prisoner**.

After Samson had been in prison for a long time, his hair became long again. One day, the Philistines were having a great **feast**. They said, "Let's call for Samson from the prison so we can rejoice even more as we see him **bound** in ropes and blind."

Samson stood between two great **pillars** of their temple. The people were laughing and shouting **cruel** things at him. Then Samson prayed to God, "O Lord God, remember me, I pray! Make me strong just one more time!" Samson pushed the pillars with all of his strength. The temple crashed down on top of all the Philistines there. God had given Samson one last victory for Israel.

Word and Phrase Meanings

celebrate: to be happy and cheer on a special day

prisoner: someone who is not free

feast: a big dinner

bound: tied up

pillars: large posts that hold up a building

cruel: mean and hurtful to others

Guided Prayer Thought

Dear God, We always want to use our strength in the way that will be good and help others. Please show us what is right.
Amen

Questions:
Thinking & Remembering

1. **Whom had the Philistines made their prisoner?**
   Samson

2. **What did they do to celebrate?**
   they had parties and praised their own gods

3. **What happened after Samson had been in prison for awhile?**
   his hair became long again

4. **Whom did the Philistines call for during their feast?**
   they called for Samson, who was bound in ropes and blind

5. **Where was Samson standing?**
   between two great pillars of their temple

6. **How was Samson treated by the Philistines?**
   they laughed and shouted cruel things at him

7. **What did Samson ask the Lord?**
   to make him strong one more time

8. **What did Samson do with the strength God gave him?**
   he pushed the pillars to make the temple fall down

 # Bible Words To Remember

Be strong in the Lord and in the power of His might. Ephesians 6:10
O Lord God, remember me, I pray! Judges 16:28

Choosing God's Way

God Confidence

What if you woke up tomorrow and found out that you could not run anymore? Remember Samson? That is what happened to him. He laughed at God and said, "I am strong all by myself!" He forgot that God was the One who made him strong. He was sorry that he forgot and he asked God to remember him and make him strong one more time. God listened to his prayer, and Samson had his strength back to help his people. Always remember, God gives you strength everyday, too!

What happened when Samson forgot that it was God who made him strong?
Who makes us strong so that we can do the right things?

Bible Beginnings

Ruth: The Book of Ruth

❤ Bible Love Lesson ❤

"Mom, I'm so hungry!" Have you ever said that? When mom hears that, she usually will say, "Let's get lunch ready." Then you can help her make a sandwich or something else good to eat. Rain makes food grow so that we will have delicious things to eat.

Bible Story: A Family Moves

Key Points

❖ The people in Bethlehem were very hungry because the food did not grow.

❖ One man took his family to another place where there was food.

❖ The family wanted to go back to their home someday.

❖ Naomi's husband and sons died before they could return to Bethlehem. God took care of Naomi.

In Bethlehem the people could not get food. The land around them in Israel was very dry for a very long time. There was no rain.

Finally, one man decided that he and his family would leave their home and go to a place called Moab. "We will go where there is food," Elimelech told his wife, Naomi. "Get our two sons ready for the **journey**."

The happy family left Bethlehem, knowing that they were going to a place where there was food to eat. They planned to go back to their home when the **crops** were growing again.

After they had been in Moab for a while, a sad thing happened. Elimelech died. The two sons married women from Moab and the family was again happy for a while. But then both of Naomi's sons died. Naomi felt **lonely** without her husband and sons. God knew how sad Naomi was. He had a plan to take care of her.

Word and Phrase Meanings

finally: after waiting a period of time

repay: to give back something

refuge: a place where it is safe

journey: a long trip

crops: food growing on the land

lonely: a feeling of being alone

reward: to be given something because you have done the right thing

under whose wings: an expression of safety and protection

Guided Prayer Thought

Thank You God, for showing us that You care about us. Thank You for taking care of this family in the Bible and that even when sad things happened, You were there to comfort them.

Amen

Questions:
Thinking & Remembering

1. Where could the people not get food?
   in Bethlehem

2. Why was there no food in the land of Israel?
   it was dry because it had not rained.

3. What did one man decide to do?
   he took his family to Moab

4. What were the names of the man and woman?
   Elimelech and Naomi

5. What did the family think they would do when there was food again?
   go back to Bethlehem

6. What sad thing happened after they had been in Moab for a while?
   Elimelech, Naomi's husband, died

7. What did the sons do?
   married women from Moab

8. What happened again that was sad for Naomi and her son's wives?
   the son's died

9. Who cared that Naomi was sad?
   God

 # Bible Words To Remember

. . .Your God will be My God.   Ruth 1:16

The Lord **repay** your work, and a full **reward** be given you by the Lord God of Israel, **under whose wings** you have come for **refuge**.
Ruth 2:12

Praise Hymn

Sing or say these words
Resource: My First Hymnal Pg. 29

PEACE LIKE A RIVER

I've got peace like a river,
I've got peace like a river,
I've got peace like a river in my soul.
I've got joy like a fountain,
I've got joy like a fountain,
I've got joy like a fountain in my soul.
I've got love like an ocean,
I've got love like an ocean,
I've got love like an ocean in my soul.

♥ Bible Love Lesson ♥

God wants us to love our families and our homes. He knows that by loving each
other and loving Him, it will be the very best place for us to learn how
He wants us to live and to know how much He loves us.

Bible Story: Longing for Bethlehem

Key Points

❖ **Naomi decided to go back to
  Bethlehem to the people who
  loved God.**

❖ **The wives of Naomi's sons
  who had died loved Naomi.**

❖ **Ruth and Orpah traveled with
  Naomi to make sure she was
  safe.**

Naomi was **longing for** her home in Bethlehem. The rains had
come and there was food again. She thought about seeing family
that she had left behind. She thought about all the **familiar** things
she loved. Most of all, she thought about the people who loved
God in the same way that she did.

She decided to go back to Bethlehem. She knew she would miss
her daughters-in-law, Ruth and Orpah. She had **grown** to love
them. They were kind and good to her. And they had **offered** her
much **comfort** after her husband and sons died.

She packed her **belongings** and her daughters-in law, Orpah and
Ruth traveled with her. They wanted her to be safe. They loved
her, too.

Word and Phrase Meanings

longing for:	to want something you used to have
familiar:	things that you are used to; that you know about
grown:	to care for more and more
comfort:	to make someone feel better
offered:	to give
belongings:	things that are yours, that you own

Guided Prayer Thought

Thank You, God for our families. Help us to show love to each
other in the same way that this family cared for each other.
Amen

Questions:
Thinking & Remembering

1. What was Naomi longing for?
   her home in Bethlehem

2. What had changed in Bethlehem?
   there was rain so food could grow
   again

3. What had Naomi been thinking about?
   her family and the things she loved

4. What was most important to her?
   the people in Bethlehem believed
   in God

5. What did she decide to do?
   to go back to Bethlehem

6. Whom would she miss?
   her daughters-in-law, Ruth and Orpah

7. What is said about these two women?
   they were kind and good and
   comforted her

8. Why did Orpah and Ruth travel with her?
   they wanted her to be safe because
   they loved her too

 # Bible Words To Remember

. . .Your God will be My God.   Ruth 1:16

The Lord repay your work, and a full reward be given you by the Lord God
of Israel, under whose wings you have come for refuge.
Ruth 2:12

Choosing God's Way

Loving Home
and Family

It is so much fun to go on a holiday or vacation! You pack your bags with clothes and a few favorite things and go on an adventure to see places and do things you have not done before. After a few days or weeks, though, you begin thinking about the pet you left behind. You remember how soft your own bed is. You miss your friends and all the things that are comfortable. You want to go back home! God wants us to love our homes. He wants us to be happy there with our families.

What do you miss when you go away from your home?
Where does God want us to be happy?

❤ Bible Love Lesson ❤

God can make love very strong in a family. Moms and dads, grandmas and
grandpas, brothers and sisters, aunts and uncles---this makes a family.
Doing things for each other and with each other shows
God's love to others, too!

Bible Story: Back to Bethlehem

Key Points

❖ **Naomi was sad to leave her daughters-in-law, but she wanted them to stay with their own families.**

❖ **Ruth and Orpah cried because they did not want to leave Naomi.**

❖ **Orpah returned to her people. Ruth stayed with Naomi.**

When the three women came close to Israel, Naomi said to Orpah and Ruth, "You have been very kind. But it is time for you to return to your own mother's house. You will get married again and may the Lord grant you rest."

She kissed them and they began to **weep**. "We will go with you to Bethlehem." But Naomi said, "Why should you go with me? You both **deserve** some happiness after the sadness in our lives. Please find joy in having husbands again **among** your own people."

They hugged each other and wept together as they thought of leaving each other and being **separated**. Then Orpah, one daughter-in-law, kissed her mother-in-law and turned toward her own country and family.

Word and Phrase Meanings

weep:	to cry with tears
deserve:	to be worthy of
among:	surrounded by
separated:	to be apart
cooperate:	to work together

Guided Prayer Thought

It is very hard to be separated from the people we love, God. Help us know that You will be with us when we cannot be with each other.
Amen

Questions:
Thinking & Remembering

1. **What happened when the women came close to Israel?**
   Naomi told Orpah and Ruth to return to their home

2. **What did she say about the way they had treated her?**
   that they had been very kind

3. **What did Naomi think the two women should do?**
   get married again

4. **What blessing did she give?**
   "The Lord grant you rest."

5. **What did they do when she kissed them?**
   they began to weep

6. **What did they say they would do?**
   go with her to Bethlehem

7. **Why did Naomi think they should go back to their own family?**
   to be happy and have husbands in their own land

8. **Which daughter-in-law left to go back?**
   Orpah

 # Bible Words To Remember

. . .Your God will be My God. Ruth 1:16

The Lord repay your work, and a full reward be given you by the Lord God of Israel, under whose wings you have come for refuge.
Ruth 2:12

Choosing God's Way

Cooperation

Families don't stay the same size. Every time a new baby is born in a family, it gets bigger. When someone gets married, there is one more person that is part of the family. Not only does the family get bigger in size, it grows in love! God wants families to care for each other and help each other. The kind of love God puts inside of us for our family cannot be broken. It will be strong if we ask God to help us.

How do families get bigger?
*How does God want us to **cooperate** and care for each other?*

♥ Bible Love Lesson ♥

Your mom and dad always love you---even when they are away from you for a while. God always loves you, too. He will be with you wherever you are. Nothing can separate you from God's love!

Bible Story: Don't Ask Me to Leave You!

Key Points

❖ Naomi knew that life in a new country would be hard for Ruth.

❖ Ruth said she wanted to go and that she believed in Naomi's God.

❖ Ruth and Naomi went to Bethlehem together.

Ruth stayed with Naomi as her sister-in-law Orpah began to go back to her own home. Naomi said to Ruth, "You must go also. Life will be **difficult** for you in a new country. It is a **different** way of life in Israel. We worship one God, while your people worship many gods. It will be hard for you to **change**."

But Ruth said, "Please don't keep telling me to go back. I want to go with you. I will live where you live. Your people will be my people. Your God will be my God."

When Naomi saw how **determined** Ruth was, she stopped speaking. She and Ruth went to Bethlehem together. On their **arrival**, the whole city was excited because they had come back from Moab.

Word and Phrase Meanings

difficult:	hard to do; not easy
different:	not the same
determined:	to want to do something strongly
refused:	to not accept what someone wants you to do
encourage:	to give hope; to try to get someone to do something
arrival:	to get to a place
willing:	to want to do something
secure:	safe; protected

Guided Prayer Thought

Dear God, We know that You are the One True God. In the story of Ruth, we see how much she wanted You to be her God. Help us to show Your love to others, like Naomi did, so they will want to love You, too.

Amen

Questions:
Thinking & Remembering

1. Which daughter-in-law stayed with Naomi and **refused** to go back home?
   Ruth

2. What did Naomi **encourage** her to do?
   to return with her sister-in-law Orpah

3. Why did Naomi think Ruth should stay in Moab?
   because life would be difficult for her in a new country

4. How would everything be different?
   the Israelites worshiped one God; they worshiped many

5. What did Ruth beg of her mother-in-law?
   "Don't keep telling me to go back."

6. What did she say she was **willing** to do?
   "Live where she lived." "Your people will be my people." "Your God will be my God."

7. What happened next?
   the two women went to Bethlehem together

8. How did the people in Bethlehem act when they saw them coming?
   they were excited

 # Bible Words To Remember

...Your God will be My God. Ruth 1:16

The Lord repay your work, and a full reward be given you by the Lord God of Israel, under whose wings you have come for refuge.
Ruth 2:12

Choosing God's Way

Being Secure

Do you feel sad when your mom or dad is away? That's because you love them! They will miss you, too. When they return you are so happy to see them. That's because of love. You feel their love and know that they will protect you. You are **secure** knowing that they are there to take care of you. That is what God does, too. And God does it best. He will be there with you always. When you are lonely, ask God to let you feel His love!

How do you feel when your parents are away from you? Who will always be with you and take care of you?

❤ Bible Love Lesson ❤

God takes care of you in so many special ways! God is never too busy to care about you. You are very important and God loves you very much!

Bible Story: Love Story

Key Points

❖ Ruth was kind and took care of Naomi.

❖ Boaz saw how much Ruth loved her mother-in-law. He knew she was special.

❖ Boaz and Ruth loved each other and were married.

❖ Ruth and Boaz had a baby son.

When Naomi and Ruth began a new life in Bethlehem, Ruth took good care of her mother-in-law. She had left her own mother and father and the land she was born in and come to the land of Israel where people **believed** in God.

A very wonderful man, named Boaz, **noticed** Ruth and how much she loved Naomi. He was kind to Ruth and when she was out in the field **gathering** grain, he made sure that his workers helped her and gave her food and water.

Ruth told Naomi how kind and gentle Boaz had been. "God is so good!" Naomi said. "He has taken care of us. You will be very safe with Boaz." Soon, Boaz asked Ruth to be his wife. They loved each other very much and had a beautiful baby son.

Word and Phrase Meanings

believed:	to think that something is true
noticed:	to look at and pay attention to
gathering:	to come together into one place
repay:	to give back something
reward:	to be given something because you have done the right thing
refuge:	a place where it is safe

Guided Prayer Thought

Dear God, You really are so wonderful! You were taking care of Naomi and Ruth all of the time, making sure that they were safe. You will keep us safe too. Even when there are sad times, there is always a happy ending when we love You and believe in You.   *Amen*

Questions:
Thinking & Remembering

1. When Naomi and Ruth began a new life in Bethlehem, who took care of Naomi?
   Ruth

2. Whom had she left?
   her own mother and father

3. In whom did she believe?
   in the God of the Israelites

4. Who noticed Ruth?
   a man named Boaz

5. How did Boaz treat Ruth?
   with kindness

6. How did he make sure she had enough food and water?
   he told his workers to take care of her

7. Was Naomi happy with the attention Boaz gave Ruth?
   Yes. She knew Ruth would be safe.

8. What is the happy ending to this story?
   Ruth and Boaz were married and had a baby boy

 ## Bible Words To Remember

. . .Your God will be My God.   Ruth 1:16

The Lord **repay** your work, and a full **reward** be given you by the Lord God of Israel, under whose wings you have come for **refuge**.
Ruth 2:12

Choosing God's Way

You are Important to God

You may think that God has too many important things to do to think about children, but God is a very big God. The Bible tells us that God knows how many hairs you have on your head! God cares about the little things and the big things. Everything you do is important to God. Everything you think is important to God. Everything you feel is important to God.

Who is important to God?
Does God always have time to care about you?

Bible Beginnings

Lesson 16 - DAY 1

Samuel: 1 Samuel

♥ Bible Love Lesson ♥

Because you were born, your mom and dad can feel a special kind of love.
You bring love and joy and happiness to your parents. You are God's
amazing gift to them, with little hands and feet that grow stronger
every day and arms that hug them. You are wonderful!

Bible Story: Hannah's Prayer

 Key Points

❖ Hannah wanted to have a baby.

❖ Her husband loved her and wanted her to be happy.

❖ Hannah prayed and asked God for a child.

Hannah was very sad. Other women had babies to love and care for. But Hannah didn't even have one!

Hannah's husband loved her very much. He couldn't **understand** why she was so unhappy. He told her, "I love you---please don't cry. Doesn't it help to know that I care about you?"

Hannah loved God and she knew that God would **listen** to her prayer for a baby. "I will go to the **temple**," she thought, "and I will ask God to give me a baby."

Word and Phrase Meanings

understand:	to know the reason why
listen:	to hear what someone says
rejoices:	to have joy; be very happy
temple:	a place to worship God in special ways (church)
heavenly hosts:	the many angels in heaven
blessings flow:	all of God's gifts and the wonderful things that keep happening

Guided Prayer Thought

Dear God, sometimes we cry when we are sad. We know that You care how we feel. Help us to know that You want what is best for us.
Amen

Questions: Thinking & Remembering

1. How did Hannah feel?
   very sad

2. What did other women have to love and care for?
   babies

3. What did Hannah not have?
   even one baby

4. Who loved her very much?
   her husband

5. Give the reason that he didn't understand why she was unhappy?
   he loved her

6. Did he think that should be enough to make her happy?
   Yes. He thought that should be enough.

7. Whom did Hannah know would listen to her prayer for a baby?
   God

8. Where did Hannah go to pray?
   the temple

Bible Words To Remember

My heart **rejoices** in the Lord. 1 Samuel 2:1

Speak, my Lord, for Your servant hears. 1 Samuel 3:10

Praise Hymn

Sing or say these words
Resource: My First Hymnal Pg. 43

PRAISE GOD FROM WHOM ALL BLESSINGS FLOW

Praise God, from whom all **blessings flow**:
Praise Him all creatures here below;
Praise Him above, ye **heavenly hosts**;
Praise Father, Son, and Holy Ghost.
Amen

❤ Bible Love Lesson ❤

Mothers and fathers who love God, want their children to know God's love, too.
They are happy when their children learn and grow in all of God's ways. It is
a very special time when they can see that you want to help
God in important ways.

Bible Story: God Listens

Key Points

❖ Hannah went to the temple
and prayed to God for a
child.

❖ Hannah promised to teach
her child about God.

❖ God heard Hannah's prayer
and she had a baby boy
named Samuel.

❖ Hannah kept her promise and
took Samuel to the temple
to be a helper.

Hannah and her husband visited the **temple** and she **prayed** to
God. "Dear God, please give me a baby boy. I will **promise** to take
care of him and **teach** Him about Your love. He will love You and
be Your **helper**. He will work in the temple."

God listened to Hannah's prayer! God knew that Hannah would
be a very good mother. He knew that she would teach her child
about Him. God answered Hannah's prayer. Soon she had a little
baby son to love. The baby's name was Samuel. Hannah didn't
forget her promise to God. She took care of Samuel and taught
him about God. She told him that God loved Him and told him
about God's commandments. Hannah also remembered that she
had promised God that she would take him back to the temple
when he was old enough and let him be a special helper there.

Word and Phrase Meanings

temple:	a place to worship God in special ways (church)
helper:	working to serve in a good way
pray:	to talk with God
teach:	to tell what another needs to know and help them learn important things
rejoices:	to have joy; be very happy
promise:	doing what you say you will do

Guided Prayer Thought

Dear God, We know that You will listen whenever we talk to You. We are thankful for our church, God's house, where we can say special prayers to You.   Amen

Questions:
Thinking & Remembering

1. Where did Hannah and her husband go?
   the temple

2. What did Hannah pray and ask God for?
   a baby boy

3. What promise did Hannah make to God?
   that she would teach him about God

4. Where would he be a helper?
   at the temple

5. Did God hear Hannah's prayer and answer it?
   Yes. She had a baby boy.

6. What was the boy's name?
   Samuel

7. What promise did Hannah keep?
   she told him that God loved Him and taught him God's commandments

8. Where did she take Samuel when he was old enough?
   to the temple to be a helper there

 # Bible Words To Remember

My heart **rejoices** in the Lord.   1 Samuel 2:1

Speak, my Lord, for Your servant hears. 1 Samuel 3:10

Choosing God's Way

Being a Good Listener

Parent's sometimes promise God at the church that they will be careful to teach you about God and His love for you. When you listen to your parents and do what God tells in His word to do, you are helping your parents keep their promise to God.

What do parents promise God?
How can you help your parents keep their promise to God?

♥ Bible Love Lesson ♥

Your mom and dad like to make things for you that will make you happy. They love to
see the smile on your face when your dad puts a swing in the backyard. Think
of some special things your mom and dad have done for you.
Remember to say "thank you!"

Bible Story: A Helper in God's House

Key Points

❖ Samuel loved God and was a
good helper.

❖ Samuel heard a voice calling
him in the night. It wa☺
God's voice!

❖ God had a very special plan
for Samuel.

Samuel was a good **helper** in the temple. He learned many
wonderful things about God. Every year, his mother, Hannah,
brought him a beautiful new coat to wear. The priest saw that
Hannah missed her son and asked that God would give her more
children so she would not be lonely. God gave her three more
sons and two daughters!

The priest knew that he could call Samuel whenever he needed
him and he would always come to help. One night, Samuel heard
a voice **calling** him in the night. Samuel ran to Eli, the priest and
said, "Here I am!" The priest said, "I didn't call you," go back to
sleep.

Then Samuel heard the voice calling him again. Samuel ran to Eli
the second time. Eli said, "I haven't called you." Samuel went to his
bed and again a voice said "Samuel!" When Eli saw the boy, he
now **knew** it was God calling Samuel. He told Samuel, when you
hear the voice again say, "Speak, Lord, I am listening!" God told
Samuel that He had special plans for him to help the people of
Israel.

Word and Phrase Meanings

calling:	speaking in a way that can be heard
helper:	working to serve in a good way
important:	something that has value
cheerful:	bright, happy and joyful
obedient:	to be willing to do what is asked
knew:	(past tense of know) to be absolutely sure

Guided Prayer Thought

Dear God, Thank You for listening to me when I pray to you.
Help me to hear Your voice and listen for Your calling.
Amen

Questions:
Thinking & Remembering

1. **What kind of helper was Samuel at the temple?**
   a good helper

2. **What did he learn at God's House?**
   wonderful things about God

3. **What did his mother bring to him every year?**
   a new coat

4. **What was the priest's prayer for Hannah?**
   that she would have more children

5. **How did God answer the priest's prayer for Hannah?**
   He gave her three more sons and two daughters

6. **What would Samuel do when Eli, the priest called for him?**
   he would go to help him

7. **How many times did Samuel go to Eli when he heard the voice?**
   three times

8. **Whom did Eli know was calling Samuel after the third time?**
   it was God

9. **What did Eli tell Samuel to do?**
   to say, "Speak Lord, I am listening!"

10. **What did God tell Samuel?**
    that he had special plans for him to help the people of Israel

 # Bible Words To Remember

My heart rejoices in the Lord.   1 Samuel 2:1

Speak, my Lord, for Your servant hears. 1 Samuel 3:10

Choosing God's Way

Being a Helper

Samuel was just a young boy when he listened to God calling him to do **important** work for Him. You are never too little to be God's helper. You can do important things for God right now. You can be **obedient** and **cheerful**. Others will watch you and see the love of Jesus in you!

Do you think you are too young to be a helper for God?
Do you think, "Maybe when I am big or grown up I can do something important?"
How can you be God's helper right now?

♥ Bible Love Lesson ♥

You are God's miracle! There is no one else exactly like you. Whether you have blue eyes or brown eyes, blond hair or black hair, you are unique and very special. and your parents think that you are the best ever. God loves you very much, too, so smile your very own smile!

Bible Story: God's People Want a King

Key Points

❖ Samuel told the people about God and His commandments.

❖ Samuel knew that God could help everyone, even with hard questions.

❖ The people decided that they wanted a king when Samuel was old.

❖ God was sorry that the people wanted a king who would not love them like He did.

Samuel became a good leader. He taught the people how to love God and remember His commandments. Everyone loved Samuel because they knew he did the right thing and was always listening to God, just as he did as a boy helper in God's House.

Whenever the people had hard questions, they would go to Samuel. He was **fair** and **honest** in his answers because he believed that God would help him know what was best. When Samuel was getting older, the people said, "We need a **king** to lead us!" Samuel was very sad. He didn't **understand** that the people were fighting against God, not him.

God was sorry, too. He wanted the people to know that He was their king. They didn't need anyone else to rule over them. Samuel tried to tell the people that they would be sorry when they had a king who did not care about them and love them like God did. But they would not believe Samuel this time.

Word and Phrase Meanings

king: a ruler (someone who tells people what to do)

fair: to treat with equal (the same) respect for everyone

honest: being truthful (telling what is true)

warning: to tell that something bad will happen before it actually does happen

understand: to know the reason why

diligent: working hard to learn

Guided Prayer Thought

Dear God, You love us more than any king or important person on earth can love us! Help us to know what is right to do and love You more.
                                                Amen

Questions:
Thinking & Remembering

1. Why was Samuel a good leader?
   he taught the people how to love God and remember His commandments

2. How did the people feel about Samuel?
   they loved him because he knew the right things to do

3. How did Samuel know what was right?
   he listened to God

4. When the people had hard questions, what did Samuel do?
   he was fair and honest in his answers

5. Whom did Samuel ask to help him?
   God

6. What did the people want when Samuel was getting old?
   a king to lead them

7. Who did Samuel tell the people their king was?
   God

8. What **warning** did Samuel give them about having a king?
   that a king would not care about them and love them like God did

 # Bible Words To Remember

My heart rejoices in the Lord.   1 Samuel 2:1

Speak, my Lord, for Your servant hears.   1 Samuel 3:10

Choosing God's Way

Being Diligent

As you grow and learn more about God and His love, you will know what the right thing to do is. God tells you to be kind. If you feel like being mean and hurting someone, you can be sure that God is not pleased--you don't need to ask Him things He has told us in His word. He will never tell you it is OK to bite someone! It will never be OK to tell someone you hate them.

What will happen when you learn more about God and His love?
How do we know what God wants us to do or not do?

❤ Bible Love Lesson ❤

Some days you might feel extra strong. You think that you can do lots of hard things. Learning at school or playing can be hard work. God will help you and be with you when you need to think hard and be extra strong.

Bible Story: A King

Key Points

❖ God told Samuel to choose a king for the people.

❖ The man he chose was what the people wanted. He was tall and strong.

❖ Saul, the new king, listened to God at first.

❖ When Saul forgot that it was God who made him strong, God said he could no longer be king.

God was Israel's **real** king. They said they wanted a **king** like all the other people around them. So God let them have a king. Samuel had told them what it would be like. It would be **different** than a loving God. Man cannot love in the same way that God loves His people.

God showed Samuel the man who would be Israel's king. He was a tall, strong man who looked the way the people wanted a king to look. His name was Saul.

In the **beginning**, Saul listened to God. He went to fight the enemies of Israel and because he believed God, He won the battles. But Saul began to forget God. He thought that he was strong and didn't need God any longer. He no longer followed God's commandments and did only what he thought was right. He did not pray to ask for God's help and did not listen to Samuel. God said that he would choose a new king.

Word and Phrase Meanings

real:	actual and true
king:	a ruler (someone who tells the people what to do) *An earthly king is not perfect. God is a perfect king and knows what is right and best. We can always trust Him to ask us to do what is good.*
different:	not the same
beginning:	at the very first
change:	to be different

Guided Prayer Thought

Dear God, Sometimes we think that we know what is right without asking You.
Help us to listen to Your word and follow Your commandments.
Amen

Questions:
Thinking & Remembering

1. Who was Israel's real king?
   God

2. What kind of a king did the people want?
   they wanted a king like all the
   other people around them

3. Did God let them have what they wanted?
   Yes

4. How would this king be different than God?
   he could not love them in the same
   way

5. What did the king look like and what was his name?
   he was tall and strong and his name
   was Saul

6. Did the king listen to God in the beginning?
   Yes

7. How did Saul **change**?
   he began to forget God and didn't
   follow His commandments

8. What did God say He would do?
   choose a new king

 # Bible Words To Remember

My heart rejoices in the Lord.   1 Samuel 2:1

Speak, my Lord, for Your servant hears. 1 Samuel 3:10

Choosing God's Way

Doing the Right Thing

Sometimes being a special helper for God is not a lot of fun! When you want to do the right thing, there are times that others will laugh at you for doing what God says. They might say, "It's okay to tell your mom NO". You will have to choose to do what God wants you to do and not listen when someone tells you to do the wrong thing.

Is choosing God's way always easy and fun?
What will you do when someone tells you to do the
wrong thing?
Tell about a time when you chose to do the right thing.

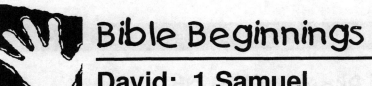

❤ Bible Love Lesson ❤

The people (even those who loved God) sometimes made mistakes. When something is wrong you need to choose to make it right and not stay sad and cry. Ask God to forgive you and help you do the right thing next time! He loves you very much!

Bible Story: God Chooses a New King

 Key Points

❖ Samuel was very sad that Saul would not listen to God.

❖ God told Samuel to stop being sorry and go choose a new king.

❖ God promised Samuel that He would show him who the king would be.

Samuel kept **hoping** that God would **change His mind** about **choosing** a new king. He was so sad that Saul had **turned** from the Lord God. God was sorry that He had made Saul king over Israel.

God said to Samuel, "How long are you going to **grieve** about Saul because I have **rejected** him from being the king of Israel? I want you to go to Bethlehem. I have chosen the new king from one of the sons of a man named Jesse."

"How can I go? If Saul hears that I have done this, he will kill me." God said again, "Go, and I will show you what to do and help you know the one that I am choosing. I will name him to you."

Word and Phrase Meanings

hoping: to believe that something good will happen

choose: to decide between more than one thing

grieve: great sadness

rejected: to turn against

turned: to change from one thing to another

changed his mind: to decide something different than what was said

outward appearance: what someone looks like that you can see

Guided Prayer Thought

Dear God, Samuel didn't even want to think of getting a new king. He was afraid of Saul's anger. Help us to know that You always know what is best and obey You.
                    Amen

Questions:
Thinking & Remembering

1. What did Samuel want God to do?
   change His mind about choosing a new king

2. Why was he sad?
   because Saul had turned from the Lord

3. Why was God sorry?
   that He had made Saul king over Israel

4. What did God want Samuel to stop doing?
   grieving about Saul

5. What did God say He had done?
   rejected Saul from being the king

6. Where did God say Samuel would find the new king?
   in Bethlehem from the sons of Jesse

7. What was Samuel afraid of?
   that Saul would kill him

8. How would God help Samuel know who the new king would be?
   God said, "I will name him to you."

 # Bible Words To Remember

The Lord does not see as man sees; for man looks at the **outward appearance**, but the Lord looks at the heart.   1 Samuel 16:7

Praise Hymn

Sing or say these words
Resource: My First Hymnal Pg. 73

STANDIN' IN THE NEED OF PRAYER

It's me, it's me, it's me, oh Lord--
standin' in the need of prayer.
It's me, it's me, it's me, oh Lord--
standin' in the need of prayer.
Not my brother,
Not my sister, but it's me, Oh Lord,
standin' in the need of prayer.

❤ Bible Love Lesson ❤

Your mom and dad and your friends can see what you look like on the outside. They know if you are wearing a blue shirt or a red dress.   They can see if your face is clean or if it still has peanut butter on it. But God can see inside. He can see your heart and know if you feel love inside. Make God smile when He sees inside you!

Bible Story: Samuel Goes to Bethlehem

 Key Points

❖ **God told Samuel the place to go to find the new king.**

❖ **The new king would love God.**

❖ **God said it was more important to love God than look good on the outside.**

❖ **God can see what is inside a person's heart.**

Samuel obeyed the Lord and went to Bethlehem. The leaders of the town were afraid when they saw him coming. They asked, "Are you coming in **peace**?" Samuel was an important man of God and they didn't know why he would come to their town. Samuel told them, "I have come in peace."

Then he told Jesse and all his sons to **gather** to **sacrifice** to the Lord. When they had come, Samuel looked carefully at each of Jesse's sons. The oldest one was tall and **handsome**. Samuel thought, ' This must be the one God has chosen.'

The Lord said to Samuel, "Do not look at the one who is good-looking and tall, because I have **refused** him. I do not see the same thing that a man sees. A man looks and sees what someone looks like on the outside (**appearance**). I look at the heart of a person."

── Word and Phrase Meanings ──

peace:	a time of quiet and rest; an absence of fighting and war
gather:	to come together in one place
sacrifice:	an offering to God
refused:	to say no to something
handsome:	good looking
appearance:	what someone looks like; a part of a person you can see on the outside
notice:	to look at and pay attention to

Guided Prayer Thought

Dear God, we sometimes think we can tell what a person is like by looking on the outside. You can look at the heart and You know what people are like on the inside. Help us to have a clean heart.
                                                    Amen

Questions:
— Thinking & Remembering —

1. **Where did Samuel go to find the new king?**
   to Bethlehem

2. **What did the leaders in the town ask when he came?**
   "Are you coming in peace?"

3. **What did Samuel invite Jesse and his sons to come to?**
   a sacrifice for the Lord

4. **What did Samuel do when he saw them?**
   he looked carefully at each one

5. **What did he notice about the oldest son?**
   that he was tall and handsome

6. **Did Samuel think that this would be the one?**
   Yes

7. **What did God say that man sees when he is looking?**
   outside appearance

8. **What does God see?**
   the heart

 ## Bible Words To Remember

The Lord does not see as man sees; for man looks at the outward appearance, but the Lord looks at the heart. 1 Samuel 16:7

Choosing God's Way

Beauty

The words grown-ups often use to describe children are: "You're so adorable!", or "You're such a beautiful child!" It feels good to have people say nice things about the way you look, but it is truly wonderful when they say nice things about the way in which you behave, how kind you are, or how pleasant you are. God not only sees how you look on the outside, He sees how you treat your mom and dad and He looks inside to see what you are thinking. He looks at your heart to see the love there.

What is the very best way for people to notice you?
What does God see that people cannot see?

♥ Bible Love Lesson ♥

God has important things for you to do. He tells us in the Bible, "I have plans for YOU!"
Put your very own name in the 'you' spot, because God chooses you for a certain
thing that needs to be done. It doesn't matter if you are little right now. Think
about God and His plan for you.

Bible Story: A Shepherd Boy

 Key Points

❖ Samuel looked at all of the sons of Jesse. One son was missing.

❖ David was out in the fields with the sheep. He was the one God wanted to be king.

❖ David went to King Saul's palace and played his harp because Saul was sad.

❖ David sang and played songs about God.

After Samuel had seen Jesse's sons, God had said, "I have chosen none of these." Samuel said to Jesse, "Are all of your sons here?" Jesse said, "There is one left. He is out in the field taking care of the sheep." Samuel said, "Send someone to bring him." David came. His eyes were bright with excitement and he was good-looking. God said to Samuel, "This is the one!"

David **continued** taking care of his father's sheep until one day, he was called to King Saul's **palace**. Saul had become very sad and **confused** now that **God's spirit** was not with him. He wanted to hear music to make him feel better. David played the **harp** to comfort the king. He sang songs about God as he played.

─ Word and Phrase Meanings ─

continued:	to keep doing
palace:	a very beautiful place where a king or queen lives
confused:	to be mixed up in thinking about what is right
harp:	a musical instrument with strings
God's spirit:	the Helper that makes God's love strong inside us

Guided Prayer Thought

Dear God, it is very sad when someone forgets You and does not want to let You help them. Help us never to forget Your love and to come to You for help. *Amen*

Questions:
Thinking & Remembering

1. What did God say about Jesse's sons that were there?
   "I have not chosen any of these."

2. What question did Samuel ask Jesse?
   "Are all of your sons here?"

3. Which one of his sons was missing?
   the one taking care of the sheep

4. What was this son's name?
   David

5. What did God tell Samuel?
   "This is the one."

6. What do you think was the most important reason that God chose David----because he was good-looking or that he had a good heart?
   he had a good heart---a heart that loved God

7. Why did David go to the palace?
   to sing and play his harp for Saul

8. Why was Saul sad and confused?
   God's spirit had left him

 # Bible Words To Remember

The Lord does not see as man sees; for man looks at the outward appearance, but the Lord looks at the heart. 1 Samuel 16:7

Choosing God's Way

Being Important

Can you imagine how excited you would be if the most important leader in your church came to your house and asked for YOU? What if you were playing outside and that person said to your dad, "Bring him into the house, now. God has chosen your child for a very important job." It might be a little scary because you are just a child right now. But God makes everyone He chooses 'right' for the job!

Who has chosen you for a very important job?
Who will help you be 'right' for the job He has for you?

❤ Bible Love Lesson ❤

When someone is bigger and stronger than you are, you may feel like some of the soldiers did in the Bible story today. A giant wanted to fight them and they were afraid. Everyone was afraid except one boy. He knew that God was stronger than the giant. You can always remember how strong God is and how much He loves you.

Bible Story: David and the Giant

 Key Points

❖ The giant of the Philistines wanted to fight God's people.

❖ All the soldiers were afraid to fight the giant. David was not afraid.

❖ David knew that God was stronger than the giant.

❖ David killed the giant because the Lord God was with him.

"You will never believe how big Goliath is!" David's brothers were with Saul's army, fighting the Philistines. David was visiting his brothers, who were afraid of this **enemy giant**. They were not the only ones who were afraid. All of Saul's army was afraid. No one would go out and fight him.

David said, "Goliath is not stronger than our God! I will go out and fight this giant!" David took five stones and a **sling** to **aim** at this giant of a man. It was the **weapon** he had used as a shepherd to kill a lion and a bear who were attacking his sheep.

When Goliath saw that David was just a boy, he laughed loudly. David shouted, "I come to you in the name of the Lord!" The first stone went into his sling and flew through the air hitting Goliath in the forehead. The giant fell to the ground, dead. The Philistine army ran away when they saw what had happened to their **champion**.

God was with David and Israel was saved from the Philistines.

Word and Phrase Meanings

enemy:	one who wants bad things to happen and hurt someone
giant:	a huge person with great strength
sling:	a strap in which a stone can be thrown
aim:	to point to a mark
weapon:	something that will harm or kill
champion:	someone who is the strongest and best in a contest

Guided Prayer Thought

No one can be stronger than You, Dear God! Help us remember that we do not need to be afraid because You will help us be brave.
Amen

Questions:
Thinking & Remembering

1. **What size was Goliath?**
   big (he was more than nine feet tall - I Samuel 17:4)

2. **Where were David's brothers?**
   with Saul's army

3. **Who was the enemy they were fighting?**
   the Philistines

4. **Who was afraid of the giant Goliath?**
   all of Saul's army

5. **Why was David surprised that they were afraid?**
   because God is stronger than a giant

6. **What did David say he would do?**
   go fight the giant

7. **What did David use to fight the giant?**
   five stones and a sling

8. **What did Goliath do when he saw that a boy had come to fight him?**
   he laughed

9. **What did David say to the giant?**
   "I come to you in the name of the Lord!"

10. **Who was with David to help him kill the giant?**
    God

 # Bible Words To Remember

The Lord does not see as man sees; for man looks at the outward appearance, but the Lord looks at the heart. 1 Samuel 16:7

Choosing God's Way

Being Strong

Do you know what a giant is? Sometimes it may seem like it is just something or someone bigger and stronger than you. The giant in the Bible was even taller than your dad. But sometimes the 'giant' for you is just something hard that you have to do. It seems like a big job to help plant a garden, or make your bed when it is messed up. Whatever you have to do or whomever you have to face (the big kid next door who says he will take your ball away), God will help you with your giant!

What is a giant?
Tell about something that seemed like a 'giant' to you.
Who is stronger than any giant?

❤ Bible Love Lesson ❤

Learning to share your very favorite toy is hard to do. God wants you to be able to love friends in a way that will make sharing easy. Friends are much more important than toys! God will help you share with others.

Bible Story: A Best Friend

Key Points

❖ The king's son, Jonathan, wanted David to be his friend.

❖ They promised each other that they would always be friends.

❖ The king was angry because David would be the next king. He tried to kill David.

❖ God took care of David. Jonathan helped protect David.

After David killed the Philistine giant, King Saul wanted David to live at the palace all the time. David became friends with the king's son, Jonathan. They loved each other as best friends and made a promise that they would always be friends. Jonathan gave David his own robe that only a **prince** would wear. He gave David his **armor**, his sword and his bow and belt.

Then Saul decided he didn't want David at the palace any longer. He even tried to kill David! Saul was **jealous** of David because he knew that David was going to be the next king. Jonathan **protected** Him and told him to stay away from the king.

Jonathan and David hoped the king would **change his mind** and not be angry at David anymore. Jonathan told David that he would give him a **signal** if it were safe to come back to the palace. He shot an arrow **beyond** the rock which meant that David should run for his life. It was no longer safe to be at the palace. But God would take care of David until it was time for him to become king.

Word and Phrase Meanings

prince:	the son of a king
armor:	a shield(cover) to protect the soldier
jealous:	wanting to keep what one has (Saul wanted to still be king and knew that God had chosen David to be king)
protected:	to take care of and keep safe
signal:	a warning sign
beyond:	past a certain point
change his mind:	to make a different decision and think something else

Guided Prayer Thought

Dear God, please remember our special friends today. Help us to show the same kindness that David and Jonathan showed to each other.
Amen

Questions:
Thinking & Remembering

1. Where did David live after he killed the giant?
   at the palace

2. Who became best friends?
   Jonathan and David

3. What did they promise each other?
   that they would always be friends

4. What five things did Jonathan give David?
   his robe, armor, sword, bow and belt

5. How did Saul change?
   he didn't want David to live at the palace and tried to kill him

6. Why was Saul jealous of David?
   he knew that David was going to be the next king

7. Who protected him and told him to stay away from the king?
   Jonathan

8. What was the signal Jonathan gave David to run for his life?
   he shot an arrow beyond the rock

 # Bible Words To Remember

The Lord does not see as man sees; for man looks at the outward appearance, but the Lord looks at the heart.   1 Samuel 16:7

Choosing God's Way

Being a Good Friend

A best friend will come to your house to play, even if you don't have the new toy that all the kids like! He plays with you because he likes YOU! Even when you do something he doesn't like, he will still be your friend. Jesus is our very BEST friend because He always loves us, even when we are mad. He wants you to be someone's best friend too, and show the kind of love He has for you!

Why will your best friend play with you?
How can you be someone's best friend?
Tell about a friend and why you like each other?

David, the King: 2 Samuel

♦ Bible Love Lesson ♥

Nothing is too hard for God! There are no problems that are too big for Him to handle.
There are no problems that are too small for Him to care about. And when God
says He will be with you--and He did--He will!

Bible Story: The City of God

Key Points

❖ David wanted to honor God by building a wonderful city while he was king.

❖ The city would be built in the land God promised the Israelites.

❖ The people in that land thought that the Israelites were not strong enough to *conquer* them.

❖ God was with David. God helped the Israelites take the city.

David was the king of all Israel. He wanted a city that would **honor** God and His kingdom on earth. Jerusalem was the perfect place. The city was set high on a **ridge** with hills around it. God wanted the Israelite's to make this their city when they had first entered the **promised land**.

It was time to take this city and make it a special place for Israel in the land that God had promised them. The people that were in this city laughed at David and said, "You will never be strong enough to take the city of Jerusalem!"

King David and his men went to Jerusalem and God helped them win against the armies that were there. Then David moved into the city and became great because God was with him.

Word and Phrase Meanings

honor:	to think about in a very special way; with respect and worship (God)
promised land:	the place God gave His people to live
ridge:	a place above; hill
conquer:	to fight and win over
weapons:	things to fight with; swords

Guided Prayer Thought

Dear God, We know that we cannot be strong all by ourselves. It is because You will make us strong when we believe and trust in You.
Amen

Questions:
Thinking & Remembering

1. Who was the king over all of Israel?
   David

2. What kind of a city did he want?
   one that would honor God and His kingdom

3. What city did David decide would be right for this?
   the city of Jerusalem.

4. Who wanted this to be a city in Israel when the people entered this promised land?
   God

5. What did the people who were in that city do when they heard that David was coming to take the city?
   they laughed

6. What did they say to try and frighten David?
   "You will never be strong enough!"

7. Who helped the Israelites win against the armies in Jerusalem?
   God

8. Did David become great because he was strong and had **weapons**?
   No. He was strong because he believed that God would help him.

 ## Bible Words To Remember

You are great, O Lord God. There is none like You, nor is there any God besides You.   2 Samuel 7:22

...Your words are true.   2 Samuel 7:28

Praise Hymn

Sing or say these words
Resource: My First Hymnal Pg. 20

GOD MADE ME

God made me, God made me,
In my Bible-Book it says that
God made me.
God loves me, God loves me,
In my Bible-Book it says that
God loves me.
God helps me, God helps me,
In my Bible-Book it says that
God helps me.

♥ Bible Love Lesson ♥

You can trust God for everything! Little things and big things are important to Him.
If your dog is lost, tell Him. If your little finger hurts, tell Him. God understands
all our hurts and even when He knows it is not best to fix everything,
He will be there to help you through it.

Bible Story: Peace for Israel

Key Points

❖ God's people rested and were happy when they obeyed God.

❖ David was a good king who believed and trusted in God.

❖ God said that David's son would build a temple in the city of Jerusalem.

Finally, there was a time of peace and **contentment** for God's people, the Israelites. They had been at war for many years and they were happy for the rest, a time when they could live with their families and be together. David was a strong king who believed in God and was not afraid to trust God for everything.

David wanted to do something great for God and build a beautiful **temple** for worship. He told the **prophet** of God, Nathan, about what he wanted to do.

Nathan said that God did not want David to build the temple. David's son Solomon, who would be the next king, would build it. David wanted to do this special thing for God but he was happy that God would let his son be king after him.

Word and Phrase Meanings

contentment:	feeling happy about what you have right now
temple:	a building for worship to God (church)
successful:	doing the right things to make good things happen
disappointed:	wishing that something could happen that didn't
prophet:	someone who tells what will happen

Guided Prayer Thought

Dear God, thank You for peace and contentment. Thank You for giving us the rest we need. Help us to remember to trust and believe in You always.
Amen

Questions:
Thinking & Remembering

1. What changed in Israel when David became king?
   there was peace and contentment

2. What had been happening for many years?
   Israel had been at war

3. Can families be together if there is war?
   No. In Bible times the men were out fighting.

4. Why was David a strong and **successful** king?
   he believed in God and was not afraid to trust Him

5. What did David want to do for God?
   build a temple for worship

6. Whom did he tell that he wanted to do this?
   the prophet, Nathan

7. Whom did Nathan tell David would build the temple?
   David's son, Solomon

8. Why was David happy, even though he was **disappointed**?
   because God would let his son be king after him

Bible Words To Remember

You are great, O Lord God. There is none like You, nor is there any God besides You.　2 Samuel 7:22

. . .Your words are true.　2 Samuel 7:28

Choosing God's Way

Having Contentment

There are many happy moments you can think of like riding the merry-go-round, going to the park to feed the ducks or having a special visit with grandma to bake cookies. But sometimes after you do one special thing, you want to do another right away. It is hard to keep still, but you can learn to do it. The Bible tells us to be still and know that He is God. Think about His love for you. Be still and enjoy and be content with your happy times.

Think about a special and happy time you have had.
Can you stop and just enjoy a happy moment without always wanting more?
What does the Bible say about being still?

♥ Bible Love Lesson ♥

It is so wonderful to have a special friend to talk with and play with! Friends stick with you all the time and they keep their promise to be your friend. Not everyone is a true friend. God will help you keep your promises and be a good friend to others.

Bible Story: David Remembers a Promise

Key Points

❖ David often remembered his friend Jonathan.

❖ David kept his promise to take care of anyone from Jonathan's family.

❖ Best friends remember their promises to each other.

David often thought about his wonderful **friend**, Jonathan. He wished that he could be with him and talk to him as they had in the palace when Saul was king.

One day he asked his servant to find out if anyone from Jonathan's family was still alive. "I made a **promise** to Jonathan to take care of his family", he said. "I want to keep my promise."

The servant found out that there was one boy who was saved from all of Jonathan's family. A **nurse** had tried to **protect** him but as she was running away with him, she fell, and the boy was hurt. Both of his feet were **lame**. David's servant brought Jonathan's son to him. David said, "I want to take care of you and give you all that you need." Your father was my best friend and we promised that we would care for each other's family.

Word and Phrase Meanings

friend:	someone who likes you and is on your side; someone you can trust
promise:	doing what you say you will do
nurse:	one who takes care of others
protect:	to keep safe from harm
lame:	a body part (like legs or arms) that are weak or do not work properly

Guided Prayer Thought

Dear God, we thank You for our friends. Help us to keep our promises to always be kind to each other and care for one another.
Amen

Questions:
Thinking & Remembering

1. **Whom did David think about?**
   his friend Jonathan

2. **What did he ask his servant to do?**
   to see if there was anyone from Jonathan's family still alive

3. **What was his promise to Jonathan?**
   that he would take care of his family

4. **What did David want to do?**
   keep his promise

5. **What did the servant find out?**
   that there was only one boy who was still alive

6. **What had happened to this boy?**
   he was hurt and his feet were lame

7. **How did this happen?**
   the nurse was running away with him to keep him safe

8. **What did David tell Jonathan's son?**
   that he would take care of him and give him all that he needed

 ## Bible Words To Remember

You are great, O Lord God. There is none like You, nor is there any God besides You.   2 Samuel 7:22

. . .Your words are true.   2 Samuel 7:28

Choosing God's Way

Keeping Promises

Sometimes you think maybe it isn't important to keep a promise. Maybe you told your grandpa when he was visiting you that you would make a picture for him. Your mom said she would send it in the mail. But after grandma and grandpa go back to their home which may be far away, you forget or think it is not important. It is important! God wants you to do what you say you will do. Keep your promises. God always keeps His!

What promises have you made to other people?
Why are promises important to keep?
Who always keeps promises?

♥ Bible Love Lesson ♥

Choosing to love and be kind to everyone is important. It is hard to think of others and not yourself all the time. It is something you can learn to do with God's help and your parents. Ask God to help you think kind things, say kind things, and do kind things.

Bible Story: David Disobeys God's Law

 Key Points

❖ The Israelites had war again while David was still king.

❖ David disobeyed God's commandment.

❖ Because of David's sin, there was sadness.

❖ God was very sorry that David had done wrong.

The **peace** of Israel did not last long. Soon they were at war again. One time, David stayed at the **palace** while his men went out to **battle**.

David could not sleep one night and went out on his **rooftop** into the night air. He saw a woman who was the wife of one of his commanders. Her name was Bathsheba. David did not think about God. He only thought about how beautiful this woman was. David took this woman to his room and did not obey God's law about loving someone who belonged to someone else. God wants a man and woman to keep themselves special for only the person they are married to. Now David had broken God's law. God was very sorry David had **disobeyed**. There was sadness for David after that.

Word and Phrase Meanings

peace:	a time of quiet and rest
palace:	a very beautiful place where a king or queen lives
battle:	fight; conflict
rooftop:	a patio (like a porch) on the top of a house
disobeyed:	to do what you have been told not to do
compassion:	to show love and sympathy

Guided Prayer Thought

Dear God, When we forget Your Word, we think only of what we want and what we think will make us happy. Help us not to forget that we can only be happy when we follow Your laws.

Amen

Questions:
Thinking & Remembering

1. What did not last very long in Israel?
   peace

2. Where did David stay one time while his men were in battle?
   at the palace

3. Where did David go one night when he could not sleep?
   he went out on his rooftop

4. Whom did he see when he was there?
   the wife of one of his commanders

5. Was David thinking about God?
   No. He was thinking about how beautiful the woman was.

6. What did David do that was wrong?
   he loved a woman who was not his wife and belonged to another man

7. What does God want a man and woman to do?
   keep themselves special for the person they are married to

8. When David did this wrong thing, how did God feel?
   He was sad

 # Bible Words To Remember

You are great, O Lord God. There is none like You, nor is there any God besides You. 2 Samuel 7:22

...Your words are true. 2 Samuel 7:28

Choosing God's Way

Showing Compassion

A good way to decide how God wants you to act is to ask, "What would Jesus do?" How would Jesus want you to treat a child who is in a wheelchair? Would Jesus laugh and say, "Why can't you run and walk like I can?" That would make them sad. Be kind and loving to children who are different than you. God will help you know what they need and being kind makes God smile!

What question can you ask to know how God wants you to act?
To whom should we show kindness and love?
Who will help you know how to treat others?

♥ Bible Love Lesson ♥

When you do the wrong thing, or say the wrong thing, tell the person you hurt that you are sorry that you hurt them. Tell God you are sorry. Even if the person does not forgive you and stays mad, you can know that God will still love you and forgive you.

Bible Story: David Is Sorry-- God Forgives

Key Points

❖ David could not make right what he had done wrong.

❖ The king whom God had blessed was unhappy and troubled.

❖ God's prophet helped David understand how *serious* his sin was.

❖ David asked God to forgive him.

David sent the husband of Bathsheba, the woman he loved and wanted, into battle. The woman's husband and a commander in David's army was killed. David married Bathsheba and they had a child. David was never at **peace** now. God could not bless him for disobeying His laws.

Nathan, the **prophet** of God, came to David to tell him a story. He told him that a rich man had taken a baby lamb from a poor man who had little money. The lamb was the only thing the man had left. The story made David angry. He said, "That man should die because of what he did!" Nathan said, "Oh king, you are that man! You have taken what did not **belong** to you. God gave you so much, and you took something from a man who had little."

David was so **sorry**. He knew he had done wrong. He said, "I have **sinned** against God." Nathan said, "God forgives you, but your child will not live."

Word and Phrase Meanings

peace:	a time of quiet and rest
realize:	to know and understand
prophet:	someone who tells what will happen
belong:	to be someone's own things; to own
sorry:	being sad for something said or done
sinned:	doing wrong against God's laws and commandments

Guided Prayer Thought

Dear God, we know that we cannot be happy when we do wrong things. Please help us to remember how much You love us, even though we sin. We will ask You to forgive us.

Amen

Questions:
Thinking & Remembering

1. What happened to the husband of the woman David loved?
   he was killed

2. What did David do after he died?
   married the woman

3. What could God not do because of David's sin?
   bless him

4. Who came and told David a story?
   the prophet Nathan

5. What did the story tell David?
   that he had taken something that did not belong to him

6. What did this story make David **realize**?
   that he had done a great sin

7. How did David feel?
   he was sorry, he knew he had done wrong

8. Against whom had David sinned?
   against God

9. What did Nathan tell David?
   that God would forgive him

10. What happened to the baby?
    the baby did not live

 Bible Words To Remember

You are great, O Lord God. There is none like You, nor is there any God besides You.   2 Samuel 7:22

. . .Your words are true.   2 Samuel 7:28

Choosing God's Way

Knowing Who to Obey

Do you remember who it was that wanted Adam and Eve to disobey God in the Garden of Eden? Satan never gives up trying to make us do the wrong thing. But we know that God is much stronger and more powerful than Satan. When Satan tries to make us afraid or tries to get us to do wrong things, we can talk to God. Tell God you want to obey Him.

Where did people first begin to disobey God?
Who tries to make us do wrong things?
Who is more powerful and will help us do the right things?

Solomon: The Book of 1 Kings

❤ Bible Love Lesson ❤

God always has a perfect plan! Sometimes we think *our* plan is **perfect**. Then we find that things don't work out and everything goes wrong. God sees all things from the beginning to the end. Talk to God every day and ask Him to show you His plan. He will help you do the right things.

Bible Story: David's Son, Solomon

 Key Points

❖ **King David was old and very sick.**

❖ **David's oldest son wanted to be king, even though he knew that Solomon had been chosen by God.**

❖ **The oldest son planned a celebration to make himself king.**

❖ **God's prophet was not invited to the celebration.**

King David could not get warm! He was getting old and could not get out of bed. David did think about God and what God had told him about who would be the new king. God had said that his son, Solomon, would be king.

But David had other sons and his oldest son thought that he should be king because he was older than Solomon. One day, Adonijah decided that it was time for him to be **crowned** king of Israel.

A big **celebration** was planned. Many were **invited**, but some were not invited. Someone very important was not **welcome** to come. It was the prophet, Nathan. Nathan knew who God had chosen. It was not Adonijah, it was Solomon.

Word and Phrase Meanings

perfect:	the very best it can be
celebration:	a very special party
crowned:	to put a beautiful covering of gold or jewels on someone's head to show that they are a king or queen
invited:	to be asked to come
welcome:	to accept someone with kindness

Guided Prayer Thought

Dear God, we know that You have a plan. Help us to remember that what You plan is best.
Amen

Questions:
Thinking & Remembering

1. Which words tell that King David was getting old and was sick?
   he could not get warm, he could not get out of bed

2. Who did David think about?
   God

3. Did David know who would be the next king? Who was it?
   Yes. It would be his son Solomon.

4. What did one of his sons think?
   that he should be king

5. Which son decided to be king?
   Adonijah

6. What did he plan?
   a celebration

7. Who was not invited?
   the prophet, Nathan

8. Whom did Nathan know that God had chosen?
   God had chosen Solomon

 # Bible Words To Remember

As for God, His way is perfect.   2 Samuel 22:31

God is my strength and power, and He makes my way perfect.
2 Samuel 22:33

Praise Hymn

Sing or say these words
Resource: My First Hymnal Pg. 15

WHAT A MIGHTY GOD WE SERVE

What a mighty God we serve!
What a mighty God we serve!
Angels bow before Him,
Heaven and earth adore Him.
What a mighty God we serve.

❤ Bible Love Lesson ❤

Sometimes children forget what their mom or dad tells them to do. But sometimes children *choose* to just not remember. Choosing not to remember results in unpleasant and unhappy times. Always choose to remember so your parents don't have to remind you again and again.

Bible Story: Solomon Is King

Key Points

❖ When God's prophet heard that a celebration was being planned for the wrong son to become king, he wanted to let King David know.

❖ Solomon's mother reminded David about whom God wanted to become king.

❖ David kept his promise to make Solomon the next king.

Nathan heard about the celebration Adonijah was having. He knew that he had not been invited. He knew that Solomon had not been invited. He knew that King David did not know about his older son's plan to take over his **throne.**

So Nathan went to Solomon's mother and told her to go to the king. King David was not too sick to remember what God had told him. Then Nathan also talked to the king to **remind** him of what God had told them about who would be king.

King David said, "I will keep my **promise** that I made to God that Solomon would be king. Blow the trumpet and shout, 'God save King Solomon! He will sit on the throne of Israel.'" All the people played flutes and were so happy that the earth seemed to burst with joy.

― Word and Phrase Meanings ―

throne: a special and fancy chair for a king or queen to sit in

remind: to tell something again to someone

promise: doing what you say you will do

perfect: the very best that can be

Guided Prayer Thought

Dear God, we are glad that You like celebrations!
Help us to be joyful when we are doing what is right.
Amen

Questions:
Thinking & Remembering

1. Who heard about the celebration of David's son?
   Nathan

2. Who had not been invited?
   Nathan or Solomon

3. Did this son tell King David about the celebration to take the throne?
   No

4. Whom did Nathan tell about the plan first?
   Solomon's mother

5. What did David remember?
   what God had told him---Solomon would be king

6. What did David say when Nathan reminded David?
   I will keep my promise

7. What words did David say they should shout when the trumpet blew?
   "God save King Solomon!"

8. How happy were the people?
   so happy that the earth seemed to burst with joy

 # Bible Words To Remember

As for God, His way is **perfect.** 2 Samuel 22:31

God is my strength and power, and He makes my way perfect.
2 Samuel 22:33

Choosing God's Way

Being Dependable

There are times that we need a reminder of what we promise to do. Maybe you promised mom you would go to bed right after you finished watching a video. Then you begin watching another video! Your dad needs to say to you, "You promised to..." You are reminded! Always do what you say you will do. When you do that, your mom and dad will be very proud of you. They will say, "We can trust you!" God will be pleased, too.

What should you always do when you make a promise? How will your parents feel when you don't need to be reminded?

♥ Bible Love Lesson ♥

God cares about you so much that He **considers** what will be best for you. His love
is so perfect! There are many things you will learn that may be difficult. If
you go too fast on your tricycle and fall, you will learn that you need
to go slow at first. God will be saying, "It's OK! Try again!"

Bible Story: David Instructs the New King

Key Points

❖ Even though David made
mistakes when he was king,
he loved God.

❖ David remembered to ask
God to forgive him when he
was wrong.

❖ David told Solomon to always
obey God's laws.

❖ Solomon wanted to be a
good king and do all that
God commanded.

David loved God. He had made **mistakes** as king of Israel but he
asked God to **forgive** him. He learned many **lessons** about what
a king should do. He told Solomon that he must always obey
God's laws. . . . this was the most **important** thing to remember.
Solomon listened carefully to his father. He wanted to be a good
king.

After David died, Solomon had a lot of work to do as king. He
heard about all the **problems** the people had and tried to be **fair**
when he told them what to do. Being a king was harder than he
thought it would be!

Solomon knew that he could not do the work of a king all by
himself. He went alone to be with God. He wanted to do what God
asked of him.

Word and Phrase Meanings

mistakes: to be wrong about something

forgive: to excuse someone for doing wrong

lessons: learning from experiences

important: something that has value

problems: things that are hard or difficult to figure out

fair: honest; treating two or more people equally

consider: think about carefully

Guided Prayer Thought

*Dear God, We know that we can never do all the right
things all by ourselves. We need Your help!*
Amen

Questions:
Thinking & Remembering

1. Which king loved God?
   David

2. Why was David not a perfect king?
   he made mistakes (he was like all of us!)

3. What made David different from the king before him, king Saul?
   he asked God to forgive him

4. What had David learned?
   many lessons about what a king should do

5. What did David tell Solomon was most important?
   to obey God's laws

6. Why did Solomon listen carefully to his father, David?
   he wanted to be a good king

7. What did Solomon try to do after David died and he was king?
   he tried to be fair and listen to people's problems

8. What did Solomon find out about being a king?
   it was hard to do by himself---he needed God's help

 # Bible Words To Remember

As for God, His way is perfect. 2 Samuel 22:31

God is my strength and power, and He makes my way perfect.
2 Samuel 22:33

Choosing God's Way

Following God's Rules

God tells parents to make sure that you know God's commandments. God did not make rules to make you unhappy. Following God's rules will make you happy. Some children think that 'rules' are made so that they can never do what they want to do, when they want to do it. Don't forget that God knows what is best for you!

Who does God put in charge of making sure you know His commandments?
Why is it important to follow God's rules?

♥ Bible Love Lesson ♥

God loves you enough to give you thoughts and words so you can know right from wrong. There will be times when your mom or dad is not 'right there' to say, "No, that will hurt you." That is when you will have 'God thoughts'. Listen! God is telling you what is right to do.

Bible Story: God is With Solomon

Key Points

❖ God asked Solomon what he wanted so he could to be a good king.

❖ Solomon asked God to make him wise.

❖ God gave Solomon wisdom and riches.

❖ God promised Solomon that he would live a long time if he obeyed Him.

Solomon had a dream at night after he prayed and **offered** gifts to God. God came to Solomon and asked him, "What shall I give you?" Solomon thought of the many things that he did not know how to do. He told God that His people were a great people and he would need to be able to have an **understanding heart** to know what was good and what was **evil**. He asked that God would make him **wise**.

God was very **pleased** that Solomon had asked this. He said, "You could have asked to be rich and powerful or to live a very long time. But you have chosen to ask for the best thing, to be wise. "

God told Solomon, "I will give you a wise and understanding heart, so that there will never be anyone as wise as you. I will also give you riches. And if you **obey** me, you will live a long life.

Word and Phrase Meanings

offered:	to give to someone to accept or reject
understanding heart:	knowing what the right thing to do is and doing it in a kind way
evil:	bad and sinful behavior
wise:	knowing and understanding what is right
pleased:	happy, satisfied
obey:	to listen and do what is asked

Guided Prayer Thought

Dear God, When we remember to keep You the most important in our lives, You will help us to be wise and make the right choices.
                                        Amen

Questions:
Thinking & Remembering

1. What happened when Solomon was praying to God?
   he had a dream

2. What had Solomon been doing?
   praying and offering gifts to God

3. What question did God ask Solomon?
   "What shall I give you?"

4. What did Solomon think about himself?
   that there were many things that he did not know

5. What did Solomon think he would need most in being King of God's people?
   an understanding heart

6. What would he know if he had an understanding heart?
   he would know what was good and what was evil

7. What did God say that he could have asked for?
   to be rich and powerful or to live a very long time

8. What did God give Solomon because he had chosen the best thing?
   wisdom and riches and also a long life

Bible Words To Remember

As for God, His way is perfect.   2 Samuel 22:31

God is my strength and power, and He makes my way perfect.
2 Samuel 22:33

Choosing God's Way

Being Wise

In the Bible, King Solomon asked God to make him wise. He didn't ask for a big house or lots of money. He knew that the most important thing was to know what was the right thing to do. We need God to help us know what is right to do. There are so many things to choose to do and so many things you can choose to be. You can know that God will help you choose what is best!

What would you ask for if you could have anything you wanted?
What is the most important thing you can want to have?

❤ Bible Love Lesson ❤

Even when you are a child, you decide what you will do many times each day. Maybe your
mom tells you to decide what to wear, the red shirt or the yellow shirt. You can also
decide whether or not to obey what your parents tell you to do. What is Best?
What will you decide?

Bible Story: Solomon is Wise

 Key Points

❖ **Solomon knew that God was with him.**

❖ **God helped Solomon make wise decisions.**

❖ **Solomon wrote down the wise things that God told him.**

❖ **Solomon built a wonderful temple for the worship of God.**

After Solomon's dream, he knew that God had been with him and
had been speaking to him. He knew that God would help him make
the right **decisions** and help him be a good king.

Solomon was so **wise** that all the other **nations** heard about the
decisions he made, and they were very good decisions! One time
two women came to the king with one baby. Each woman said that
the baby was hers. The king told his soldiers to cut the baby in half!
Of course the real mother did not want the baby to be hurt and cried
out, "Do not **harm** the baby!" Then the king knew who the mother
was and gave the baby to her.

Solomon wrote many wise sayings that we have in our Bible called
the **Proverbs**. These words tell many important things about the
right way to act and live.

King David had told Solomon before he died that he would be the
one to build a great and beautiful temple for God. When the house of
God was finished, there was music and singing. They sang, "Praise
the Lord, because He is good. His love will last forever!" Solomon
thanked God for letting him be a good king for Israel.

— Word and Phrase Meanings —

decisions: thinking about and making a choice between two or more things

wise: knowing and understanding what is right

nations: groups of people living together in the same land or country

harm: to hurt in some way

proverb: a short wise saying that helps one know what to do

humble: not bragging about how great you are

Guided Prayer Thought

Dear God, when we ask You to help us, You will answer our prayers.
Help us to be good servants. Thank You for loving us forever!
                                        Amen

Questions:
Thinking & Remembering

1. What did Solomon know?
   that God had been speaking with him.

2. What was he sure that God would do?
   help him make the right decisions,
   help him be a good king

3. What special thing did God give Solomon?
   wisdom

4. Tell what kind of decisions Solomon made because he was wise.
   very good decisions

5. What was one hard decision Solomon had to make?
   to choose the mother of the baby

6. How did he know which woman was the baby's mother?
   the real mother did not want the baby harmed

7. What did Solomon write that is in the Bible?
   wise sayings (Proverbs)

8. What had king David told Solomon to do?
   build a great and beautiful temple for God

9. Tell the words of the song the people sang.
   "Praise the Lord, because He is good. His love will last forever!"

10. What did Solomon thank God for?
    for letting him be a good king for Israel

 ## Bible Words To Remember

As for God, His way is perfect.   2 Samuel 22:31

God is my strength and power, and He makes my way perfect.
2 Samuel 22:33

Choosing God's Way

Being Humble

We can find out what is happening in the world by reading the newspaper or watching the news on TV. In the Bible when kings did great and wonderful things people knew what happened because people told other people as they traveled from place to place. King Solomon was famous. People went all over telling of his greatness. The King said, "It was God who made me great."

How do you find out what is happening in the world? How did people in the Bible find out about the great king Solomon? What did king Solomon say?

Elijah: The Book of 1 Kings

❤ Bible Love Lesson ❤

It is so wonderful to know that we have a God who loves us and cares about us. God will keep telling us in many different ways that He loves us, too! Look for the reminders of His love every day--- the world He made and the people who take care of you and love you.

Bible Story: Israel Forgets God

Key Points

❖ After King Solomon died, his son did not follow God.

❖ The prophet Elijah tried to remind the people of God's laws.

❖ Elijah told them to remember their powerful God.

❖ God protected Elijah when the king wanted to kill him.

After King Solomon died, his son became the new king. He did not follow God. The people began to **worship** other gods and disobeyed God's law. A **prophet** of God tried to **remind** Israel of God's **promises** to them to be His people.

The prophet's name was Elijah. One day he went to the king and said, "There will be no rain in the land for two years. You will know that the God of Israel is the one true God. He has power over everything, even though you have forgotten Him."

The king was so angry that he wanted to kill Elijah. God told Elijah to hide by a **brook** and He would sent a **raven** to feed him. God took care of Elijah.

Word and Phrase Meanings

worship:	to make a special time to show respect and honor
prophet:	someone who speaks for God and tells what will happen
remind:	to tell something again to someone
brook:	a small stream of water
promises:	doing what you say you will do; and agreement
raven:	a large black bird that has a loud call

Guided Prayer Thought

Dear God, It must have been very hard for Elijah to tell the king something that would make him angry. Help us not be afraid to tell others what the truth is.

Amen

Questions:
Thinking & Remembering

1. **What kind of a king was Solomon's son?**
   he did not follow God

2. **What two things did the people do?**
   worshiped other gods and disobeyed God's law

3. **What did the prophet of God try to do?**
   remind them that they were God's people

4. **What was the prophet's name?**
   Elijah

5. **What did Elijah tell the king?**
   that there would not be rain for two years

6. **What did he say that the people of Israel would know?**
   that there is one true God

7. **What did the king want to do to Elijah?**
   kill him

8. **How did God feed Elijah and take care of him?**
   He told him to hide by a brook and he would send a raven to feed him

Bible Words To Remember

The Lord was not in the wind, earthquake or fire. God spoke
in a still, small voice.   1 Kings 19:11-12

Praise Hymn

Sing or say these words
Resource: My First Hymnal Pg. 61

O WORSHIP THE KING

O worship the King,
all glorious above,
And gratefully sing
His wonderul love:
Our Shield and Defender,
the Ancient of Days,
Pavilioned in splendor,
and girded with praise.

❤Bible Love Lesson❤

God's words in the Bible tell us how much He loves us. That is the most wonderful
thing we can know! God's words also tell us God's best plan for each of us.
Learn God's words and say them again and again so that you will
remember and know what is important.

Bible Story: Food that Lasts

 Key Points

❖ **Elijah did what God told him to do.**

❖ **God told Elijah to ask a woman to give him food and water.**

❖ **The woman believed God and shared her last bit of food with Elijah.**

Elijah stayed by the brook until the water dried up. God told him to go to a certain **town.** There would be a woman there who would give him food and take care of him.

When he came to the town, he saw the woman that God had told him about. He asked her for a drink of water. Even though there was very little water the woman was **kind** and brought him water. Then he also asked her for something to eat.

The woman looked very sad. She said, "My son and I will die after I cook this one last **meal** for us." Elijah said, "Do not be afraid. When you give me food, God has told me that you will never run out again until the rains come." God took care of the woman and her son and the food **lasted** until the rain came!

── Word and Phrase Meanings ──

town: a place where a small group of people live

kind: a nice person who cares about others

meal: a time when food is eaten

lasted: to keep on having something

Guided Prayer Thought

*Dear God, Thank You for this story about the kind woman. She shared
what she had, even though it was almost gone! You will always
take care of us when we believe Your Word.*
Amen

Questions:
— Thinking & Remembering —

1. **Where did Elijah stay when there was no rain?**
   by a brook until it dried up

2. **Why did God tell him to go to the town?**
   there would be a woman there who would give him food

3. **When he saw the woman, what did he ask her to give him?**
   water

4. **How did the woman treat Elijah?**
   she was kind

5. **When he asked for something to eat, what did she tell him?**
   that she only had enough for one more meal

6. **What did she think would happen after this meal?**
   she and her son would die

7. **What did Elijah tell her?**
   not to be afraid she would never run out of food.

8. **How long did her food last?**
   until the rain came

 # Bible Words To Remember

The Lord was not in the wind, earthquake or fire. God spoke
in a still, small voice.   1 Kings 19:11-12

Choosing God's Way

Sharing

Can you share what you have---even if it is your very last piece of candy? Most of the time, we want to keep things for ourselves. There is a wonderful story about a woman who shared her last bit of food. Because she was kind and wanted to share, God did something very special. God will help you want to share your things, too.

What have you chosen to give to someone that you wanted to keep for yourself?
What happened because the woman loved God and shared her food?

❤ Bible Love Lesson ❤

It is so wonderful to be able to run into your mom or dad's arms and get extra hugs
and kisses when you feel lonely or afraid. If you get hurt, your parents
are there to fix it with something that will make it better. This
love is what God planned for you to have!

Bible Story: God is Very Powerful

Key Points

❖ **Elijah told the king that there would be no rain until the people came back to God.**

❖ **The people called to their god, but their god could not hear them.**

❖ **Elijah proved that God was the one true God.**

Elijah sent someone to tell the king that he wanted to see him. The king was still angry at Elijah for telling him that there would be no rain.

The king came to Elijah and said, "It was you who brought all this terrible trouble to Israel!" "No" said Elijah, "It was because you and your people have forgotten God and His commandments."

Elijah said that he could **prove** who was the one true God. He told The king that there would be a **contest**. They built two **altars**. One altar to the false god, Baal, one altar for the true God. He told them to ask their god to send fire to burn up the offering, and he would do the same. The people prayed to their false god and nothing happened. They screamed and cried but their god did not hear.

Elijah prayed to God. "O God of Israel, send down fire from heaven and show Your power!" **Immediately** fire burned up all the wood on the altar and even the water that was poured around it. The people cried, "The Lord is the true God. He is the only God of Israel!"

📖 Word and Phrase Meanings

prove:　　　　to show that something is true

contest:　　　a test to find out who is greater

altar:　　　　a place where sacrifices are offered in worship

immediately:　right away or something done right now

Guided Prayer Thought

Dear God, We know that You are the true God! Help us not to try to test You and disobey Your Word. You have shown Your love to us in so many ways.   *Amen*

Questions:
Thinking & Remembering

1. Whom did Elijah want to see?
   the king

2. Why was the king still angry with Elijah?
   because he told him there would be no rain

3. Who did the king blame for there not being any rain?
   Elijah

4. Who did Elijah tell him was to blame?
   the king and his people--they had forgotten God and His commandments

5. How did Elijah want to prove that God was the true God?
   by having a contest

6. What test would show the true god's power?
   the one that sent fire to burn up the offering

7. Did the god the people and king prayed to answer their screams?
   No

8. When did they believe that the God of Israel was the true God?
   when fire came from heaven and burned the offering and the water

 # Bible Words To Remember

The Lord was not in the wind, earthquake or fire. God spoke
in a still, small voice.   1 Kings 19:11-12

Choosing God's Way

Accepting Responsibility

When things go wrong, like falling and getting hurt, it is easy to blame something or somebody. It is hard to say, "Ooops! It was my fault. I didn't watch where I was going." What you can learn is to be more careful next time so you don't get hurt. Try to learn something every day. God does not want you to be sad or to feel bad. He will help you as you learn and grow.

What happened to you that made you feel bad or get hurt?
What did you learn that will help you?

♥ Bible Love Lesson ♥

God knows everything! He knows what will happen to you today. God wants you to know that He loves you. Then whatever happens, He will be there with you to help you and He will help you think, "God loves me, He knows where I am, and He cares!"

Bible Story: Clouds in the Sky!

Key Points

❖ The king knew that God was very powerful.

❖ Elijah prayed and asked God to send rain.

❖ When God sent rain, Elijah was so excited he ran faster than the king's horses and chariots.

The king was ready to listen to Elijah. He had seen the power of the God of Israel when He sent fire from heaven to burn up an offering. After the people said that they would **choose** to serve God, Elijah said, "It will rain very soon."

Elijah and his servant climbed to the top of a mountain. Elijah prayed and listened to God. He told his servant to go and look toward the sea. He came back with the **news**---there is nothing to see. Elijah sent him back six times. The seventh time the servant rushed back and said, "I do see a very small cloud in the sky."

Elijah said, "Go and tell the king to get in his **chariot** and go home before the rains come." The sky became black with clouds, the wind blew and there was a heavy rain. God gave Elijah great strength. He was so excited, he ran faster than the chariots and arrived at the palace before the king!

Word and Phrase Meanings

choose: to decide between more than one thing

news: something that is told to someone else

chariot: a cart with two wheels that important people could ride in;

horses pulled the cart, called a chariot

report: to tell what has happened

Guided Prayer Thought

You are so powerful and wonderful, God! Thank You for hearing and answering prayers.
Amen

Questions:
Thinking & Remembering

1. After the king saw God's power, what was he ready to do?
   listen to Elijah

2. What news did Elijah give when the people said they would serve God?
   "It will rain very soon."

3. Where did Elijah and his servant go?
   to the top of a mountain

4. What did Elijah do on the mountain?
   prayed and listened to God

5. What did he tell his servant to do?
   go and look toward the sea

6. How many times did he come back to Elijah and **report** that he saw nothing?
   six

7. What did he see the seventh time?
   a small cloud in the sky

8. Why did Elijah send his servant to the king?
   to tell him to go back home before the rains

9. What three things happened?
   (1)the sky became black with clouds
   (2)the wind blew
   (3)there was a heavy rain

10. Why did Elijah arrive at the palace before the kings chariots?
    God gave him strength and he was so excited

 ## Bible Words To Remember

The Lord was not in the wind, earthquake or fire. God spoke in a still, small voice.   1 Kings 19:11-12

Choosing God's Way

Being Adaptable

God is very powerful! He is the only one who really knows what the weather will be like tomorrow. People try to study the clouds and the sky to tell what will happen. But sometimes the wind blows a different way and they are surprised. They thought they knew what would happen. We can be happy knowing that God is in control!

Who knows exactly what will happen and where it will happen?
Can people ever know for sure what the weather will be like?

♥ Bible Love Lesson ♥

If you listen to your mom or dad when they talk to you softly, they will not need to use a loud voice to tell you what you should do. God will help you to be quiet and hear Him, too, in your thoughts. He will give you very special messages that tell you of His love for you.

Bible Story: A Still, Small Voice

 Key Points

❖ The queen hated Elijah for destroying her god.

❖ Elijah thought God was the only one who loved him.

❖ God talked to Elijah in a very still, small voice.

❖ God sent a helper to Elijah who believed in God too.

Elijah was not **welcome** at the **palace**. The queen was angry that Elijah had destroyed her god. She gave **orders** to kill him. Elijah was so sad that he just wanted to die. He told God that he felt like he was the only one left who loved Him.

When Elijah stopped speaking, there was a great and **furious** wind! Elijah waited, he thought that it was God in the wind. But God was not in the wind. The earth started shaking and again, Elijah thought he would see God. But God was not in the earthquake. Suddenly fire **sprang up** over the ground around him. But God was not in the fire.

The fire was gone. Elijah listened. There was a still, small whisper of a voice. It was the voice of God. "Why are you here, Elijah? You are not the only one in Israel who believes in Me. I have chosen a helper for you who will be the next prophet. Go to him and don't be sad any longer."

Word and Phrase Meanings

welcome: to accept someone with kindness

palace: a very beautiful place where a king or queen lives

orders: what is told to do

furious: very angry

sprang up: to suddenly appear

Guided Prayer Thought

Dear God, Help us to hear Your still small voice.
Amen

Questions:
Thinking & Remembering

1. Why was Elijah not welcome at the palace?
   the queen was angry because he had destroyed her god

2. What did she order to happen to Elijah?
   to be killed

3. How did Elijah feel?
   He was so sad, he wanted to die. He felt like he was the only one left who loved God.

4. What three things happened next?
   a. wind
   b. earthquake
   c. fire

5. Was God in any of these things?
   No

6. In what way did God speak to Elijah?
   in a still, small, voice

7. What question did He ask Elijah?
   "Why are you here?"

8. What did God tell Elijah to do?
   to go and get a helper that would be the next prophet

 # Bible Words To Remember

The Lord was not in the wind, earthquake or fire. God spoke in a still, small voice.   1 Kings 19:11-12

Choosing God's Way

Being Reflective

When you are listening to God, He knows! He is always ready to speak to your heart. Can we hear God's out-loud voice? We do not hear a great voice from heaven. First, God gives us His words in the Bible. Then, God sent Jesus to be God on earth to show His love. When Jesus went to heaven, God, the Holy Spirit came to work in our minds and thoughts and our heart. When you pray, God is speaking in a soft, still voice. It is so exciting to discover and learn about our wonderful God!

How can we hear God's voice and know what He wants to tell us?
When did you know that God was telling you something?

Elisha: The Book of 2 Kings

❤ Bible Love Lesson ❤

Do you have a big brother or sister that you think is great? You think that they can do so many things that you cannot do. You want to be with them and stay with them or go where they go so you can learn to be like them. God wants us to learn from others who are following in His way.

Bible Story: The Great Whirlwind

Key Points

❖ Elijah was finished with his work and Elisha was God's new prophet.

❖ Elisha didn't want Elijah to leave. He wanted to learn how to be as great as Elijah.

❖ God took Elijah to heaven in a chariot of fire.

❖ Elisha knew that God would help him do the work Elijah had been doing.

The prophet Elijah was ready to give his job to Elisha, the helper God had given him. Elijah started to journey toward the river where he would meet God. Elisha didn't want him to leave. He wanted to learn more from him. He followed close beside him. "I just want to be as great as you!" Elisha said.

Suddenly, there was a great **whirlwind** and in it was a chariot of fire! Elijah was taken into heaven and Elisha watched in **wonder**. He was sad because he would not see his friend again on the earth.

Elisha looked down at his feet, and the **cloak** that Elijah had been wearing was lying there. He knew that this meant that it was time for him to do God's work, just as Elijah had done.

Word and Phrase Meanings

victory: to win and be successful

whirlwind: a mass (large amount) of air swirling to a center like in a tornado

wonder: something wonderful and amazing; seeing a miracle

cloak: cape; a coat without sleeves

Guided Prayer Thought

Dear God, Even when we are separated from people we love on earth, we know we will see them in heaven if they believe in You and we believe in You, too.   *Amen*

Questions:
Thinking & Remembering

1. Who was going to be the next prophet after Elijah?
   Elisha

2. Where did Elijah go to meet God?
   to the river

3. Why didn't Elisha want Elijah to leave him?
   he wanted to learn more from him

4. What did Elisha want to be?
   as great as Elijah

5. How did Elijah go to God?
   in a chariot of fire

6. Why was Elisha sad?
   he would not see his friend again on the earth

7. What did Elijah leave behind?
   the cloak he had been wearing

8. What did Elisha know that he must do?
   God's work

Bible Words To Remember

Yours, O Lord, is the greatness, the power and the glory, the **victory** and the majesty. 1 Chronicles 29: 11

Praise Hymn

Sing or say these words
Resource: My First Hymnal Pg. 11

RISE AND SHINE

Rise and shine
and give God the glory, glory,
Rise and shine
and give God the glory, glory,
Rise and shine
and give God the glory, glory,
Children of the Lord.

♥ Bible Love Lesson ♥

God thinks about you and cares about you all the time! If you can always remember that God is with you, it will make it easy to think about your family and friends. It will make you feel happy when you are kind to them. Because God loves you, you can love others!

Bible Story: Elisha Helps a Poor Woman

Key Points

❖ Everyone loved Elisha. He was very kind and cared about people.

❖ God helped Elisha know how to do what was right.

❖ God did a miracle for a woman who needed help because she believed in Him.

Elisha was very kind as he went about doing the work God had for him to do. People everywhere knew how much He cared about them. Whenever they had problems, they knew they could go to Elisha and he would help them.

One woman was frightened and sad. Her husband had died and **owed** money to some men. They came to her and said, "Give us the money or we will take your sons away."

The woman told Elisha about her problem. He knew he didn't have any money, but he thought about what God could do. "What do you have left in your house?" he asked. She only had a jar of oil. Elisha told her to find as many empty jars as she could find and pour oil from her jar into the empty jars. He said that she could fill all the empty jars with the one she had that was full. The most wonderful thing happened! All the jars were filled with oil, it was a **miracle**! Elisha then told her to sell the oil and pay the money her husband had owed.

── Word and Phrase Meanings ──

owed:	what needs to be paid to someone
miracle:	something only God can do
majesty:	greatness, worthy as a king
solve:	knowing the answer; to figure out what to do

Guided Prayer Thought

*Dear God, We cannot **solve** all of our problems. We can't stop bad things from happening sometimes. But You can do a miracle when we believe and obey You.*
Amen

Questions:
Thinking & Remembering

1. How was Elisha kind to people?
   he cared for them and helped them

2. Why was the woman frightened and sad?
   her husband died and had owed money to some men

3. What terrible thing did they say would happen if she didn't pay the money owed to them?
   they would take her sons away

4. Whom did the woman tell about this problem?
   Elisha

5. Whom did Elisha know could help her even though he couldn't?
   God could

6. What happened to her one jar of oil when she did what Elisha told her to do?
   all the empty ones were filled

7. What did Elisha tell her to do with the oil?
   to sell it to pay the money her husband owed

8. What had God done?
   a miracle (something only God can do)

 ## Bible Words To Remember

Yours, O Lord, is the greatness, the power and the glory, the victory and the **majesty**. 1 Chronicles 29: 11

Choosing God's Way

Perseverance

What kinds of problems do you have? When you are little, zipping your coat can be a problem. Tying your shoes is a hard thing to do! Grown-ups have different problems—driving to work in traffic and getting to work on time. Big and little, we can give problems to God. He won't do everything for us, though. When we ask Him, He helps us think and figure out things and is there with us when we ask Him.

Think about one big problem you have had. Think about a little problem.
What kind of problems can we ask God to help us with?

❤ Bible Love Lesson ❤

Have you ever been sick with a **fever** and you hurt all over? Your mom and dad probably looked very worried. They put you in your bed and covered you with warm blankets. They also cover you with their love. They pray and ask God to take special care of you and make you better.

Bible Story: God Heals a Sick Boy

 Key Points

❖ Elisha was given a room to stay in by a kind woman and her husband.

❖ The man and woman did not have any children. Elisha told them that God would give them a son.

❖ When the boy got sick and died, Elisha prayed that God would make him alive again.

There was a kind woman in one of the towns where Elisha visited. The woman asked her husband if they could make a room in their house for him to rest when he came to do God's work. "This man is a special man of God," she said. Soon the room was ready and Elisha and his servant had a comfortable place to stay.

The woman and her husband had many things, but they did not have any children. Elisha told them that soon they would have a son. This made the man and his wife very happy! When the child became a young boy, he went out with his father as he worked. One day he suddenly cried out, "My head, my head!" The servants rushed him to his mother. He was very sick and he died in his mother's arms.

His mother laid him on the bed and said, "I will go see the man of God." When Elisha saw her coming, he knew a terrible thing had happened. She told Elisha that the boy was dead. Immediately, Elisha went to the house. Elisha prayed to the Lord. He asked God to make the boy alive. The boy sneezed and opened his eyes. God made him alive again! It was another **miracle**.

— Word and Phrase Meanings —

fever:	feeling hot; body temperature higher than normal
miracle:	something only God can do
victory:	to win and be successful

Guided Prayer Thought

Dear God, We know that You can do anything----You even made a boy that died come alive! Thank You for caring for us and we believe and love You, too.   Amen

Questions:
Thinking & Remembering

1. **What special place did a woman and her husband make for Elisha?**
   a room for him to rest in their house

2. **Whom did the woman say that Elisha was?**
   a special man of God

3. **What did the man and his wife not have?**
   children

4. **What did Elisha tell them they would have?**
   a son

5. **What happened when the boy was working with his father?**
   he cried and said that his head was hurting

6. **What happened after the servants took him to his mother?**
   he died in her arms

7. **What did the mother do?**
   went to find Elisha

8. **How did Elisha make the boy alive again?**
   Elisha prayed to God, and God made the boy alive

 # Bible Words To Remember

Yours, O Lord, is the greatness, the power and the glory, the **victory** and the majesty. 1 Chronicles 29: 11

Choosing God's Way

Trusting

God wants to show His people how much He cares for them. He cares if you are sick. He cares if you fall and get hurt. God showed His power by even making a boy alive again! If our God is this great, we do not need to be afraid and worry about the things that happen. He wants us to believe that He loves us enough to take care of us. If you worry, you are not trusting Him to do what is best. Tell Him you want to have faith to trust Him completely!

How did God show how much He cared for the sick boy in the Bible story?
Are there things that are too hard for God to do?

❤ Bible Love Lesson ❤

God can do what no one else can do! When someone does not know about God, they
do not know what wonderful things He can do. If someone you know is
sad or sick, tell them about the amazing things God does.

Bible Story: A Girl Wants to Help Her Master

Key Points

❖ Naaman was sick, but didn't know that God could heal him.

❖ The servant girl said that God could make him well.

❖ Naaman went to see Elisha so he could pray and ask God to heal him.

There was a man named Naaman. He was a **captain** of a large **army** and was very important. One day Naaman became very sick. He went to the doctor but the doctor could not help him. Naaman didn't know about God, so He couldn't ask God to make him well.

The little girl who lived at his house helped Naaman's wife clean and sew, and she knew all about God's love. She loved God and knew that God could help Naaman. She told Naaman's wife, "I know a man who loves God who could make my master well."

Naaman took his **chariot** and horses, along with his servants. He took gifts to this man of God. He thought that he was such an important man, that he would be made well **immediately**. He would be very surprised when he found out what the prophet Elisha asked him to do!

Word and Phrase Meanings

captain: leader who gives orders to one group of men in an army

army: large group of soldiers

chariot: a cart pulled by horses

immediately: at once

Guided Prayer Thought

Dear God, You love everyone the same----people who are poor as well as people who are rich. What really matters is how important You are to them and how much they love You.

Amen

Questions:
Thinking & Remembering

1. What was the man's name who was sick?

   Naaman

2. Why was this man important?

   he was a captain of a large army

3. Could the doctor help him?

   No

4. Why didn't he ask God to make him well?

   he didn't know about God

5. What did the little girl know who helped Naaman's wife?

   all about God's love

6. What did she tell Naaman's wife?

   that she knew of a man who loved God who could make Naaman well

7. What did Naaman take when he went to see the prophet Elisha?

   his chariot and horses, servants and gifts

8. What did he expect Elisha to do for him?

   make him well immediately

 # Bible Words To Remember

Yours, O Lord, is the greatness, the power and the glory, the victory and the majesty. 1 Chronicles 29: 11

Choosing God's Way

Confidence

Sometimes when people are very important (like the president) or have a lot of money and are rich, you might think that they couldn't have the same problems as everyone else. But they get sick and are sad sometimes, too. Even though they have enough money to go to the doctor and get medicine, it does not always help. God helps everyone. He does not care if you have a lot of money or are important to other people. Everyone is important to God!

Who will God always help?
Which people are important to God?

❤ Bible Love Lesson ❤

God does not always ask you to do something very hard. He may ask you to do something you do not like. But believing God is doing what He asks---then you will be **wondrously** surprised at the wonderful things that will happen!

Bible Story: A Surprise Cure

 Key Points

❖ Elisha gave Naaman a message to wash in the river seven times.

❖ Naaman was not happy with the message.

❖ Naaman's servant told him that what Elisha told him to do was not hard.

❖ When Naaman obeyed, God made him completely well again.

Naaman stood at the door of Elisha's house. Elisha did not come to see this captain of a great army. He sent his servant to give Naaman a **message**. When he got the message, it was not what he wanted to hear.

"Go and wash in the Jordan river seven times, and then your skin will be like new and you will be well." Naaman was furious! "I will not wash myself in that dirty river!" He turned and went away in a **rage**.

His servants came and said to him, "Captain, if God's prophet had asked you to do something difficult you would have done it. He just asked you to do a simple thing. Why not do as he said?" Naaman went to the water and dipped seven times and the **disease** was completely gone! Naaman ran to thank Elisha and said, "Now I know that there is no God in all the earth like your God!

Word and Phrase Meanings

wondrously:	in awe (feeling that something is terrific)
cure:	something that makes someone well
message:	to tell something to someone
rage:	extremely angry
disease:	sickness

Guided Prayer Thought

Dear God, You really only ask us to believe and love You. It is not a hard thing to do. Help us to understand Your great love.
                                                        Amen

Questions:
Thinking & Remembering

1. **Where did Naaman go to get healed?**
   to Elisha's house

2. **Who did Elisha send to give Naaman a message?**
   his servant

3. **What was the message?**
   to wash in the Jordan river

4. **How many times was Naaman told to dip into the water?**
   seven times

5. **What did Naaman think about this message?**
   He was furious. (went off in a rage) He would not do it.

6. **What did his servants tell him they could not understand?**
   that it was not a hard thing to do; if it were hard he would do it

7. **Did Naaman go to the river then?**
   Yes

8. **What happened after the seventh time?**
   Naaman was healed

9. **What did Naaman do?**
   he ran to thank Elisha

10. **What did Naaman say about God?**
    There is no God in all the earth like your God!

 # Bible Words To Remember

Yours, O Lord, is the greatness, the power and the glory, the victory and the majesty. 1 Chronicles 29: 11

Choosing God's Way

Listening and Obeying

It matters to God that we will listen when He speaks to us. He speaks to us through the Bible. The words in this wonderful book tell us how He wants us to live. He also speaks to us in our thoughts. God will help us know the right way to go. It may not be what we want to do, but God will know what is best. Say "yes" to what God tells you!

What matters to God?
How does God speak to us today?
Think about a time when you did what God wanted you to do.

Two Young Kings: Joash and Josiah
The Book of II Kings

❤ Bible Love Lesson ❤

God gave us rules for a reason. He is the One who made us and knows what is right and best for us! Sometimes people try to change the rules God made or make them easier to follow. That is not God's plan.

Bible Story: Kings and Queens

 Key Points

❖ **Not many kings and queens loved and listened to God.**

❖ **The people began worshiping other gods and forgot how much God loved them.**

❖ **The people could not be happy until they remembered God and His love.**

There were many **kings** and **queens** that ruled in Israel, but many did not love God. They did not like the **prophets** of God telling them what to do. These rulers were **cruel** and killed many people to have their own way. It was just as God had told them would happen many years before. Maybe some of the people in Israel remembered that God told them not to want an earthly king.

The kings and people worshiped other gods. The commandments of God were forgotten. They chose to turn away from God because they wanted to live in a way that would not please God. They lived in disobedience to the God who loved them.

There was a wicked queen who killed all of her family so that no one could take her place to rule. She did not know that one child had **escaped**. The baby was hidden from her and saved by an aunt who loved God.

Word and Phrase Meanings

king:	a man ruler
queen:	a woman ruler
cruel:	mean and hurtful to others
prophet:	one who reminds the people about what God says and what will happen
escaped:	to get away from someone
evil:	very wrong and bad; sinful
endures:	to continue and last (never end)

Guided Prayer Thought

*Dear God, We know that **evil** things happen when people do not love and obey You. You want what is good for everyone because You love us. Help us to love You and remember to obey.*

Amen

Questions:
Thinking & Remembering

1. Were there many kings in Israel who loved God?
   No, many did not love God

2. Why didn't they like the prophets of God?
   because they told them what to do

3. What had God told the people a long time before about having kings?
   that they would be cruel and show their power to have their own way

4. Who did they worship during these times away from God?
   other gods

5. What did they choose to do?
   turn away from God

6. What were they doing that would not please God?
   disobeying God's word and commandments

7. What did a wicked queen do?
   killed all of her family

8. What did she not know?
   that a baby was hidden

 # Bible Words To Remember

For the Lord is good, His mercy **endures** forever.

2 Chronicles 5:13

Praise Hymn

Sing or say these words
Resource: My First Hymnal Pg. 70

REJOICE IN THE LORD ALWAYS

Rejoice in the Lord always
and again I say rejoice!
Rejoice--rejoice--
and again I say rejoice!
Rejoice--rejoice--
and again I say rejoice!

❤ Bible Love Lesson ❤

God never forgets about the people He made. All the children in the world are in His care. That means YOU! God thinks about your family, too. He knows you. He knows your name. He loves you!

Bible Story: The Little Prince

Key Points

❖ One little boy was protected from a wicked queen.

❖ God was taking care of this little boy so that he could become a king.

❖ When the boy was found, the priest put a crown on his head.

❖ The queen could no longer hurt the people.

The boy who **escaped** the wicked queen's **order** to be killed was taken care of by a kind aunt. He was hidden in the temple, where the queen would never look. She had led the people to worship Baal as a god.

This baby grew and became a boy without anyone finding out the secret. The name of the prince was Joash. When he was only seven years old, the **priest** at the temple decided it was time for him to take the throne to become king and stop the evil queen from the awful things she was doing to the people.

He brought Joash, the young prince, into a room with the palace guards and captains. He told them who Joash was---a king! They put a crown on the boy's head and **protected** him from the wicked queen.

Word and Phrase Meanings

escaped: to get away from someone

order: command to do something

priest: someone special in God's house (temple; church) who tells what God's words mean; a minister or pastor

protected: to take care of and keep safe

Guided Prayer Thought

*Dear God, You had a plan for Joash to be safe until he was king.
You love us in the same way. We pray that we will ask You to
protect us when we are in danger.*

Amen

Questions:
── Thinking & Remembering ──

1. **Who had protected the little prince?**
   his kind aunt

2. **Where was he hidden?**
   in the temple

3. **Why was he safe there?**
   *the queen would never look there
   because she worshiped Baal*

4. **What was the name of the prince?**
   Joash

5. **How old was he when he became king?**
   seven

6. **Why did the priest not wait any longer?**
   *the queen was doing awful things to
   the people*

7. **Who did the priest tell that the king was
   still alive?**
   the palace guards and captains

8. **What did they do to show that he was
   king?**
   put a crown on his head

 ## Bible Words To Remember

For the Lord is good, His mercy endures forever.

2 Chronicles 5:13

Choosing God's Way

Decisiveness

God's plan is wonderful and perfect! At times things seem like they are turned upside down and you think God forgot to take a look at what is happening. But He knows every single thing! In the Bible story, the people had forgotten God. God protected a little baby who would love him and become king. Remember God and His plan for you. He will never forget you! Decide to follow God's plan.

Was there ever a time when you thought that maybe God forgot you?
Does God forget us or do we forget Him?

❤ Bible Love Lesson ❤

Do you remember in our Bible about the little boy who was king? Even though you are little, you have a big heart to love and do what God wants you to do. God loves you and is watching over you! God will protect you and there will always be someone to teach you how to love Him.

Bible Story: The Boy King

Key Points

❖ The young king was protected by captains and guards.

❖ The queen was very angry that the people wanted a king.

❖ Joash was a good king and followed God's laws.

❖ The temple was made beautiful again so the people could worship God.

When Joash was **crowned** king, the people were so excited! They clapped their hands and shouted "Long live the king!" Joash was **surrounded** and protected by the captains and guards.

The wicked queen heard all the noise and came to see what was happening. She screamed and tore her clothes. The soldiers took her outside the temple area and killed her for all the wickedness she had done.

The people promised to follow God and they destroyed all the idols and gods they had been worshiping. Everything was done to follow God's laws. Joash was a good ruler as he grew to be a man. The priest helped him until he was old enough to make **decisions**. The temple was **repaired** and made beautiful again so that the people could worship. Everything was good in the land of Israel at last.

— Word and Phrase Meanings —

crowned: to put a beautiful covering of gold or jewels on someone's head to show that they are a king (or queen)

surrounded: to circle around someone

decisions: to choose a plan

repaired: to fix and make like new

Guided Prayer Thought

Dear God, It must make You so sad when people turn away from worshiping you and make other things more important. Help us to love You and remember what You have done for us.

Amen

Questions:
Thinking & Remembering

1. What did the people shout when Joash was crowned king?
   "Long live the king!"

2. How was Joash protected?
   he was surrounded by captains and guards

3. What did the wicked queen do when she found out about the new king?
   she screamed and tore her clothes

4. What did the soldiers do to the queen?
   killed her for all the wickedness she had done

5. What did the people promise to do?
   to follow God and His laws

6. What did they destroy?
   the idols and gods

7. What kind of a king was Joash?
   a good king

8. What did he do about the temple so the people could worship there?
   he repaired it and made it beautiful again

 Bible Words To Remember

For the Lord is good, His mercy endures forever.

2 Chronicles 5:13

Choosing God's Way

Protection

God chose special people to protect the baby who one day became king in Israel. These people kept the baby safe from harm. They also told him about God and His love. God wants you to be special in the same way. You can protect and take care of your baby sister and brother and tell them about God's love, too.

How can you be one of God's special people? Tell some ways that you can protect someone younger than you are.

❤ Bible Love Lesson ❤

Moms and dads, sisters and brothers, grandmas and grandpas, aunts and uncles, pastors and teachers and ministers---there are always special people who want you to be what God wants you to be. They love you and will teach you and help you learn God's way.

Bible Story: Another King Listens to God

 Key Points

❖ There was another boy who loved God that became king.

❖ Josiah learned about God from his grandfather.

❖ The temple needed to be fixed again, because there had been bad kings since Joash had been king.

❖ Josiah read God's words and told the people that they must follow God.

Josiah was only eight years old when he became king! By the time he became king there had been other kings who had again turned from the Lord God and followed other gods. One king even made altars to the false gods in God's own **temple**.

Josiah had been taught by his grandfather about God and he loved God. When he was king, he wanted to make the temple beautiful again. Money was collected from all the people to pay for the workers to repair all the **damage**.

After they had started working, the high **priest** found a **scroll** with God's **laws** written on it. The king wanted the priest to read the laws that God had given to his people. When he heard them read, he was so sad that he tore his clothes. He said to the people, "We have not followed God's rules for a long time."

Word and Phrase Meanings

temple: a building where people can worship God; church

damage: what is broken or ruined

priest: like a minister, pastor; one who teaches about God

scroll: a roll of special paper with God's laws written on it

laws: rules that we must follow

Guided Prayer Thought

Dear God, Help us not to forget to follow Your laws. We want to live to please You and do the right things.
Amen

Questions:
Thinking & Remembering

1. How old was Josiah when he became king?
   eight years old

2. What had other kings done?
   turned from the Lord God and followed other gods

3. What had one king done?
   made altars to false gods in the temple

4. Who had taught Josiah about God?
   his grandfather

5. What did Josiah want to do when he became king?
   make the temple beautiful again

6. How did they get the money to repair the damage?
   they collected it from all the people

7. What was found in the temple?
   a scroll with God's law written on it

8. What did the king do when the words were read to him?
   he was so sad that they had not followed God's rules, he tore his clothes

 # Bible Words To Remember

For the Lord is good, His mercy endures forever.
2 Chronicles 5:13

Choosing God's Way

Willingness to Learn

The words that God gave in the Bible are true. They are not pretend stories and we can learn from all of the words in the Bible. There are many people who read and study these words to understand how much God loves us and how He wants us to live. We cannot know God's laws unless we are willing to listen to the words in the Bible. The king in the Bible story knew that the people needed to know what God said. We will only be truly happy when we know what God says and then do what God says.

How do we know how God wants us to live?
When will we be truly happy?

❤ Bible Love Lesson ❤

God makes promises. We read about them in the Bible (someday you will read them yourself!). God keeps His promises. Children and grown-ups make promises, too. But children and grown-ups can forget promises. Isn't it wonderful to know that God loves you and that He will never forget?

Bible Story: Peace at Last

Key Points

❖ The people listened to God's words. They were very sorry that they had not followed God.

❖ Josiah reminded the people that God had kept all of His promises to them.

❖ The people promised that they would keep God's laws.

King Josiah wanted all the people to know what God said. He read to them from the scroll. He told them about God's promise to them. He **reminded** them that God had brought them out of the land of Egypt to follow Him. He said that God had kept all of His **promises** but the people had broken their promises to God.

Josiah ordered that all the **idols** be **smashed** into pieces and burned. The people could no longer make **human sacrifices**. There were many things that they had done that made God very sad.

The people cried for all their sins and said, "We will promise again to obey God and keep His laws." They had a **Passover feast** to remember what God had done for them in bringing them out of the land of Egypt.

Word and Phrase Meanings

reminded: to tell something again - not the first time

promises: doing what you say you will do; an agreement

idols: things (objects) worshiped instead of God

smashed: broken into little pieces

human sacrifices: people killed to please false gods

Passover feast: the dinner the Israelites had to remember how God took them out of Egypt and slavery

Guided Prayer Thought

Dear God, We forget, just like the people of Israel, how much You love us and how much You have done for us. Help us not to forget Your commandments and to remember to ask You to forgive us.
Amen

Questions:
Thinking & Remembering

1. What did King Josiah do so that the people would know what God said?
   he read God's words from the scroll

2. What did he tell them about that they had forgotten?
   about God's promise to them

3. Of what did he remind them?
   how God had brought them out of the land of Egypt

4. What had God done?
   kept His promises

5. What had they done?
   broken their promises

6. What did Josiah order to be done to the idols?
   smashed and burned

7. What else had the people done to make God sad?
   made human sacrifices

8. What did the people promise to do?
   obey God and keep His laws

9. What did they do to celebrate?
   had a Passover feast

10. What were they remembering?
    what God had done for them

 # Bible Words To Remember

For the Lord is good, His mercy endures forever.

2 Chronicles 5:13

Choosing God's Way

Remembering Important Things

God loves you so much that He will keep reminding you of His words. He will not give up, even when you forget a lot! God sent special people in the Bible to remind His children that He loved them. When they did not listen, He helped them understand in other ways so that they would remember how much He loved them and come back to Him. God wants you to think about how much He loves you every day.

How can you remember God's words?
Will God ever give up reminding us of how much He loves us?

❤ Bible Love Lesson ❤

God made homes for us to have a wonderful and special place to be with our families. Knowing that there is lots of love in that place makes you feel important and accepted. Remember to say thank you to God for your home and family. Remember to say thank you to mom and dad, too!

Bible Story: Remembering Home

 Key Points

❖ **Even though the people of Israel promised to follow God, they soon forgot their promise.**

❖ **The kings and people only remembered God when they were in trouble.**

❖ **The people became slaves in a land far away from their home.**

❖ **The king in Babylon finally let the people go back to Jerusalem so they could fix the temple and worship God.**

The people of Israel were taken away from their homes. They had **continued** to **disobey** God even when there were kings and prophets who tried to tell them what would happen to them if they did not follow God's commandments. Many of the kings did not love and believe in the God of Israel. They just wanted God to help them when they were in trouble. When everything was going well, they forgot God again.

The people became slaves in Babylon. Many could not **remember** living in the land that God had given them. They were far away from home. The grandfathers and grandmothers remembered; some of the fathers and mothers remembered. They told the children about the city of Jerusalem and the beautiful temple where people worshiped God.

Then there was a new king in Babylon. He knew that the Israelites would be happier in their own land. He said to them, "Go back to Jerusalem; return and rebuild your temple." The people were very happy. They were excited to be going back to the Promised Land.

Word and Phrase Meanings

continued: to keep doing

disobey: to do what you were told not to do

remember: think about again; to not forget

rise: get up from sitting, kneeling or lying

Guided Prayer Thought

*When we forget Your promises, when we forget to obey, when
we forget Your commandments, forgive us, God.*
Amen

Questions:
Thinking & Remembering

1. Why had the people of Israel been taken from their homes?
   they disobeyed God and did not follow His commandments

2. Did many of the kings love and believe in God?
   No

3. When did they ask God to help them?
   when they were in trouble

4. Where had the people gone as slaves?
   Babylon

5. Who remembered their home in the Promised Land?
   grandfathers, grandmothers, fathers and mothers

6. What did they tell their children?
   about the city of Jerusalem and about the temple

7. What did the new king in Babylon decide?
   that the people would be happier in their own land

8. What did he tell them they could do?
   go back to Jerusalem and rebuild their temple

 # Bible Words To Remember

Let us **rise** up and build. The God of heaven will help us. Nehemiah 2:18, 20
I will go to the king. . .and if I perish, I perish! Esther 4:16

Praise Hymn

Sing or say these words
Resource: My First Hymnal Pg. 13

I'M GONNA SING, I'M GONNA SHOUT

I'm gonna sing and sing and sing,
I'm gonna shout, shout, shout.
I'm gonna sing, I'm gonna shout,
Praise the Lord!
When those gates are open wide,
I'm gonna sit at Jesus' side,
I'm gonna sing, I'm gonna shout
"Praise the Lord!"

♥ Bible Love Lesson ♥

God wants you to choose to love Him. He does not make you love Him. It makes Him very sad when people love other things more and decide not to believe Him. He tells us in so many ways that He loves us. Tell God that you want to love Him more each day!

Bible Story: A Lot of Work To Do

 Key Points

❖ Jerusalem was no longer a beautiful city.

❖ The people celebrated when they started rebuilding the temple.

❖ A prophet told the people to love and worship God.

❖ The people promised again to serve God.

The people of Israel returned to the city of Jerusalem. It was not at all like they remembered. The temple had been burned down. The walls of the city were broken. It would take a lot of work to make everything beautiful again. One of the most important things the people did was to **rebuild** the temple. When the **foundation** was laid, the people **celebrated**. The priests blew their trumpets and there was music and singing. They sang, "The Lord is good and His love for Israel is forever!"

Ezra was a prophet of God who **reminded** the people of what God had commanded them to do. They must love and worship only God. Ezra heard that some of the people still worshiped idols and married people who did not believe in God. He was very sad. He knew that the people could **choose** to serve and obey God. They could also choose to disobey and turn away from God.

Ezra knelt down to pray and he cried for all the people who had chosen their own way instead of God's way. The people gathered around him while he was praying. One man said, "Ezra, there is still hope for Israel. We want to return to God." They promised to serve God that day.

Word and Phrase Meanings

rebuild:	put back together; build again
foundation:	the base
celebrated:	to be happy and cheer on a special day
remind:	to tell something again to someone
choose:	to decide between more than one thing
worship:	to make a special time to show respect and honor

Guided Prayer Thought

Dear God, We know how sad it makes You when we choose to go our own way and not follow You. Help us remember how much You love us and help us to serve You.
Amen

Questions:
Thinking & Remembering

1. Was Jerusalem like the people remembered it had been?
   No

2. What had happened?
   the temple was burned down and the walls were broken

3. What would the people need to do to make it like it used to be?
   do a lot of work

4. What was the most important thing to do before anything else?
   rebuild the temple

5. What words did they sing when the foundation was laid?
   "The Lord is good and His love for Israel is forever!"

6. What did Ezra hear about?
   that some people were worshiping idols; some were marrying people who did not believe in God

7. Could the people choose who they would love and serve?
   Yes, God does not make people love Him

8. When Ezra was praying, what did the people promise?
   to serve God

 # Bible Words To Remember

Let us rise up and build. The God of heaven will help us. Nehemiah 2:18, 20
I will go to the king. . .and if I perish, I perish! Esther 4:16

Choosing God's Way

Praising God

God made a special place for His people to go to pray and worship Him. People went to the temple in Bible times to worship. Now people can go to a building called a church to worship. It is wonderful for us to be with others to listen to the words of God and sing praises to Him. We can also worship God wherever and whenever we think of Him. He loves us! When we praise Him we show Him how much we love Him!

Where does your family go to worship God?
Is a church building the only place you can worship?
In what ways can you show God how much you love Him?

❤ Bible Love Lesson ❤

Sometimes you are doing what mom or dad asked you to do, and you get tired before you get it finished. Or you say, "I don't want to do this---this isn't fun". Work is not always fun, but it needs to be finished! Show your love by doing the whole job to the end!

Bible Story: The Walls Are Fixed

 Key Points

❖ Nehemiah was sad when he knew the walls around Jerusalem were still broken down.

❖ Nehemiah prayed that God would forgive the people for disobeying so often.

❖ Nehemiah told the people not to be afraid because God was with them.

❖ The people worked together to finish the wall around Jerusalem.

After the temple was finished, the walls around Jerusalem were still broken. This news came to a man named Nehemiah, who was a special servant for the king in Babylon. He loved God and was sad because the building of Jerusalem wasn't finished.

He prayed to God and said, "God, our people have disobeyed You so often, we don't even **deserve** Your love for us. Please help us. We want to turn back to You!"

The king told Nehemiah he could go back to Jerusalem to help the people rebuild the walls. There were enemies who tried many times to stop the work but Nehemiah thought of a plan to keep them away so they could finish the wall. He told the workers, "Don't be afraid. God will fight for us." When the wall was finished, the city of Jerusalem and the Israelites were safe again.

Word and Phrase Meanings

condition:	the way something looks
permission:	to allow someone to do something
deserve:	to be worthy of
perish:	to die; to be completely destroyed

Guided Prayer Thought

Dear God, Help us to know that if we will remember to keep
YOU most important, YOU will be with us.
                                        Amen

Questions:
Thinking & Remembering

1. What work still needed to be done after the temple was finished?
   the walls needed to be repaired

2. What was the name of the man in Babylon who heard about the **condition** of the wall?
   Nehemiah

3. What did he tell God the people of Israel did not deserve?
   God's love

4. Why did he think they did not deserve God's kindness?
   they had disobeyed God

5. What did he ask God for?
   His help

6. What did the king give Nehemiah **permission** to do?
   go back to Jerusalem to help rebuild the walls

7. What made the job more difficult?
   there were enemies who tried to stop the work

8. What did Nehemiah tell the workers?
   "Don't be afraid. God will fight for us."

 # Bible Words To Remember

Let us rise up and build. The God of heaven will help us. Nehemiah 2:18, 20

I will go to the king. . .and if I perish, I **perish**! Esther 4:16

Choosing God's Way

Persistence

Some jobs are so big that everyone must work together to get them done. The work would not get finished if even one person says, "This job can get done without me. It's not important. I think I'll just play today." When you start a job, be cheerful about working until it is done. God says to work hard, work together, and do your best.

Think of a time when there was a big job that you were helping with.
Were you cheerful about working until the job was finished?

❤ Bible Love Lesson ❤

When you are loving and kind to your mom and dad, you show God's love. When you are loving and kind to your teachers, you show God's love. It is easy to share God's love with other people. God loves you and you should love others!

Bible Story: The Queen Who Helped Her People

Key Points

❖ **Esther was a Jewish girl who loved God.**

❖ **Esther's cousin, Mordecai, took Esther to the palace.**

❖ **The king in Persia chose Esther to be his queen.**

❖ **God had a special plan for Esther to help the Israelites.**

The king of Persia was choosing a new queen. His servants **gathered** all the beautiful girls in the **kingdom** to come before the king. Although many Jewish people had returned to Jerusalem, some had remained in this land.

There was an Israelite named Mordecai who worked in the palace for the king. Mordecai had a beautiful cousin living at his home. Her name was Esther. He wanted her to be **presented** before the king. He knew that when the king saw how beautiful she was that he would **certainly** want her for his queen.

Esther was excited to be among the young women who would come before the king. She waited her turn. Then it was time for Esther to go before the king. The moment the king saw her, he chose her to be his queen. God had a plan for Esther. She would someday be able to help her people, the Israelites.

── Word and Phrase Meanings ──

gathered: to come together in one place

kingdom: an area ruled by a king

presented: to give something in a special way

certainly: something that is thought to be sure to happen

Guided Prayer Thought

Dear God, Even though the Jews were living in a land that did not believe in You, it was in Your plan to protect Your special people. We are Your special people, too. Thank You for taking care of us.

Amen

Questions:
Thinking & Remembering

1. **Who was going to choose a new queen?**
   the king of Persia

2. **How would he choose a new queen?**
   all the beautiful girls in the kingdom would come before the king

3. **Why were there Jewish people in this land?**
   not all of them had returned to Jerusalem

4. **Who was Mordecai?**
   an Israelite who worked at the palace for the king

5. **Who was living in his home?**
   his cousin, Esther

6. **What did Mordecai want Esther to be?**
   the new queen

7. **Was Esther willing to be chosen as a queen?**
   Yes

8. **Who was chosen to be queen?**
   Esther

Bible Words To Remember

Let us rise up and build. The God of heaven will help us. Nehemiah 2:18, 20

I will go to the king. . .and if I perish, I perish! Esther 4:16

Choosing God's Way

Attitude

We can sometimes help God best in quiet ways. You can show God's love to others by being obedient to your parents and teachers. You can show God's love by your attitude and behavior when you are with other people. Be considerate of those around you, and they will know you love God. Is this easy for a child to do? You can ask God to help you, it is not easy to do all by yourself!

How can you help God and show His love to your parents and teachers?
Who will help you have a good attitude?

❤ Bible Love Lesson ❤

You can be sure that God loves you! He loves you every day and in every way. Your parents love you too. They will tell you the words in the Bible that will help you grow in God's way.

Bible Story: The Brave Queen

Key Points

❖ Someone was trying to kill all the Jews!

❖ Haman convinced the king he should give an order against God's people.

❖ Esther told the king that she was a Jew who would be killed with her people.

❖ The king did not want Esther to die. He commanded that all the Jews be saved.

There was a man in the king's court who hated the Jews. He thought of a way to get rid of all the Jews in Persia. "The Jews are all over this land," he told the king. "They are becoming stronger. They don't follow your laws and do whatever they please. Write an order to have them all killed and I will pay **silver** to the ones who do the killing." The king told this **evil** man, Haman, "Do whatever you please."

Mordecai sent word to Esther, the queen, asking for help to stop this awful plan. "Please go to the king and speak for your people, the Jews." He knew that Esther would not escape death. Even the queen would be in danger when Haman carried out his plan to destroy the Jews.

Esther said, "I will go to the king; If I **perish**, I perish!" It was against the law to go to the king without being **invited**. When Esther went before the king, she looked very beautiful. He said, "I will give you anything you wish." She answered, "I ask for the lives of my people, who are to be destroyed." The king immediately wrote a new law and Haman was killed instead. The queen had saved her people.

Word and Phrase Meanings

silver:	an amount of money; payment
perish:	to die; to be completely destroyed
evil:	wrongdoing; sinful
invited:	to be asked to come
plead:	to beg; to ask with great feeling

Guided Prayer Thought

Dear God, help us to be brave in doing what is right.
Amen

Questions:
Thinking & Remembering

1. What reason did the man named Haman give to kill the Jews?
   that *they were strong and they didn't follow the king's laws*

2. What did Haman offer as payment for killing the Jews?
   he would pay silver

3. What did the king answer Haman?
   "Do whatever you please."

4. What did Mordicai, Esther's cousin, ask the queen to do?
   to speak to the king for her people

5. Why was it dangerous for her to speak to the king?
   it was against the law to speak without being invited

6. How did she show how brave she was?
   she said she would die for her people, "If I perish, I perish!"

7. What did the king say when he saw Esther?
   "I will give you whatever you wish."

8. How did Esther save the lives of the Jewish people?
   she asked that the Jews be able to live

 # Bible Words To Remember

Let us rise up and build. The God of heaven will help us. Nehemiah 2:18, 20
I will go to the king. . .and if I perish, I perish! Esther 4:16

Choosing God's Way

Praying for Others

There are people who do not love God. That is very hard to understand when you know how much God loves everyone. Those who do not love God even try to make you think that God is not real. Just listen to God and ask Him to protect you. Ask Him to give you the words to tell others about His love. Love the people who don't know God and pray for them.

Even though God loves everyone, does everyone love God?
What can you do to help your friends and others know about God?

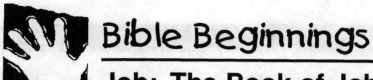
Job: The Book of Job

❤ Bible Love Lesson ❤

It is easier to thank God for your food when it is your favorite kind? Maybe you just remember to say thank you when the sun is shining. Some children remember to thank God when everything is 'just right'. Be thankful all the time because God loves you all of the time, not just some of the time!

Bible Story: A Man Who Loved God

Key Points

❖ **Many people in the Bible loved God even when bad things happened to them.**

❖ **Job loved God and served Him every day.**

❖ **Job prayed every day for his family and asked God to help him be faithful.**

In the Bible, there are many people who followed God's word. These people loved God even though there were bad things that happened to them. There was a man named Job who was like this.

To Job, loving God was life itself. He did not wake up each morning and think, "Do I love God today?" When things in his life were going the wrong way, he did not say, " I'm not going to love God."

Job thanked God every day for all of the good things he had. Every morning, he would offer a **sacrifice** to God before he started his work. He thought about God throughout the day. He would pray for his family and he would ask God to make him **faithful**.

Word and Phrase Meanings

sacrifice: an offering to God

faithful: true to

trouble: something that goes wrong

charge: complaint

Guided Prayer Thought

Dear God, Please make us faithful to You. Help us to think of all You have given to us and remember to say "Thank You."
Amen

Questions:
Thinking & Remembering

1. Did all of the people in the Bible disobey God and forget to follow Him?
   No, there were many who followed Him

2. Did the people who loved God have everything go 'just right'?
   No, some bad things happened to them

3. What was the name of the one man who loved God all the time?
   Job

4. What was 'life itself' to Job?
   loving God

5. What did Job thank God for every day?
   all the good things God had given him

6. How would he start his day?
   offering a sacrifice to God

7. What did he do throughout the day?
   he thought about God

8. What did he do so that he could stay close to God?
   he prayed and asked God to make him faithful to Him

Bible Words To Remember

Job said, "Blessed be the name of the Lord." In all his **trouble** Job did not sin nor **charge** God with wrong. Job 1:21, 22

Job said to God, "I know that You can do everything." Job 42:2

Praise Hymn

Sing or say these words
Resource: My First Hymnal Pg. 31

KUM BA YAH*

Kum ba yah, my Lord,
Kum ba yah,
Kum ba yah, my Lord,
Kum ba yah!
Oh, Lord, Kum ba yah!

*African way to say, "Come by here." When we sing or say these words, we are asking Jesus to stay by us.

♥ Bible Love Lesson ♥

God has given you so many wonderful things. His world is beautiful and His love is amazing. Choose to see all the good things around you. Choose to love the people close to you. You will soon love those who are far away, too.
God has already chosen to love you!

Bible Story: Trouble!

 Key Points

❖ **Satan wanted to make trouble for Job to see if he would stop loving God.**

❖ **God knew that Job would keep loving Him, even if he didn't have riches.**

❖ **Satan tried to prove that God was wrong.**

❖ **After many terrible things happened to Job, he kept praying to God.**

One day Satan, who had **noticed** what a good man Job was, came to talk to God himself. We know that Satan wants people to be bad and he was not happy about Job. Satan said to God, "The only **reason** that Job is good is because of all the things you give him. You have let him be so **successful** and he is very rich. He lives a comfortable life. If all of that were gone, he wouldn't love You!"

God said to Satan, "You may **test** My servant, but you may not take his life." God knew Job very well. He knew that Job would not turn away from loving Him, even if all his riches were gone.

Satan wasted no time in trying to **prove** to God that Job would begin to hate Him if bad things happened. Satan killed all of Job's cattle and sheep. Then he destroyed Job's servants and his land. Even that did not keep Job from loving God! Then Satan killed Job's children. Still, Job did not stop praying to God.

Word and Phrase Meanings

noticed:	to look at and pay attention to
reason:	why something is done
successful:	doing the right things to make good things happen
prove:	to show that something is true
test:	examine, to prove what is right

Guided Prayer Thought

Dear God, Help us to remember that it is because of You that we have wonderful things. Even if bad things happen, You will always be there loving us. Amen

Questions:
Thinking & Remembering

1. What had Satan noticed?
   that Job loved God and was a good man

2. What does Satan want?
   for people to be bad

3. Why did Satan think that Job loved God?
   because of all the good things God had given him

4. What did God allow Satan to do?
   test Job

5. What did God not allow Satan to do?
   to take Job's life

6. What was Satan trying to prove?
   that Job would not love God if bad things happened to him

7. What three things did Satan do?
   a. *killed Job's cattle and sheep*
   b. *destroyed Job's servants and his land*
   c. *killed Job's children*

8. What did Job do after all these bad things happened?
   kept praying to God

 # Bible Words To Remember

Job said, "Blessed be the name of the Lord." In all his trouble Job did not sin nor charge God with wrong. Job 1:21, 22

Job said to God, "I know that You can do everything." Job 42:2

Choosing God's Way

Being Thankful

Job was a man in the Bible who loved God and thanked Him every day for all that God gave him. He had lots of things! He had a wonderful family and life was really great in every way. But he did not say, "I am great because of my riches," He said, "God is great!" When everything is just 'great', don't forget to thank God for the wonderful things He has given you.

Are we ever great just because we might have riches? Who has given us all that we have?

❤ Bible Love Lesson ❤

Love happens when we are feeling well. Love can happen when you are not feeling so great. You can love God whether the sun is shining or whether it is raining.
God loves you all the time(even when you're grumpy).
God loves you wherever you are!

Bible Story: More Trouble

Key Points

❖ Satan did not give up trying to make Job hate God.

❖ Job was loyal and loved God.

❖ Satan thought that if Job were very sick, he would stop loving God.

❖ God knew Job would keep loving and worshiping Him.

Satan **visited** the Lord again. The Lord asked Satan, "From where do you come?" Satan answered the Lord and said, "From going to and fro on the earth, and from walking back and forth on it." He was always trying to **tempt** people into not believing God.

The Lord spoke again about his servant Job and reminded Satan that he was good and had stayed **loyal** to God, even though Satan had tested him. Satan told God that Job would not keep loving Him if he were sick.

God said, "Job will still worship Me. You may try again and **test** him but you may not take his life."

Word and Phrase Meanings

visited: to come to see

tempt: to try to get someone to do something

loyal: to be true to someone

test: examine, try

Guided Prayer Thought

Dear God, Satan will always try to get us to do wrong. He will try to make us stop loving You. Help us to say NO to Satan and YES to God.
Amen

Questions:
Thinking & Remembering

1. **Who visited the Lord again?**
   Satan

2. **What question did the Lord ask Satan?**
   "From where do you come?"

3. **What did Satan answer the Lord?**
   "Going to and fro on the earth walking back and forth on it." (looking for someone he could tempt to get into trouble)

4. **What did the Lord remind Satan of?**
   that Job was good and had stayed loyal

5. **What had Satan done to Job?**
   tested him

6. **What did Satan think would make Job turn away from God?**
   if he were sick

7. **What did God know?**
   that Job would still worship Him

8. **What did God give Satan permission to do without killing Job?**
   test Job again

 ## Bible Words To Remember

Job said, "Blessed be the name of the Lord." In all his trouble Job did not sin nor **charge** God with wrong. Job 1:21, 22

Job said to God, "I know that You can do everything." Job 42:2

Choosing God's Way

Being Consistent

There is a lot of trouble in the world. But it isn't because of God and it isn't because He doesn't care. There is trouble because of the world's enemy, Satan. He loves trouble and what he likes best is when God's people have trouble. He thinks that they will stop believing in God if things aren't going right for them. Choosing to do and think the right thing will make you strong.

Why is there trouble in the world?
What does Satan think will happen if you have problems?
What will happen if you choose to do the right thing?

♥ Bible Love Lesson ♥

It is good to remember that it is God who gives us good gifts. We enjoy what He has given us. We also accept what He has given us. When something bad happens, we should be patient and know that God will take care of us.

Bible Story: Job is Sick

Key Points

❖ Even when Job was very sick, he did not say anything wrong about God.

❖ Job's wife tried to blame God for Job's trouble.

❖ Job reminded his wife that God had given them many good things.

❖ Job's friends told him that he must have done something wrong to deserve all his trouble. They just made Job sad.

After Satan left the Lord's **presence**, he immediately made terrible sores all over Job's body. It was so painful, Job could not even sleep. Still, Job did not speak evil of God.

His wife said to him, "This is all God's **fault**! Why do you **continue** to love God with all this trouble? Why don't you just give up and die?" Even in his pain, Job said to her, "We have been happy with all that God has given us and accepted many good gifts. We should accept the bad things that happen and be **patient**. We will wait for things to get better."

All the people around them talked of Job's troubles. Three of his friends came to see him. They did not **comfort** him. They said that maybe he was being **punished** for something he did wrong! Job knew he had done nothing evil. He said to them, "You are not helping me. You have just made things worse."

— Word and Phrase Meanings —

presence: being near or close to

fault: mistake; wrong

continue: to keep doing

patient: to wait without complaining

comfort: to make someone feel better

punished: to have to suffer for doing wrong

suggest: to tell an idea that can be accepted or rejected

Guided Prayer Thought

Dear God, You are the giver of all good things. Satan is the evil one.
Help us to be patient in our troubles and know that You will help
us when we are sick or sad.
                                        Amen

Questions:
Thinking & Remembering

1. What terrible thing happened to Job?
   he had sores all over his body

2. How did Job feel?
   he was in very great pain

3. Did Job blame God?
   No

4. Whom did Job's wife blame for their trouble?
   God

5. What did his wife **suggest** that Job do?
   give up and die

6. What did Job remind his wife of?
   all the good things that they had accepted from the Lord

7. What did he say was the right thing to do?
   to accept what had happened and be patient

8. Were Job's friends of any help to him? Did they comfort him?
   No, they made things worse

 # Bible Words To Remember

Job said, "Blessed be the name of the Lord." In all his trouble Job did
not sin nor charge God with wrong. Job 1:21, 22
Job said to God, "I know that You can do everything." Job 42:2

Choosing God's Way

Being Strong and Having Courage

God's enemy and our enemy, Satan, does not like to give up! He will try again and again to make you stop believing that God loves you. If something in your mind is telling you that God does not really care about you, that is Satan. You can say, "STOP!" Satan will know that you are choosing God and he will leave.

What will Satan try to make you think?
What will happen if you are strong and choose God?

❤ Bible Love Lesson ❤

If something or someone makes you unhappy, or you are sad and sick, some people will say it is God's fault! God does not make anything bad or evil. He only makes what is good. Remember the beginning of the world? God made everything perfect. He loves you very much!

Bible Story: Job Trusts God

Key Points

❖ **God made a great storm and then He talked to Job.**

❖ **God helped Job remember how great and powerful He was.**

❖ **Job knew that God cared about him.**

❖ **God made Job well and gave him back all the things he had lost because of Satan.**

Job and his friends stopped talking. Suddenly, a great storm came. The lightening flashed and thunder roared. The rain came down harder and harder. Then God talked to Job from the **midst** of the storm.

God reminded Job of all His creation. He said, "Who has given **wisdom** in the mind? Or who had given **understanding** to the heart?" Job knew that God was much greater than all things. He was more powerful than man can understand. Even though God is so mighty He listens to us and cares about us.

Job said, "You are more wonderful than I can understand and know!" The Lord made Job well again. He became rich once more and he even had more children. God took care of Job and he lived a long time.

Word and Phrase Meanings

midst: center or middle of

wisdom: much knowledge; good sense

understanding: knowing the reason why

charge: complaint

Guided Prayer Thought

Dear God, You are more wonderful than we can even imagine.
Thank You for caring about our problems and help us to
remember all the good things You give us every day.
                                    Amen

Questions:
Thinking & Remembering

1. **What happened after Job and his friends stopped talking?**
   there was a great storm with lightning and thunder and rain

2. **Who talked to Job from the midst of the storm?**
   God

3. **What did God remind Job of?**
   all of His creation

4. **What did God say He had given to the mind?**
   wisdom

5. **What did God say He had given to the heart?**
   understanding

6. **What did Job know?**
   that God was greater and more powerful than anything

7. **Even though God is mighty, what does He still do?**
   He listens to us and cares about us

8. **What did God do for Job because he believed and was faithful?**
   He healed him; gave him riches again; gave him more children

 ## Bible Words To Remember

Job said, "Blessed be the name of the Lord." In all his trouble Job did
not sin nor charge God with wrong. Job 1:21, 22
Job said to God, "I know that You can do everything." Job 42:2

Choosing God's Way

Being Sure of God's Love

God will be with you, even when bad things happen! He
will help you through it. God is very powerful and He
cares about you! We cannot begin to understand how
great He is. We wonder how He can be the maker of all
the universe and still care that we are sad because our
grandma is sick. But God does care! Keep your eyes on
God and He will show you the brightness of His love!

When will God be with you?
Think about a time when something bad happened, and
God helped you.

Songs to God: The Book of Psalms

❤ Bible Love Lesson ❤

The words in the Bible tell us that God loves each one of us. There are many ways
to show God that we love Him too! Sing songs about Him, pray to Him,
and tell your friends that God loves them.

Bible Story: Praises to God!

Key Points

❖ Songs are one way the people in the Bible told God how much they loved Him.

❖ Some words in the songs tell God when someone is sorry for disobeying Him.

❖ We can know that God will forgive when we ask Him and will help us do the right things.

Many of the people in the Bible were so thankful to God and in **awe** of His goodness. They wanted to **express** their love to God in songs. Words can be beautiful and tell of God's wonderful love and care for His people and His children.

Not all of the songs are happy. Some songs are sad because the writers knew that they had disobeyed God and wanted to tell God how sorry they were. But the writers were joyful in knowing that God loved them and forgave them for the wrong things they did if they asked Him.

Some of the songs were telling God that the people needed Him. They made **requests** to God asking for His help for many things. Because people can never do all the right things at the right time and in the right way by themselves. We need God's help!

Word and Phrase Meanings

awesome: a word to describe God

express: to show in words or deeds

request: to ask for something to be done or for something to be given

dwell: to live

awe: wonder and amazement

Guided Prayer Thought

*Dear God, Thank You for Your love. You are an **awesome** God!*
We need You so much and You are always there for us.
Amen

Questions:
Thinking & Remembering

1. How did the people in the Bible feel about God?
   they were thankful to God; they were in awe of His goodness

2. How did they express their love to God?
   in songs

3. What do the beautiful words tell about?
   God's wonderful love and care for everyone

4. Why are some of the songs sad?
   the writers had disobeyed God

5. What did they want to tell God?
   how sorry they were

6. How could they have joy?
   by knowing that God loved them and would forgive them

7. What were other songs written for?
   telling God that they needed Him

8. Can people ever be good enough and not need God's love and help?
   No, we will always need God to help us

 # Bible Words To Remember

Show me Your ways, O Lord; teach me Your paths.   Psalm 25:4

I will lie down in peace, and sleep; for You alone, O Lord, make me **dwell** in safety. Psalm 4:8

Praise Hymn

Sing or say these words
Resource: My First Hymnal Pg. 27

THE LORD IS MY SHEPHERD

The Lord is my shepherd,
I'll walk with Him alway.
He knows me and He loves me,
I'll walk with Him alway.
Alway, Alway,
I'll walk with Him alway.

❧ Bible Love Lesson ❧

Can you think of your very own words to sing how you feel about God? A young boy
in the Bible sang songs to God about all the things he could see and feel. Look
at all of God's creation and remember how much God cares for you.
Sing a song to tell Him you love Him!

Bible Story: David's Song

Key Points

❖ David remembered that God
gave him what he needed.

❖ David remembered that God
would take care of him. He
did not need to be afraid.

❖ David remembered that God
would give him even more
than he needed. He would
give him things that he
wanted.

God is just like a **shepherd** to me. He gives me whatever I **need**.
When I am tired He takes me to green grass to lie down. When I
am thirsty He takes me to still waters to drink. When I am
discouraged He lifts me up and makes me glad. He helps me do
the right thing because of His Name.

When I am in danger I do not need to be afraid. God is with me. He
protects me with His rod and staff which comforts me. I can know
that I am always safe with Him.

God gives me food even though I have enemies. God treats me
like a guest and gives me even more than I **want** or need. I know
that God's goodness to me will never end as long as I live. I will
always stay in God's house!

Word and Phrase Meanings

shepherd:	one who takes care of sheep; protects and gives them what they need
discouraged:	to feel sad about something; not cheerful
need:	something we must have to stay alive
want:	something you would like to have

Guided Prayer Thought

*Dear God, We want to stay at Your house forever! Help us
and guide us in the path You have for us.*
Amen

Questions:
Thinking & Remembering

1. **What did David say God is like?**
   a shepherd

2. **What does God give?**
   whatever I need

3. **What does God do that a shepherd would
   do for his sheep?**
   *takes me to green grass to rest and to
   still waters to drink*

4. **What happens when I am sad or
   discouraged?**
   He lifts me up and makes me glad

5. **What will God help us do? Why?**
   the right thing, because of His Name

6. **Why did David say that he never needed to
   be afraid?**
   *God is with him to protect him, he is
   always safe*

7. **What else does God give?**
   food

8. **How does God treat us like a guest?**
   *He gives even more than we can want
   or need*

 # Bible Words To Remember

Show me Your ways, O Lord; teach me Your paths.   Psalm 25:4

I will lie down in peace, and sleep; for You alone, O Lord, make me

dwell in safety. Psalm 4:8

Choosing
God's Way

Praising God

Isn't God's Word, the Bible, wonderful? In these words
of God we can know who He is and who we are because
of Him! When we feel God's love we want to find a way
to tell Him in special ways. We can sing words to God
about whatever we are feeling. David did this in the
Bible. He made up songs to tell God. You can do this
too!

What do we know from the words in the Bible?
How can we show God how we feel?

❤ Bible Love Lesson ❤

It is so nice to feel safe. You can know that God will take care of His own children even when there are **scary** things all around. You can sleep knowing that God is protecting you. He puts His angels on guard for those who love Him.

Bible Story: The Lord Keeps His Own Safe

 **Key Points**

❖ **When others try to say that God does not love us, we can know that He does. David knew and believed that God cared.**

❖ **David knew that God would listen to his prayers and help him.**

❖ **David knew that God would protect him while he was asleep.**

One of the songs that David wrote tells God that there are many enemies who have caused him trouble. David said that there were those who were against him who said that God would not help him.

But David knew His God. He said to God, "When I ask You to help me, You will hear me!" David said that he did not need to be afraid of ten thousands of people who were against him when God was with him. He said he could go to sleep knowing that God was **guarding** and **protecting** him.

David said that God had put **gladness** in his heart more than anything else that he could have. Whenever he felt afraid or troubled about what might hurt him, he knew he could talk to God and God would listen. He said, "The Lord will hear when I call to Him."

── Word and Phrase Meanings ──

scary:	things that make you afraid
guarding:	watching over
protecting:	taking care of and keeping safe
gladness:	joy, happiness

Guided Prayer Thought

Dear God, When we lay down to go to sleep at night, we know that You will be with us. You will guard and protect us.

Amen

Questions:
Thinking & Remembering

1. What tells that David knew that not everyone was his friend?
   he said he had many enemies who caused him trouble

2. Did his enemies think that God would help David?
   No

3. What did David know about God?
   that God would help him when he asked him

4. Did David ever think that God would be too busy to listen to him?
   No, he knew that God would hear him

5. Why was David not afraid to go to sleep at night?
   He knew that God was guarding and protecting him.

6. How many people did David say might be against him?
   ten thousands

7. What did David say that God had put in his heart?
   gladness

8. What would David do whenever he felt afraid?
   talk to God

 ## Bible Words To Remember

Show me Your ways, O Lord; teach me Your paths.   Psalm 25:4

I will lie down in peace, and sleep; for You alone, O Lord, make me dwell in safety. Psalm 4:8

Choosing God's Way

Loyalty

David knew that there were people who did not like him. Even though it feels wonderful to be liked in every way, there will be those who are unkind to you. It will make you feel bad and hurt you not to be liked and loved the way your parents love you. God will be listening when you tell Him how you feel. He cares and He will show you what matters more than what other people say and do. Be loyal and true to others and then let God take care of the rest!

Will everyone always love you the way your parents love you?
Who will be listening when you tell Him how you feel?
What matters more than what others say and do?

❤ Bible Love Lesson ❤

God does not just love you when you are good and do all the right things.
God loves you even when you are mad at your mom for making you go to bed.
God loves you when you have been disobedient, even though it makes
Him sad. Tell God that you are sorry. He will forgive you.

Bible Story: God Will Forgive When We Ask Him

Key Points

❖ Even though David did wrong things, he knew that God still loved him.

❖ David was very sad that he had hurt God by doing wrong. He asked God to forgive him.

❖ David knew that he needed God's Word in his heart so that he would know the right thing to do.

❖ God heard David's songs and prayers and forgave him.

When David **sinned**, he was very sad. He knew that God still loved him, but his sin had not only hurt God but had hurt himself and others. David wanted to have the same **friendship** with God that he had before he had done wrong.

He said to God in this song, "Wash me completely from my sin, and make me clean. Wash me, and I will be whiter than snow." He asked God to let him hear joy and gladness again. He felt **broken** from the sin he had done. David asked God to 'create a clean heart' in him. Another song writer in Psalms said, "Your word I have hidden in my heart, that I might not sin against You."

David knew the Lord heard him weeping for his sins. God **forgave** David and said that He (God) had covered his sin. "The Lord will receive my prayer. My voice You will hear in the morning, O Lord; and I will look up."

Word and Phrase Meanings

sinned: doing wrong against God's laws and commandments

friendship: being friends with another person

broken: very sad or depressed

forgave: excused someone for doing wrong

Guided Prayer Thought

Dear God, When we sin against You, we also hurt others. Help us to hide Your Word in our hearts so we will not sin. Help us to remember that when we are sorry and ask You to forgive us, You will!
Amen

Questions: Thinking & Remembering

1. **How did David feel when he sinned?**
   very sad

2. **Did God stop loving him because he sinned?**
   No, He still loved him

3. **What happens when we sin?**
   it hurts God, it also hurts others

4. **What did David want?**
   to have friendship with God

5. **How did David tell God he was sorry?**
   he asked God to wash him and make him clean

6. **What did he ask God to do with his heart?**
   to create in him a clean heart

7. **What can we do so that we will not sin?**
   hide God's word in our heart

8. **When the Lord forgives, should we still be sad?**
   No, we should look up and be happy!

Bible Words To Remember

Show me Your ways, O Lord; teach me Your paths.   Psalm 25:4

I will lie down in peace, and sleep; for You alone, O Lord, make me dwell in safety.   Psalm 4:8

Choosing God's Way

Forgiveness

God still loves you, even when you do wrong things. You can try your best to do everything just right, but you will still make mistakes. You need God's help every day. What God does want, is for you to be sorry when you have done wrong and ask Him to forgive you. And He will!

Will we ever be able to do everything just right all by ourselves?
Think about something you have done wrong or someone you have hurt. Did you ask God to forgive you? Did you ask the person you hurt to forgive you?

❤ Bible Love Lesson ❤

It is wonderful when a whole family can be together and love each other. That is the way God planned for homes to be. But sometimes sad things happen and love gets broken. God can help families love again. He can fix anything! But He will love and care about you, even during 'broken' times.

Bible Story: Hope

Key Points

❖ When we feel sad, we can remember all the good things God gave us and He will help us be happy again.

❖ God wants us to always think of His love.

❖ God even cares about the birds. Think how much more He cares for you!

❖ God gives angels to watch over you.

One writer in the Psalms wrote about feeling sad. He asked himself why there should be sadness. He said that there was only **hope** in God. When we praise God for His goodness and His help, we will feel glad again.

We need to always **remember** what God does for us. There are often people who want to look for all the bad things in life to make everyone feel **miserable**. They forget to look for and remember God's love and all that He has given.

Another song tells about God's care for the birds. The words say, "Even the sparrow has found a home, and the swallow a nest for herself." If God cares for the birds, He will care for you even more. "He will give His angels **charge** over you, to keep you in all your ways." Isn't that a wonderful promise?

Word and Phrase Meanings

hope: count on, trust

remember: to think about again; to not forget

miserable: very unhappy

charge: control over

Guided Prayer Thought

Dear God, Knowing that You love us gives us a great hope and is a great promise that You will always be with us. If you even care for each bird, how much You must care about us!

Amen

Questions:
Thinking & Remembering

1. **What did one of the writers in the Psalms write about?**
   feeling sad

2. **What question did he ask?**
   "Why should there be sadness?"

3. **What did he say there was because of God and His goodness?**
   hope

4. **How can we know that God loves us?**
   because of all He does for us and because He tells us in His word

5. **What can we remember when others try to make us miserable with all the bad things?**
   remember God's love and all He gives you

6. **What did one of the songs tell about?**
   God caring for the birds

7. **Would God care more for the birds than for the people He made?**
   No, He will care for us, too

8. **What wonderful promise is given in one of the songs?**
   God will give us angels to watch over us

 # Bible Words To Remember

Show me Your ways, O Lord; teach me Your paths.   Psalm 25:4

I will lie down in peace, and sleep; for You alone, O Lord, make me dwell in safety. Psalm 4:8

Choosing God's Way

Loving Families

Sometimes there may not be a mom and dad who can be with their children to love and care for them. That can be very sad. God said that He will not let these children be alone. He will care for them in a special way and help them. It was God's perfect plan for you to be with a mother and father who would love Him and love their children. When you have two parents who love you, be very thankful. If you have only one person who loves you, be thankful. Tell them you love them!

What is God's perfect plan for families?
What did God promise for children who do not have two parents?

Wise Sayings of Solomon: The Book of Proverbs

♥ Bible Love Lesson ♥

Knowing about things is important. But being wise is even more important. God said He will give wisdom to those who ask for it. Wisdom is more than knowing something. It is understanding *why* something is important

Bible Story: The Wise King

Key Points

❖ Being wise is the best thing to want.

❖ God will make us wise if we ask Him.

❖ King Solomon wrote down the wise things God told him.

❖ Loving God and listening to His words will make us wise.

When king Solomon asked God for wisdom, God said that he had asked for the very best thing. **Wisdom** means knowing what the right thing is. It is also knowing how to do the right thing at the right time and in the right way. We will still make **mistakes** because of sin. We may go off the path God has planned for us, but He will help us back on the right path if we ask Him to make us wise.

God gave Solomon what he asked for----wisdom to know what was right and wrong. He showed him what the difference was. These wise sayings were written down in the Bible in the Book of Proverbs so that we can know what God told Solomon and learn from it.

The first thing we must all do is to **love** and **respect** God. That is the most important thing. If we do not do that, all the wise words or sayings in the world cannot make us better or happier.

Word and Phrase Meanings

wisdom:	knowing what the right thing is
mistakes:	to be wrong about something
love:	a great, warm feeling about someone
respect:	to think highly of and to treat with honor
lean:	trust or depend on
understanding:	know the reason why

Guided Prayer Thought

Dear God, We want to love and respect You first. We want to keep You important to us every day. Please help us to be wise.

Amen

Questions:
Thinking & Remembering

1. What did king Solomon ask God for?
   wisdom

2. What did God think about Solomon's choice?
   He said he had asked for the very best thing

3. What does wisdom mean?
   knowing what the right thing is

4. After knowing what the right thing is, what else can we know?
   how to do it and when to do it

5. Does this mean that we will never make mistakes?
   No, we will still make mistakes because of sin

6. When we go off the path God has planned for us, what will He help us do if we ask Him?
   get back on the right path

7. Where can we learn about the wisdom God gave Solomon?
   it is written in the Bible

8. What is first and more important than wise words or sayings?
   to love and respect God

 # Bible Words To Remember

A friend loves at all times. . .   Proverbs 17:17

Trust in the Lord with all your heart, and **lean** not on your own **understanding**.   Proverbs 3:5

Praise Hymn

Sing or say these words
Resource: My First Hymnal Pg. 6

BE CAREFUL LITTLE EYES

Oh, be careful little eyes what you see,
Oh, be careful little eyes what you see,
For the Father up above is looking down in love,
So be careful little eyes what you see.

2. Oh, be careful little hands what you do.
3. Oh, be careful little feet where you go.

❤ Bible Love Lesson ❤

There are more and more things to learn and know about. Just when you learn one thing really well, you find out there is something else that is important to learn! God will help you learn all the things you need to know. Ask Him to help you learn.

Bible Story: Friends

 Key Points

❖ The Bible tells that God knows that friends are important.

❖ Being a friend and being friendly make others want to be a friend to you.

❖ A friend is someone who loves you--even when you are having problems.

❖ Friends don't run away when you need them. They stick with you!

Everyone likes to have friends. Friends are those you can share things with, and tell your feelings to. You can tell them what is important to you and they will listen and care about what you think. It is nice to be with friends who **accept** you for just being you!

The Bible talks about friends, too. In the Book of Proverbs, there are wise words that tell how to be a friend. If you follow God's word and you are kind and love others, you will have many friends, but first of all, you will be a **friend**.

"Someone who has friends must be friendly. There is a friend who sticks closer than a brother. A friend loves at all times." Sometimes someone who says they are your friend will hurt your feelings or do something to hurt you. At those times, remember that God will always love you. He will never let you down and will be there every time you need Him!

Word and Phrase Meanings

accept: to receive with satisfaction

friend: someone who likes you and is on your side; someone you can trust

trust: to know and believe that God will do what He said

lean: depend or rely on

understanding: knowing the reason why

Guided Prayer Thought

Dear God, Thank You for being my very best friend. Help me to be a good friend and be friendly to others so that I can show them Your love.
Amen

Questions:
Thinking & Remembering

1. **Why is it nice to have friends?**
   you can share things with them and tell them your feelings

2. **What can you tell a friend that you might not tell to anyone else?**
   what is important to you

3. **What will a good friend do when you tell them these things?**
   listen and care about what you think

4. **What is most special about friends?**
   They accept you for just being you!

5. **What does the Book of Proverbs say about being a friend?**
   friends are kind and loving

6. **What must we do first of all?**
   be a friend

7. **What do good friends do?**
   stick closer than a brother; love at all times

8. **What can you remember if your friend hurts your feelings?**
   that God will always love you and will be there when you need Him

 Bible Words To Remember

A friend loves at all times. . .   Proverbs 17:17
Trust in the Lord with all your heart, and **lean** not on your
own **understanding**.   Proverbs 3:5

Choosing God's Way

Being a Friend

Does someone call you their friend? Sometimes we just think about others being our friend. We want them to be nice to us, give us the toy we want to play with, invite us to their birthday party or come to our birthday party and give us a present. The Bible tells you that it is important first of all to be a friend. You can 'be' a friend--then you will 'have' a friend.

Tell about a special friend you have.
What does the Bible say about being a friend?

❤ Bible Love Lesson ❤

God gave the important rules in the Bible so that we can learn how He wants us to care about others and how to treat others. When you love God most of all, He will help you care about everyone in just the right way. Everyone will want to be your friend.

Bible Story: Family

Key Points

❖ **God wants families to learn about the words in His book.**

❖ **Parents have a special teaching job to show their children what God's love is like.**

❖ **Children are wise (smart) if they listen to what their parents tell them.**

❖ **Families should always love each other.**

The Bible tells us a lot about families. Families are important to God. Mothers and fathers are to be important **examples** to their children and teach them God's word and His commandments. God wants parents to love their children to show them what God's love can be like. Taking care of them and helping them know what is right and wrong is a special job for parents.

But children have a job, too. If you are **wise**, you will listen to your father's **instruction**. A father wants what is best for his children. A father must also **correct** and **discipline** his children. Just as God corrects us because He loves us, fathers should do the same.

To be wise, you will not only listen, but will also obey and do things that will make your parents proud of you and happy that you are their special child. If you are **foolish**, you will make your mother sad. The proverb says, "Keep your father's command, and do not turn away from the law of your mother. A wise son will make his father glad."

Word and Phrase Meanings

example:	model
wise:	knowing and understanding what is right
instruction:	to tell how to do something
correct:	teach to do what is right
discipline:	training that corrects
foolish:	silly, senseless

Guided Prayer Thought

Dear God, We want to be wise. Help us to listen to the instruction of our parents and make them proud and glad.
Amen

Questions:
Thinking & Remembering

1. Why are families important to God?
   children learn about God from their parents

2. What does God want parents to show children?
   what God's love is like

3. What is a special job for parents to do?
   to teach their children what is right and wrong

4. What should children do when their father gives instruction?
   listen

5. What do fathers want?
   what is best for their children

6. What else must a father do that God also does?
   correct and discipline their children

7. What four things will children do if they are wise?
   make your parents proud of you; keep your father's command; not turn away for the law of your mother; make your father glad

8. What will happen if you are foolish?
   you will make your mother sad

 # Bible Words To Remember

A friend loves at all times. . . Proverbs 17:17

Trust in the Lord with all your heart, and lean not on your own understanding. Proverbs 3:5

Choosing God's Way

Self-Control

Will your mother be proud of you if you cry and **whine** all the time to get your own way? "I don't want to go!" "I don't like to play with him!" "I won't clean up my room!" God will be sad if you only think of YOU, and not others. Your family is very special. Listen to your parents and make your home a happy place to be.

Why will God be sad?
How can you make your home a happy home?

♥ Bible Love Lesson ♥

Sometimes your mom or dad needs you to notice when they are not having a great day. Tell them how much you love them. Tell them that you think they are the greatest! Thank them for all they do for you.

Bible Story: Cheerfulness

Key Points

❖ God does not want us to be "grumpy"! He wants us to be cheerful.

❖ When we are cheerful, we make others happy, too.

❖ If you think about how much God loves you, you will forget to complain and be sad.

❖ Good words are sweet like honey. Use good words that make others happy.

God does not expect or want us to be gloomy and sad! He wants us to have joy and happiness every day. He tells us in His Word that we will **especially** be happy when we have **wisdom**.

The Bible says that a **cheery** face gives joy to others! And being **pleasant** with your words is just like honey. The words are sweet and make others happy. There is joy for those who do the right thing.

When you think about what is really important and how much God loves you, you will forget to **complain** about what you don't have and you won't have time to feel sorry for yourself. Enjoy the birds singing. Enjoy the wonderful blue sky, the flowers and grass and the rain that makes it all beautiful. Enjoy your family and the love you share with each other. God has given us so many gifts!

— Word and Phrase Meanings —

especially: you are very special

wisdom: much knowledge; good sense

cheery: happy

pleasant: kind, nice, agreeable

complain: to talk about unhappiness; whine

whine: complain

Guided Prayer Thought

*Dear God, Help us to think of the important things. Help us
to remember Your gifts and be cheerful.*
Amen

Questions:
Thinking & Remembering

1. **Why should we not be gloomy or sad?**
   *God wants us to have joy and
   happiness*

2. **When will we be especially happy?**
   when we have wisdom

3. **What does a cheery face do for others?**
   gives joy

4. **What are pleasant words like?**
   like honey

5. **What do sweet words do?**
   make others happy and give us joy

6. **What will happen when you think about
   God's love?**
   *you will forget about complaining;
   you will stop feeling sorry for yourself*

7. **What things can you enjoy?**
   *birds, sky, flowers, grass and rain;
   family and love*

8. **Who has given us all of these wonderful
   gifts?**
   God

 ## Bible Words To Remember

A friend loves at all times. . .   Proverbs 17:17
Trust in the Lord with all your heart, and lean not on your
own understanding.   Proverbs 3:5

Choosing God's Way

Being Glad

Doesn't it make you feel happy when you are with others
who can laugh and be glad? It is very different when you
are with those who talk about how bad everything is , "Oh,
now it's raining, and we can't go to the zoo!" "I didn't want
carrots. I hate vegetables!" Soon, you feel as bad as
those around you who are grumpy! You can change
gloom to sunshine. Think of the bright side! "We can't go
to the zoo because it's raining. Let's play a game
instead." God will always help you to be glad!

*Tell how you feel when someone complains and is grumpy.
How can you help others feel glad?*

❤ Bible Love Lesson ❤

Some children do not have as much as you have. God tells us to be kind to those who
are lonely and sad. Be kind to people who are poor. Share the things you have,
but most of all, show them that God loves them and that you love them, too!

Bible Story: Kindness

Key Points

❖ God wants us to think of
others before we think about
ourselves.

❖ Giving to others shows God's
love in a special way.

❖ Speak softly to others. Don't
shout or use mean and
unkind words.

❖ Treat others the same way
you want them to treat you.

God's word tells that thinking of others before you think of yourself
will bring happiness. Caring about others and their feelings
shows that you know how much God loves and cares about you!
Giving to others shows that you know how much God has given
you.

When you are **kind** to those who have little, you will be happy.
Share and be good to others. Kind words make you feel happy.
Say kind words to others, too! When you speak to others, talk
softly, even when they have spoken loudly. They will stop being
angry.

When you think about what God wants and how God wants you to
treat others, He will be **pleased** and even those who are unkind
will be more **peaceful** around you. They will know that you love
God and will say, "I would like to know your God, too!"

— Word and Phrase Meanings —

kind: a nice person who cares about others

share: to give part of what you have to someone

pleased: happy, satisfied

peaceful: to be calm or quiet

Guided Prayer Thought

Dear God, Help us to show others how much You love them by being kind and showing love.   Amen

Questions:
Thinking & Remembering

1. What does God's Word tell about happiness?
   thinking of others brings happiness

2. What does it show when you care about others and their feelings?
   it shows that you know (are confident) about how much God loves and cares about you

3. Why should you give and share with others?
   because God has given you so much

4. How will you feel if you are kind to others?
   you will be happy

5. What should you say to others?
   kind words

6. Even when someone is angry and talking loud, how should you speak?
   softly

7. When you think about how God wants you to treat others, what will happen?
   God will be pleased

8. When you treat others kindly, what else will happen?
   they will know you love God and will want to know Him too

 Bible Words To Remember

A friend loves at all times. . .   Proverbs 17:17

Trust in the Lord with all your heart, and lean not on your own understanding.   Proverbs 3:5

Choosing God's Way

Knowledge

What are some of the things you already know? You probably know that you have ten fingers and toes. You know your name. You might know your address and telephone number. These are all good things to know. Are there more things to know? The wise king in the Bible said that knowing lots of things was not as important as being able to know how all of the things you know can make the world better for God.

Tell some things that you have learned and know. What is more important than knowing lots of things?

Bible Beginnings

What is Important: The Book of Ecclesiastes

♥ Bible Love Lesson ♥

You can show God and others that you believe that God has plans for you.
They are very special plans because you are very special to God.
Pray every day that He will show you the way.

Bible Story: Lots of Life Questions

Key Points

❖ King Solomon thought about what was most important.

❖ Being rich and having lots of things does not make people happy.

❖ Think and talk about what is most important to you.

The writer of the words in the Book of Ecclesiastes was king Solomon. After he was **rich** and **famous**, he started thinking again about what was most **important**. What had really made Solomon happy?

Was it having the most beautiful **palace** in all the world to live in? Was it having a large family? Was it having lots of servants getting him whatever he wanted and obeying all of his commands? Was it just being **smarter** than anyone else? Was it having lots of money to buy anything he wanted? Was it having lots of parties to invite friends to?

King Solomon started answering all these questions and you might be surprised at what he found out in his life. They are answers for you to think about and see how you might answer the questions. Even though you are very young, the answers can be very important.

Word and Phrase Meanings

rich: to have lots of money to buy many things

important: something that has value

palace: a very beautiful place where a king or queen lives

smarter: to know more than others

famous: known by many people

Guided Prayer Thought

Dear God, You have all the answers to all the questions.
Help us know what is really important.
Amen

Questions:
Thinking & Remembering

1. Who was the writer of the words in the book of Ecclesiastes?
   king Solomon

2. What did he think about after he was rich and famous?
   about what was most important

3. Were king Solomon's questions different than some questions we ask?
   No, we think about the same things

4. What question did he ask about where he lived?
   "Did having the most beautiful palace make him happy?"

5. Think about the same questions Solomon asked and pretend you had all of those things. What are your answers?

6. Can you can decide right now, while you are young, before you have lots of things what is really important?
   yes

7. Do you think that God told Solomon the answers to his questions?
   yes

8. What do you think is the most important?
   loving God and knowing that He loves you

 Bible Words To Remember

There is a time for every purpose under heaven.   Ecclesiastes 3:1
Whatever your hand finds to do, do it with your might.   Ecclesiastes 9:10

Praise Hymn

Sing or say these words
Resource: My First Hymnal Pg. 1

DEEP AND WIDE

Deep and wide,
deep and wide,
There's a fountain flowing
deep and wide.
Deep and wide,
deep and wide,
There's a fountain flowing
deep and wide.

❤ Bible Love Lesson ❤

God's love does not ever change. It is the same forever. Sometimes someone
we thought was our friend, stops liking us. But God is not like that.
He will love us always!

Bible Story: What Really Matters

Key Points

❖ **King Solomon knew that God had answers to every question.**

❖ **All the things we have are a gift from God.**

❖ **God will give us all the things we need--not all the things we want.**

❖ **God knows what is best for us to have. He will give more than we need and He wants us to enjoy what He gives.**

When King Solomon asked God for the answers to his questions
and he considered everything in his life, he found out that:
A big house was not most important,
Having servants was not important,
Having parties with lots of friends was not important,
Being rich and having more than you need was not important,
Being the wisest and smartest was not the most important,
Having a big family was wonderful, but still not the most important.

Solomon **decided** that it was God who gave us all things. God
also gives **wisdom** and **knowledge** and joy to those who are
good and walk in His ways. Everything we have is a gift from God.

Riches can buy you things you want on earth, but you will not take
anything with you when you leave to go be with God. You will not
need anything you have here in heaven. What really **matters** is
that we love and respect God and follow His commandments.

Word and Phrase Meanings

decided:	made a choice
wisdom:	much knowledge; good sense
knowledge:	to know and understand
matters:	what to give attention to; to mean something
might:	great strength; giving a task everything you can do to get it right

Guided Prayer Thought

Dear God, You have given us so many wonderful gifts. Help us to remember that it is most important to love You. It is because You love us that You have given us all the things we have to enjoy.
Amen

Questions:
Thinking & Remembering

1. What did Solomon find out about all of the things he had?
   they were not the most important

2. What else did Solomon discover about the things he had?
   it was God who gave them

3. What else did God give besides things?
   wisdom, knowledge, joy

4. To whom does He give these things?
   to those who are good and walk in His ways

5. What is everything we have?
   a gift of God

6. What can you buy if you are rich?
   things you want, but don't always need

7. Will you be able to take any of these things with you when you die?
   No

8. What really matters?
   that we love and respect God and follow His commandments

 # Bible Words To Remember

There is a time for every purpose under heaven.   Ecclesiastes 3:1
Whatever your hand finds to do, do it with your might.   Ecclesiastes 9:10

Choosing God's Way

Happiness

Maybe you know someone who lives in a big house and has a TV in their own bedroom. They may have all the clothes and shoes they want. Every time they go to the store with their mom they can buy a toy. This family goes on special vacations and gets there on an airplane. Wouldn't this be a happy child? But there are many unhappy children who have all of these things and more. What is important is loving God. That is the only real happiness. Keep looking around and you will see!

Do lots of things and lots of money always make people truly happy?
What is most important to know that will bring real happiness?

❤ Bible Love Lesson ❤

You can show that you are thankful for what God gives you by the happy expression
on your face. When others see you, they will be thankful that they know
you and will thank God for you.

Bible Story: God Is In Control

Key Points

❖ God planned everything from the very beginning to the ending of the world.

❖ Solomon said to think about all that God made and what He does.

❖ God has put everything in place. He is awesome!

Whatever God does, it will be forever. Nothing can be added to it, and nothing taken from it. Solomon also **decided** that God was in **control** of the whole universe. He is in control of the world and everything in it.

Solomon said, "**Consider** the work of God." People that are born pass away, but the earth lasts forever. The sun rises, and the sun goes down and returns where it started. The wind whirls around **continually** and comes back again. All the rivers run into the sea, but the sea is not full.

Everything that has been is what will be. The things that are done will always be done. There is nothing new under the sun. God knows all things! I'm glad He is in control!

Word and Phrase Meanings

decided:　　　choose between

control:　　　power over

consider:　　　think about carefully

continually:　　over and over again

Guided Prayer Thought

Dear God, If we were in control, we would really mess things up.
You are wise and wonderful and I'm glad You are in control!
                    Amen

Questions:
Thinking & Remembering

1. **How long will the things God does last?**
   forever

2. **Can anything be added to what God has already done?**
   No

3. **Can anything be taken away from what God has done?**
   No

4. **What did Solomon decide?**
   that God was in control of the whole universe

5. **What did Solomon say to do?**
   to consider the work of God

6. **What happens to all people that are born?**
   they pass away

7. **What does the sun do after it goes down?**
   returns where it started

8. **Is there anything new under the sun? Can man create something that was not already there because God made it?**
   No, there is nothing new

 # Bible Words To Remember

There is a time for every purpose under heaven. Ecclesiastes 3:1
Whatever your hand finds to do, do it with your might.   Ecclesiastes 9:10

Choosing God's Way

Priorities

Ask God to help you know what is most important. You are just a child, but God will help you begin to see and know! All the people in the world are not loving and happy. It is not because they don't have a great car or all of the things money can buy. It is because they do not think about God. They choose to do things their way instead of God's way.

How can you know what is most important?
Is thinking about God and not having your own way a choice?

❤ Bible Love Lesson ❤

Think about what God has made and what He has done. Then think about what He will do if we love Him and let Him. We cannot stop God's plan but what we choose to do about what God has done for us can give us peace and contentment and show others how to love God, too.

Bible Story: A Time For Everything

Key Points

❖ **God planned a time for all the things we do every day and every year!**

❖ **God will help you know what is right at the right time if you ask Him.**

❖ **Do your very best in whatever you do.**

❖ **Life is a gift from God. Remember to thank God for this wonderful gift.**

Solomon said in his heart that God would **judge** the people who are good and the people who are bad. There is a time for every plan and every work there is to do.

There is a time to cry, and a time to laugh.
There is a time to be sad, and a time to dance (be happy).
There is a time to win, and a time to lose.
A time to keep silent, and a time to speak.

God has put **eternity** in our hearts but no one can find out the work that God does from beginning to end. Nothing can be better than to **rejoice** and to do good in whatever we do. Always remember that life is the gift God gave.

Word and Phrase Meanings

judge: to make a decision about something or somebody, whether good or bad

eternity: forever; where there is no time

rejoice: to have joy; be very happy

might: great strength; giving a task everything you can do to get it right

Guided Prayer Thought

Dear God, Thank You for making a time for everything. Help us to use time wisely and do what is important to do in Your plan.
Amen

Questions:
Thinking & Remembering

1. Who will judge the people that are good and bad?
   God

2. What is there a time for?
   every plan and every work

3. Put in the word that is missing:
   There is a time to cry, and a time to _____. (laugh)
   There is a time to be sad, and a time to _____.(dance)
   There is a time to win, and a time to_____.(lose)
   There is a time to keep silent, and a time to _____.(speak)

4. Who has put eternity in our hearts?
   God

5. What can we not know that only God knows?
   what God does from the beginning to end

6. What is the best thing we can do?
   to rejoice and do good in whatever we do

7. What is some of the work you do?

8. What should we remember about life?
   it is the gift God gave

 ## Bible Words To Remember

There is a time for every purpose under heaven.   Ecclesiastes 3:1
Whatever your hand finds to do, do it with your **might**.   Ecclesiastes 9:10

Choosing God's Way

Being Joyful

Do you like to have fun? Everyone likes to have a good time with friends and family. Sometimes when a party is over and you are back home after having a wonderful time, you feel 'not so happy'. God says that being happy is that feeling of joy inside that doesn't go away after the party is over. It doesn't have anything to do with the balloons and fun. Joy comes from knowing that you have a wonderful God and knowing that you belong to HIM!

Tell about a happy time you had at a party or going somewhere special.
What is the difference between a 'happy feeling' and 'joy'?

❤ Bible Love Lesson ❤

There are some grown-ups who complain about the way children act. Sometimes there is a very good reason. Children don't always think about others needing a quiet place to talk or do their work. *You* can behave in a way that grown-ups say, "I *love* having that child around me!"

Bible Story: More Important Words

Key Points

❖ **Loving God first will help you do the right things at the right time.**

❖ **God made everyone unique and different in what they can do.**

❖ **Whatever God gives you to do--do it in the best way you can.**

❖ **Listen to God's words in the Bible. They will help you know how to use your gifts (what you do best) to love and serve God.**

Because we do not know how much time God will give us on earth, we should live carefully and obediently each day; first of all, loving God and doing the right things at the right time.

Time and **chance** happens to everyone---children, too. The words of Solomon say, the fastest one does not always win the race. The strongest one does not always win the battle. Food is not just given to those who are wise. Having money is not just for those with understanding, and not just for those with **skill**.

Whatever you find that is good to do, do it very well---as well as you can. All work, everything we do, is in the hand of God to be approved and accepted. Solomon had wise words for us. They are like **goads** (**motives**: reason or purpose) that make us want to act in the right way, God's way.

Word and Phrase Meanings

chance:	opportunity
skill:	ability to do something well
goad:	something that makes us want to do things well
motive:	reason or purpose

Guided Prayer Thought

Dear God, There are many things we can learn about how You want us to live. Help us to put You first, and You will show us how to do the rest!

Amen

Questions:
Thinking & Remembering

1. Do we know how much time God will give us on earth?
   No

2. How should we live?
   carefully and obediently---loving God first

3. What do the words tell us about time?
   do the right things at the right time

4. To whom does time and chance happen?
   to everyone

5. Do the fastest or the strongest always win?
   No

6. Do just the wise have food?
   No

7. What do the words tell us to do well?
   whatever you find that is good to do

8. Who will accept the work we do?
   God

9. What are Solomon's words like?
   goads (sticks that make us get going the right way!)

10. What do these words make us want to do?
    act in the right way, God's way

 Bible Words To Remember

There is a time for every purpose under heaven. Ecclesiastes 3:1

Whatever your hand finds to do, do it with your might. Ecclesiastes 9:10

Choosing God's Way

Doing Your Best

Do you think that you will wait until you are older---at least ten---to do good work? Maybe you are learning to make your bed. You think, 'I don't need to have the covers straight because I am still little.' God says that whatever you do, do it well. You will be learning, and everything won't be perfect the first time. But you will be trying your very best!

Do you ever use your age (how old you are) as an excuse for not doing good work?
What does God say about what you do?

The Prophets:
Isaiah, Jeremiah, Ezekiel and Daniel

♥ Bible Love Lesson ♥

There are times when you do something wrong and you just want to pretend that you didn't do it. Even if you mom doesn't know that you did something wrong, God knows. We cannot hide from God. The wonderful thing is if you tell God you're sorry, He will forgive you. He loves you!

Bible Story: Isaiah--His Message From God

Key Points

❖ God kept loving His people even when they turned away from Him.

❖ God always forgave His people when they were sorry for doing wrong.

❖ God's prophets reminded the people of God's love for them.

❖ The prophet Isaiah told about the Savior whom God would send.

Even though God's people had kept forgetting God's commandments and turning away from Him, He would always forgive them when they were sorry for what they had done. He kept on loving them. He continued to protect them from their enemies when they prayed to Him. God kept ALL of His **promises** to Israel. They did not keep their promises to God.

God sent special prophets to give the people His message to remind them of how He **expected** them to live and how much He cared for them. Isaiah told the people, "If you are willing and obedient, you will have all the good things that are in the land. But if you **refuse** and are **rebellious**, your enemies will kill you. The Lord has said this."

The very best part of what Isaiah told was how God's promise of a Savior would come. He told the people that when the Savior came, God's people would be free. Someday they would come back into the land He had given them. God had a wonderful plan for them.

Word and Phrase Meanings

promises:	doing what is said will be done
expected:	counted on
refuse:	to say that you won't do something
rebellious:	wanting to do what is wrong
adoration:	love, worship

Guided Prayer Thought

Dear God, We are sorry that we forget Your commandments, just like the people of Israel. We do the things WE want to do instead of asking for Your help. Thank You for sending Jesus, our Savior, to be with us and help us know how much You love us.
Amen

Questions:
Thinking & Remembering

1. What did God's people keep forgetting?
   God's commandments

2. When they stopped obeying the commandments what happened?
   they turned away from God

3. What did God do when they were sorry for what they had done?
   forgave them

4. What did He keep on doing?
   loving them; protecting them

5. What did God do that Israel did not do?
   kept promises

6. Whom did God send to remind them of how He wanted them to live?
   the prophets

7. What was Isaiah's special message?
   God's promise of a Savior

8. What would happen when this promise came true?
   they would be free and some day come back into the land He had given them

 # Bible Words To Remember

God said, "I have called you by your name; you are Mine."   Isaiah 43:1b
Since you were precious in My sight . . . and I have loved you.   Isaiah 43:4

Praise Hymn

Sing or say these words
Resource: My First Hymnal Pg. 63

PRAISE TO THE LORD, THE ALMIGHTY

Praise ye the Lord,
the Almighty, the King of Creation!
O my soul, praise Him, for He is thy
Health and Salvation!
All ye who hear,
Now to His temple draw near;
Join me in glad **adoration**!

❤ Bible Love Lesson ❤

God says in the Bible that YOU are precious in His sight. That means that He can see you, and what He sees is precious! Precious means dear and loved. It means that you are valuable. You are worth much more than any money or riches. Wow! That is extra special love!

Bible Story: Jeremiah--His Message From God

Key Points

❖ Jeremiah was sad because the people did not follow God.

❖ When the people did not listen to God's words, God told Jeremiah that He was with him.

❖ Jeremiah did not give up trying to tell the Israelites what God said.

Jeremiah was one of the saddest **prophets** because he lived in a time when the people were not following God. When he tried to tell them what would happen because of their disobedience, they would not listen to him.

God told Jeremiah that the people would fight against him, but they would not **succeed**. God made this promise to him, "I am with you, and will **rescue** you."

Jeremiah never stopped giving the kings and people God's **message**, even when they beat him and put him in **prison**. His messages were written down on **scrolls** so that they could be read. The people soon found out that every word that Jeremiah had spoken was from God. Everything he said came true.

Word and Phrase Meanings

prophets:	someone who speaks for God and tell what will happen
succeed:	to do well
rescue:	to make free
message:	to tell something to someone
prison:	a place where someone is not free
scroll:	a roll of special paper with God's words written on it

Guided Prayer Thought

Dear God, When we read Your messages in the Bible, we can know that they are all true. Help us to listen and obey.
Amen

Questions:
— Thinking & Remembering —

1. Why was Jeremiah one of the saddest prophets?
    the people were not following God

2. What did the people do when he told them what would happen?
    they would not listen

3. What did God tell Jeremiah?
    that the people would fight against him

4. Did the people succeed?
    No

5. What promise did God make to Jeremiah?
    that He would be with him and rescue him

6. Did Jeremiah give up when he was put in prison and beaten?
    No, he kept giving them God's message

7. How were his messages kept so they could be read?
    they were written down on scrolls

8. How do we know these messages came from God?
    they all came true

 # Bible Words To Remember

God said, "I have called you by your name; you are Mine."   Isaiah 43:1b
Since you were precious in My sight . . . and I have loved you.   Isaiah 43:4

Choosing God's Way

Promises

Does God ever say, "I'm not going to give those people what I promised. They keep forgetting what I told them!"? That would not be the God we know, would it? We know by now after reading and listening to the words in the Bible, that God does not stop loving His children. He will not turn away from them, even when they turn away from Him. God will not forget any of His promises, even when people forget their promises to Him.

Will God ever stop loving His children?
How can you show God how much you love HIm?

❤ Bible Love Lesson ❤

God will keep reminding you about how much He loves you. He doesn't want you to have to guess how much. He tells how much He loves you in the Bible. He lets you feel His love whenever you are thinking about Him.

Bible Story: Ezekiel--His Message From God

Key Points

❖ **God wanted Ezekiel to tell His words to the people.**

❖ **Ezekiel was given a special way to tell God's message.**

❖ **Because the people had not listened to God, they were slaves.**

"I want you to help My people," God said to Ezekiel. Ezekiel was a priest in the temple and had been studying God's Word. When God told him that he would be a special messenger, he **memorized** every word on the scroll. He knew that the **spirit** of God was with him.

God also told Ezekiel to give His message in a different way. Instead of speaking the messages, he **acted** them out. God wanted the people to think about what they had done and what would happen because they turned away from Him.

Jerusalem had been taken by the enemy and God's people were not in their own land. They lived in Babylon and were slaves in that country. God had warned the people through His prophets that this would happen because they did not obey Him. Ezekiel said to the people, "God always wants to take us back. He wants us to be in the land He promised to us."

Word and Phrase Meanings

memorized:	to know the words in your mind and heart
spirit:	what is not physical; the inside of a person that can feel love
acted:	pretend or perform in front of a group of people
precious:	of great value

Guided Prayer Thought

Dear God, You want us to be Your people. You give us so many chances to prove our love. You never forget us. Help us not to forget You.
Amen

Questions:
Thinking & Remembering

1. **What did God want Ezekiel to do?**
   help His people

2. **What had Ezekiel been doing?**
   studying God's word

3. **What was his job in the temple?**
   he was a priest

4. **What new job was God giving him?**
   to be His special messenger

5. **What did Ezekiel memorize?**
   every word on the scroll (God's Word)

6. **How did Ezekiel give God's message?**
   he acted out the message

7. **Why had the people been taken from Jerusalem to Babylon?**
   they had disobeyed and turned away from God

8. **What hope did Ezekiel give the people?**
   God always wanted to take them back, He wanted them to be in the land He promised them.

 ## Bible Words To Remember

God said, "I have called you by your name; you are Mine."   Isaiah 43:1b
Since you were **precious** in My sight . . . and I have loved you. Isaiah 43:4

Choosing God's Way

Gentleness

What would you do if you had a little sister who wouldn't listen to you and kept running out of the yard where she would get hurt.   You keep telling her to stay in the yard. God sent messengers in the Bible to keep telling people that they would not be safe if they did not obey God. That was hard to do! But they did not give up. God does not give up. Don't give up telling someone to do the right thing.

When did you give a message to someone?
Is it difficult to keep telling someone something when they don't listen?

❤ Bible Love Lesson ❤

Learning God's words may seem like making your mind do a lot of work. It is very important to know God's word in your mind and in your heart. There is no one who can ever take it from you. You will know His words wherever you are---whenever you need them!

Bible Story: Daniel--He Listens to God's Word

Key Points

❖ Daniel served the king in the palace.

❖ Daniel studied and learned many things, but the most important thing he learned was to love God.

❖ The king had a dream that he couldn't understand. Daniel told the king what the dream meant because God helped him.

Daniel was a young man when he was chosen by the king of Babylon to come to his **palace** to serve him. Daniel was taught many things and he was very smart! Along with three of his friends, he studied language and all the many beliefs of the land he lived in. But the religion in this land believed in many gods, not the one true God that Daniel believed in.

Daniel and his friends **decided** that they would follow God. They knew that God had chosen their people and that it was God who had given them all their **knowledge** and **understanding**. God would protect them from the wrong beliefs and help them be **true** and **loyal** to Him.

The king had a dream one night, and could not find out what it meant from any of his wise men. Daniel came before the king and told him that only God could tell him the meaning of his dream. God told Daniel what the dream meant so that he could tell the king that, even though his kingdom was great, it would be destroyed because he thought he was greater than God.

Word and Phrase Meanings

palace:	a very beautiful place where a king or queen lives
decided:	made a choice
understanding:	knowing the reason why
knowledge:	to know and understand
true:	loyal; faithful
loyal:	to be true to someone

Guided Prayer Thought

Dear God, No one is greater than You! When someone is rich and powerful like the king of Babylon, they forget that You are the giver of everything. Help us to know Your love!
Amen

Questions:
Thinking & Remembering

1. Why was Daniel chosen to come to the king's palace?
   to serve the king

2. What did Daniel and his friends learn?
   the language and the beliefs of the land

3. What did the king and people in Babylon believe?
   that there were many gods

4. What did Daniel and his friends believe?
   that there was one true God

5. What did Daniel and his friends decide they would do?
   follow God in a strange land

6. What had God given them?
   knowledge and understanding

7. Whom did Daniel say could tell the meaning of dreams?
   God

8. Why would the king of Babylon be destroyed?
   because he thought he was greater than God

 ## Bible Words To Remember

God said, "I have called you by your name; you are Mine."   Isaiah 43:1b
Since you were precious in My sight . . . and I have loved you.   Isaiah 43:4

Choosing God's Way

The Most Important Choice

God always lets you choose. He will not ever make or force you to love Him. He wants you to choose to love Him. God will show you His love in so many ways. Then He will let you decide: will you follow Him and love Him or will you choose to go away from God? Even little children can decide this important question. If you choose God early, you will be able to do so much for Him.

Will God ever force you to love Him?
How does God show you His love?

❤ Bible Love Lesson ❤

When you remember how God loves you, you will want to love Him in a special way, too. If you love Him, you will want to do what is right. God will help you know the right way if you remember to keep Him important to you.

Bible Story: Daniel--God Protects His Servant

Key Points

❖ The king thought that he was greater than God.

❖ Everyone was commanded to worship the king's statue.

❖ God protected Daniel and his friends and kept them safe, because they believed in Him.

The king did not listen to Daniel. He was **determined** to be greater than God. He wanted to be the most powerful king in all the world. When he built a **statue** of himself, he ordered everyone to bow down before it. Daniel's three friends knew that it was against God's commandments and refused to bow down. They were thrown into a fiery furnace. But God protected them and they were not burned!

Other kings came to be on the throne in Babylon. None of them believed in God, but only believed in their own greatness. Daniel was still at the palace, and he was no longer a young man. He had been true to God for many years and prayed to God every day.

The new king made a law that no one could worship anyone except the king. But Daniel kept praying to God. The **punishment** was to be put in the lion's **den**! God **protected** Daniel from the hungry lions and they just shut their mouths and did not even touch Daniel. What a wonderful and powerful God!

Word and Phrase Meanings

determined:	to want to do something strongly
statue:	an image carved out of stone, wood or bronze
punishment:	to have to suffer for doing wrong
den:	home of wild beasts; lion's cage
protected:	to take care of and keep safe
precious:	of great value

Guided Prayer Thought

Dear God, You are wonderful and powerful! When we obey You, You will protect us from harm.
                                            Amen

Questions:
Thinking & Remembering

1. Why wouldn't the king listen to Daniel?
   he wanted to be greater than God, he wanted to be the most powerful king in the world

2. What was the king's order?
   to bow down to a statue of himself

3. Why did Daniel's friends refuse to bow down to the statue?
   it was against God's commandments

4. What happened to them?
   they were thrown into a fiery furnace

5. Why weren't they burned in the fire?
   God protected them

6. What did the kings of Babylon believe in?
   their own greatness

7. What was Daniel's punishment for praying to God?
   to be put in with the lions

8. How did God protect Daniel from any harm?
   He shut the mouths of the lions

 # Bible Words To Remember

God said, "I have called you by your name; you are Mine."   Isaiah 43:1b
Since you were **precious** in My sight . . . and I have loved you.   Isaiah 43:4

Choosing God's Way

Determination

Every time someone wants to be greater than God, it turns out wrong and terrible. No one can have God's power. He will give us just what we need. When we believe God and ask Him to make us useful to His kingdom and show others the way to God, He will give us the power to do that. Daniel was not afraid to love and serve God, even though it seemed dangerous. He knew that God would take care of him and protect him if he did what was right.

What will God give people the power to do?
What will God do when we believe and trust in Him?

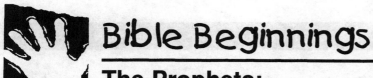

The Prophets:
Hosea, Joel, Amos and Jonah

❤ Bible Love Lesson ❤

God tells you He loves you in ways that you can understand. Even a baby can understand God's love. If someone is one hundred years old, they will understand. God makes His messages clear so we do not get confused about whether He loves us or not!

Bible Story: Hosea--His Message From God

 Key Points

❖ God's prophets told the people what God said.

❖ Hosea tried to tell the people how much God loved them.

❖ God loved the Israelites even when they didn't love Him.

Each of God's prophets or messengers listened to God. They did **exactly** what God told them to do. Sometimes the **message** was given to the people by telling them. Sometimes the message was given by writing it. One time, the prophet gave the message by acting it out. The message that Hosea was to give was the same message but given in a much different way. His messages were given in a **life picture**, and were about one important thing . . . how much God loved His people!

Hosea married a woman who thought more about herself than about God or anyone else. Her name was Gomer and she and Hosea had three children. Soon, Gomer wanted to leave her husband and her three children. She went away and was **unfaithful** to her husband and lived in sin.

God knew how much Hosea still loved Gomer. He told Hosea to go and find her and bring her back home. He forgave Gomer for the wrong things she had done. The message was like a picture of God's love for Israel. Israel was just like Gomer but God still loved them so much, He wanted them back!

Word and Phrase Meanings

exactly:	the very same
message:	to tell something to someone
life picture:	something that really happened compared to something that could happen
unfaithful:	not loyal; being untrue to one's promise
banner:	flag

Guided Prayer Thought

Dear God, we can't understand why You love us so much and are always willing to take us back. Help us to stay by You!
Amen

Questions:
Thinking & Remembering

1. Who listened to God and did exactly what God told them?
   God's prophets or messengers

2. In which ways did God give the messages through them?
   telling; writing; acting it out (Ezekiel); life picture (Hosea)

3. What were all the messages about?
   how much God loved His people

4. What problem did Gomer, Hosea's wife have?
   she cared about herself more than about her husband

5. What did Gomer do?
   left her husband and her three children

6. What happened when she went away?
   she was unfaithful and lived in sin

7. What did God tell Hosea to do?
   to find Gomer and bring her back home and forgive her

8. What was this life picture like?
   God's love for Israel

Bible Words To Remember

Hate evil, love good.   Amos 5:15

For the ways of the Lord are right; the righteous walk in them.   Hosea 14:9

Praise Hymn

Sing or say these words
Resource: My First Hymnal Pg. 21

HIS BANNER OVER ME IS LOVE

The Lord is mine and I am His,
His **banner** over me is love,
The Lord is mine and I am His,
His banner over me is love,
The Lord is mine and I am His,
His banner over me is love,
His banner over me is love.

❤ Bible Love Lesson ❤

When you go on a car trip, your dad probably uses a map to show him the way to get to the place where you are traveling. Sometimes the lines are very clear but other lines are hard to see. God will always give us the right directions and show us the way to go. He will be your guide.

Bible Story: Joel--His Message From God

Key Points

❖ Joel told the people what would happen to them if they did not turn to God.

❖ Joel tried to make the people understand before it was too late for them.

❖ Joel told the people that God would give them power to serve Him.

God told His prophet Joel to give another life picture to the people of Israel. There were more and more **locusts** coming into the land. They started eating all the plants that had food on them. Soon all the green leaves were gone. The people were hungry, but even something worse was happening. . . there was no rain and they had no water to drink.

Joel told the people that this would be like what would happen to them because they did not obey God. He told them that it would be even worse because their land would be taken away from them by an **army** of soldiers. He told the people to turn to God before it was too late.

He also told what would happen in the **future** for those who believed in God and in the Savior God would send. God would send the Holy Spirit to help people have God's power in their lives to serve Him.

Word and Phrase Meanings

locusts: large grasshoppers

future: what is told that is going to happen

disaster: something that causes great damage, loss or destruction

army: large group of soldiers

picture: to show something with your words or by painting or drawing

Guided Prayer Thought

*Dear God, Help us to see the **picture** of Your love in what is happening to us and Thank You for Hope--believing Your words.*
Amen

Questions:
Thinking & Remembering

1. What kind of message did the prophet Joel give to Israel?
   a life picture

2. What really happened in the land of Israel to all the plants?
   locusts ate all the plants

3. What other **disaster** happened?
   there was no rain and they had no water

4. What would this be like for the people of Israel?
   their land would be taken away from them by soldiers

5. Why would this happen?
   because they did not obey God

6. What did he ask the people to do?
   to turn to God before it was too late

7. What else did he tell about that would happen in the future?
   God would send the Holy Spirit to those who believed in God's Savior

8. How would the Holy Spirit help the people?
   give them power in their lives to serve God

 ## Bible Words To Remember

Hate evil, love good.   Amos 5:15

For the ways of the Lord are right; the righteous walk in them.   Hosea 14:9

Choosing God's Way

God's Message

When people cannot understand God's message in one way, He will tell His messengers to tell the message in a different way. That's how much He cares and wants people to come to Him and be in His kingdom. He knows that if we choose against Him, we will have to suffer and terrible things will happen because we wanted to go our own way.

Do you think that God would give us His message in so many ways if He didn't care about us?
How can you show God that you want to hear the right message?

❤ Bible Love Lesson ❤

Have you ever helped plant a garden in the spring? You wait and wait for the flowers or vegetable to grow. Soon you see leaves coming through the ground! The flowers are beautiful! You are like God's flower. He takes care of you and gives you all the things that you need to grow.

Bible Story: Amos--His Message From God

Key Points

❖ **God did not like the way His people treated each other. They were not kind and did not love each other.**

❖ **The people just pretended to love God. God knew their hearts.**

❖ **God told Amos to warn the people what would happen to them if they did not listen to the message God gave them.**

Amos was a shepherd who spent his time in the hills looking after his sheep. The Lord spoke to him and said, "Amos, go to my people and tell them what I will say to you." The people in Israel were not fighting with other **nations** and they were happy with their lives. But they were not following God with their heart. They tried to act like they believed God by going to the temple, but when they were in the **market-place** they were **cheating** other people and being unkind to one another.

Amos said, "God has shown me a basket of summer fruit and told me that the season for His people has ended." The fruit was beautiful now but was **spoiling** fast. It would soon be **rotten**.

The people did not like the **warnings** that Amos gave them. They would not listen because they could only think of themselves and what they wanted. They did not have time to listen to messages from God. They wanted Amos to go back to his home and leave them alone.

Word and Phrase Meanings

pretending:	to try to be someone you are not
nations:	groups of people living together in the same land or country
cheating:	being dishonest
market-place:	a place where food and other things are sold
spoiling:	something not good anymore
rotten:	spoiled; not to be eaten

Guided Prayer Thought

Dear God, Help us to listen to Your message. You love us so much that You tell us in many ways so that we will hear You.
Amen

Questions:
Thinking & Remembering

1. **What work did Amos do?**
   he was a shepherd

2. **What did the Lord tell Amos to do?**
   to go to His people and give them His message

3. **Did Amos know what he would say to the people?**
   No, God would tell him what to say

4. **Were the people happy with their lives? Why?**
   Yes, they were not fighting with other nations

5. **Were the people pretending to follow God's ways?**
   Yes, but they were not following God with their heart

6. **How were they treating each other?**
   cheating people and being unkind

7. **What picture did Amos give to the people about themselves?**
   a basket of fruit that was going to be rotten

8. **What did they want Amos to do so they wouldn't have to listen?**
   go back home and leave them alone

 # Bible Words To Remember

Hate evil, love good.   Amos 5:15

For the ways of the Lord are right; the righteous walk in them.   Hosea 14:9

Choosing God's Way

Being Sincere

Pretending is sometimes fun to do. You may put on mom's shoes or dad's hat and pretend you are all grown-up. There are some things you should never pretend, though. You should not pretend that you love God. God can see you on the inside and He knows your heart. If you only pretend that you love God, you will not have his power to love and live in His ways. That will hurt other people. They may say, "People that love Jesus aren't different. They are mean and unkind." Be sure you are real!

When is it OK to pretend?
Tell what you like to pretend to be.
What will happen if you just pretend to love God?

❤ Bible Love Lesson ❤

Do you ever think that someone you know is so mean that God should not love them?
If God just loved all the nice children, He would not be true to His promises. God
keeps His promise to love everyone. Pray for those who are unkind.
God can make them good!

Bible Story: Jonah--He Runs Away From God

Key Points

❖ The people in the city of
   Nineveh were very wicked.

❖ God told Jonah to go and tell
   them that He would destroy
   their city if they did not say
   they were sorry for the wrong
   things they were doing.

❖ Jonah was afraid to go into
   the city. He just wanted God
   to destroy them.

❖ Jonah disobeyed God and
   tried to run away.

The people in Nineveh were very wicked. God had decided that
He would destroy this city and all the people in it. Because they
were so **cruel**, those who did not live in Nineveh were afraid to go
there. These people were not Israelites and didn't even pretend to
think about God.

God told Jonah to go to Nineveh and warn the people about what
God was going to do and what would happen to them if they did
not **repent**. Jonah didn't want to go! He decided he would get on
a ship that was going the other way.

Jonah soon fell asleep on the ship and thought that God would
surely understand why he couldn't go to that place called Nineveh.
Then a terrible storm came and the ship was sinking! The men
tried everything to keep the ship on top of the water. Finally they
asked, "Has anyone on this ship done anything to **cause** God to
send such a storm?" Jonah knew it was because he was
disobeying God. He told them he was running away from God.

Word and Phrase Meanings

chances: opportunity

cruel: mean and hurtful to others

repent: to be sorry for

cause: a reason for an action

disobeying: to do what you have been told not to do

Guided Prayer Thought

Dear God, Help us know that when You ask us to do something— even something very hard, that You will be with us to help us.
Amen

Questions:
Thinking & Remembering

1. **What were the people like in Nineveh?**
   very wicked

2. **What was God going to do to their city?**
   destroy it

3. **Was Nineveh a nice place to go and visit?**
   No, the people were cruel, and they never thought about God

4. **What did God tell Jonah to do?**
   to go and tell the people in Nineveh what was going to happen (that God would destroy them if they didn't repent)

5. **Did Jonah think that going to Nineveh was a good idea?**
   No, he didn't want to go

6. **What did Jonah decide to do?**
   to get on a ship going the other way

7. **What happened when he was on the ship?**
   a terrible storm came and the ship was sinking

8. **How did they find out that Jonah had caused the storm that God had sent?**
   he told them that he was running away from God

 ## Bible Words To Remember

Hate evil, love good.   Amos 5:15

For the ways of the Lord are right; the righteous walk in them.   Hosea 14:9

Choosing God's Way

God's Love

God gives us a lot of **chances** to hear about Him. He shows us and His tells us in many ways. Sometimes we think that God shouldn't give other people so many chances. They seem to choose the bad and even love the wrong things that they do. It may be that they will never change but God will not give up until He knows that they have had a chance to hear about His love for them. We should not decide for God. We need to tell them about Jesus.

Think about what it would be like if God gave you only one chance to hear about His love?
What can you do to help others have a chance to know God?

❤ Bible Love Lesson ❤

There is a wonderful game called 'hide and seek'. Someone hides and everyone else tries to find them. It can be very exciting trying to find the hiding place. I'm glad that God does not play 'hide and seek', though. He will not hide from you. He will be there when you need Him.

Bible Story: Jonah--His Message From God

Key Points

❖ The ship Jonah was escaping on was going to tip over in a terrible storm.

❖ Jonah knew that God had sent the storm because he was running away.

❖ Jonah told God he was sorry that he didn't go where He sent him.

❖ When Jonah told the people in Nineveh what God said, they were sorry for all the wrong things they had done.

The men in the ship were **frantic**! They said, "What shall we do with this man?" Jonah knew what they must do. He said, "Pick me up and throw me into the sea. Then the sea will be **calm** again."

God sent a big fish to swallow Jonah. For three days and three nights, Jonah was inside the belly of this big fish. Jonah prayed to God in the darkness. He said he was sorry that he had not followed God's directions. He said, "I will do whatever You ask me to do, God."

The fish gave a big cough and Jonah landed on the **shore**. He got up and started for Nineveh. He told the people in Nineveh that God had seen how **evil** they were and that the city would be destroyed. God gave them forty days to **repent** and tell Him they were sorry. If they believed God, God would save them. The people cried and said that they would turn away from their evil ways and God did save their city and the people.

— Word and Phrase Meanings —

frantic:	very excited
calm:	peaceful, still
shore:	land along the edge of water
evil:	bad and sinful behavior
repent:	to be sorry for

Guided Prayer Thought

*Dear God, Thank You for caring for all people and giving everyone
a chance to repent and love You. Thank You for saving us.*
Amen

Questions:
Thinking & Remembering

1. **Were the men on the ship calm during this terrible storm?**
   No, they were frantic

2. **What did Jonah say they must do to calm the storm?**
   throw him into the sea

3. **What did God send to swallow Jonah?**
   a big fish

4. **How long was Jonah inside the belly of the fish?**
   three days and three nights

5. **What did Jonah do while he was inside the fish?**
   he prayed to God and said he was sorry he had disobeyed

6. **Where did Jonah go when he landed on the shore?**
   to Nineveh

7. **How long did God give the people to repent?**
   forty days

8. **What would God do if they believed Him and told Him they were sorry?**
   He would save them

 # Bible Words To Remember

Hate evil, love good.   Amos 5:15

For the ways of the Lord are right; the righteous walk in them.   Hosea 14:9

Choosing God's Way

Enthusiasm

Don't say "No" to God. One man who said "No" in the Bible spent three days inside a fish when He told God "No". God will never ask you to do something that is impossible for you to do. He will never ask you to do anything that is too hard. He will always be with you to help you. God wants you to care about others hearing the message of how much He loves them. If we believe in God, we will want them to know that, too. Be enthusiastic! Say "Yes" to God!

Will God ask you to do something impossible?
What does God want others to know?

The Prophets: Micah, Nahum, Habakkuk, Zephaniah, Haggai, Zechariah and Malachi

❤ Bible Love Lesson ❤

It is wonderful to have a best friend. Do you know who your best friend is? God is your best friend. He is there for you always. He is stronger than anyone. He knows everything about you. He loves to be with you.
There is no better friend than God!

Bible Story: Micah--His Message From God

Key Points

❖ The Israelites were mean and selfish. They forgot God again!

❖ God was so sad. He had given them so many chances to choose the right way and love Him.

❖ Micah told the people what God wanted them to be.

❖ Micah told them again about the Savior God was sending.

The Israelites stopped worshiping God. They stopped following the commandments of God. They stopped loving God. When people forget God, they also forget to care about each other. They only care about themselves. They become mean and selfish. They are hateful to each other.

When these things happened, God's heart was broken. He loved the people. He had taken them back again and again. Still, they would go away and not remember the promises they had made.

Micah told the people that God **expected** them to be **faithful** and **obedient**. He wanted them to be **honest** and **kind**. He wanted them to **honor** and **respect** Him. Neighbors should not live in fear of each other. God's children should set an example for others. God would send a ruler out of Bethlehem who would bring peace to the land. This ruler's name was Jesus.

Word and Phrase Meanings

expected:	counted on
faithful:	true to
obedient:	to be willing to do what is asked
honest:	being truthful (telling what is true)
kind:	a nice person who cares about others
honor:	to show respect and consideration (being thoughtful)
respect:	to think highly of and treat with honor

Guided Prayer Thought

Dear God, We are sorry that we keep breaking Your heart by sinning. Every time we go our own way, we get into trouble. Help us to remember.
Amen

Questions:
Thinking & Remembering

1. What three things did the Israelites stop doing?
   worshiping God; following the commandments of God; loving God

2. What happened when they stopped doing those things?
   they didn't care about each other; they only cared about themselves; they became mean and selfish; they were hateful to each other

3. How did God feel?
   His heart was broken

4. What had God shown the people of Israel?
   that He loved them

5. What had God done when they were sorry for turning away from Him?
   taken them back

6. Did the people keep their promise to follow Him?
   No, they did not remember

7. What did the prophet Micah tell the people that God expected?
   faithfulness and obedience

8. When would there be peace in the land?
   when God sent the one to be ruler (Jesus) out of Bethlehem

 # Bible Words To Remember

For I am the LORD, I do not change.   Malachi 3:6

The Lord will rejoice over you with gladness, He will quiet you with His Love,

He will rejoice over you with singing.   Zephaniah 3:17

Praise Hymn

Sing or say these words
Resource: My First Hymnal Pg. 75

HE'S GOT THE WHOLE WORLD IN HIS HANDS

He's got the whole world
in His hands,
He's got the whole world
in His hands,
He's got the whole world
in His hands,
He's got the whole world in His hands.

❤ Bible Love Lesson ❤

God tells us who He is. All the words in the Bible tell how wonderful our God is.
There are so many ways to describe God that we have a hard time naming
them all! God said, "I AM WHO I AM." And God does not change.
He will always be the same and love forever!

Bible Story: Nahum & Habakkuk--
Messages From God

Key Points

❖ **God is more powerful than
those who do not love HIm.**

❖ **God will help His people
when they ask Him.**

❖ **Habakkuk knew that God
would keep all of the
promises He made.**

❖ **God told Habakkuk to be
patient and wait for Him,
even when things were
terrible and sad.**

God's people had many powerful enemies. They were not more
powerful than God, but because the Israelites no longer called on
God to help them, they became **prisoners** of the enemy. God told
Nahum that these enemies would lose their strength and Israel
would **unite** and come together again to the land God had
promised. Nahum knew God was the ruler of all and would take
care of His people.

Habakkuk believed that God would keep His word and His
promise. But when he saw all the killing and destruction of God's
people, he asked God, "How long will this go on?" God told
Habakkuk that he must have **patience**.

God did not tell Habakkuk the **exact** day when it would end. God
does not tell us the exact time, either. He **expects** us to trust Him
and be patient. God's time is not the same as our time.

Word and Phrase Meanings

prisoners: people who are not free

unite: to join together

patience: to wait without complaining

expects: counts on

Guided Prayer Thought

Dear God, Help us to always be patient. Help us to remember that Your time is not the same as our time and that we can trust You.
Amen

Questions:
Thinking & Remembering

1. Did God's people have many powerful friends?
   No, they had powerful enemies

2. Were their enemies more powerful than God?
   No

3. Why were they hurt by their enemies?
   because they did not ask God to help them

4. What happened to them?
   they became prisoners

5. What did God tell Nahum?
   that Israel would come together again to the promised land

6. What did Habakkuk believe?
   that God would keep His word and His promise

7. What question did Habakkuk ask God?
   "How long will this go on?"

8. What did God tell Habakkuk?
   to be patient

 # Bible Words To Remember

For I am the LORD, I do not change.   Malachi 3:6

The Lord will rejoice over you with gladness, He will quiet you with His Love,

He will rejoice over you with singing.   Zephaniah 3:17

Choosing God's Way

Being Prepared

Many years before Jesus was born, God's messengers told that He would come. Do you like to know some things ahead of time? When you are starting a first day at school or Sunday school, you want to know which classroom you will go to, who your teacher will be, and if your friend is going to be in the same class. God does not surprise us with the things that are really important to know, either. He tells us ahead of time exactly what will happen and how we can be ready.

How do you feel when you are going to a new place? How can you prepare for what is really important?

❤ Bible Love Lesson ❤

God wants us to be ready all the time to meet Him. He told us what we need to do to be ready, but He did not tell us the exact time that Jesus will come back to earth for us. We know what God has promised. We know that He will keep His promises. We can think every day, "Maybe this day is the day! I will live in the way that God wants me to live?"

Bible Story: Zephaniah-- His Message From God

Key Points

❖ God's people pretended that they didn't remember what God wanted them to do.

❖ God's laws cannot be forgotten or broken.

❖ Zephaniah wrote down God's laws for all the people to see.

❖ God knows what everyone thinks about Him. He knows if we really love Him or if we are just pretending.

The Israelites looked at all the exciting things that the other people were doing. They had gods and idols made of gold! They had parties and danced around the streets to celebrate! God's people thought, 'maybe we can have fun and still worship our own God.' They knew that God had commanded against the worship of other gods and idols but they would just **pretend** that they had forgotten.

Zephaniah studied all of God's laws and he knew that the people would be punished for not being true and loyal to the God who loved them. Zephaniah told the people what God had said, and it was written down for everyone to see.

Zephaniah also had an important **vision** of the coming "Day of the Lord." God would **search** the hearts of everyone. Then He would **bless** those who had believed in Him, and **punish** those who had turned away from Him.

Word and Phrase Meanings

pretend:	to make believe that something is true that is not
vision:	picture seen in a dream or imagination
search:	examine and consider, look for carefully
bless:	give special favor to
punish:	to have to suffer for doing wrong
perfect:	the very best that can be
fair:	honest

Guided Prayer Thought

*Dear God, You are **perfect** and **fair** in all that You do. We want to love You more. We know that You want us to be happy, too.*
Amen

Questions:
Thinking & Remembering

1. What did the Israelites think they were missing?
   the exciting things other people were doing

2. What were their gods and idols made of?
   gold

3. What else did they do to celebrate?
   had parties and danced

4. What did the Israelite's think they could do?
   have fun and still worship God

5. What had God commanded them not to do?
   worship other gods and idols

6. Who studied God's laws and knew that the people would be punished?
   Zephaniah

7. What did Zephaniah see in his vision?
   the "Day of the Lord" when God would search the hearts of everyone

8. What would happen to those who believed in Him?
   they would be blessed

9. What would happen to those who had turned away from Him?
   they would be punished

Bible Words To Remember

For I am the LORD, I do not change.   Malachi 3:6

The Lord will rejoice over you with gladness, He will quiet you with His Love,

He will rejoice over you with singing.   Zephaniah 3:17

Choosing God's Way

Discernment

It may seem that the people who do not love God have more fun! Your mom and dad may say, "You cannot see the movie that your friend is watching." "You cannot say the words the other children are saying because they are using God's name in the wrong way. That hurts God." Parents know that there are many things that will lead you away from God. Trust them to do the right thing. God has told your mom and dad to make sure you learn to love God and grow to be like Jesus.

What will you choose to do the next time your friends are doing the wrong thing?
Whom did God put in charge of you to help you grow in His ways?

❤ Bible Love Lesson ❤

God said to always think of Him *first*. Make God more important than anything else because He is all that really matters in all of life. God will help you know what He wants you to do. His work will not always be easy but it will seem easy when He is with you, helping you.

Bible Story: Haggai & Zechariah-- Messages From God

Key Points

❖ The people wanted to build the temple as beautiful as it was when Solomon was the king.

❖ They wanted to give up when the work was too hard. They stopped working and did not finish.

❖ Haggai told the people to stop thinking of just themselves and to think more about God.

❖ Zechariah told the people to remember that God was taking care of them.

The temple in Jerusalem was burned down by the enemies of Israel. After the people had been gone a long time, they returned. The temple needed to be rebuilt. They started the work but soon they were **discouraged**. They did not believe that they could make it as beautiful as it had been in king Solomon's time. Many years later, it still was not finished. The people made a lot of **excuses** and worked on their own houses and gardens. Haggai said, "You are thinking more of yourselves than of God. Let's get busy and get the temple finished!"

Zechariah also **encouraged** the people and said that if the people were **faithful** to God, He would be faithful to them. He had a vision in which God showed him that God would rule the world in the future, not just in Jerusalem. God would love and protect all His people and they would not need walls around this city of God.

God was taking care of His people, but the most important visions were about how God was keeping His promise to send a Savior to us. He protected the family line from David so that Jesus would be born. God had a wonderful plan!

Word and Phrase Meanings

discouraged:	to feel sad about something
excuses:	to try to give reasons "why" for wrong doing
encouraged:	having hope and courage
faithful:	true to
vision:	picture seen in a dream or imagination

Guided Prayer Thought

Dear God, When a job needs to get done, help us to keep with it and get it finished. We know You will be with us to do the important things.
Amen

Questions:
Thinking & Remembering

1. What happened to the temple in Jerusalem?
   it was burned down by Israel's enemies

2. What did the people need to do when they returned to Jerusalem?
   rebuild the temple

3. Why didn't they keep working to get it finished?
   they made a lot of excuses; they worked on their own houses and gardens

4. What did Haggai say they were doing?
   thinking of themselves more than of God

5. What did he say they should do?
   get the temple finished

6. What was Zechariah's **vision**?
   that God would rule the world in the future

7. What promise was God going to keep?
   that He would send a Savior

8. From which family would Jesus be born?
   the family of David

 # Bible Words To Remember

For I am the LORD, I do not change.   Malachi 3:6

The Lord will rejoice over you with gladness, He will quiet you with His Love,
He will rejoice over you with singing.   Zephaniah 3:17

Choosing God's Way

Listening

How do you hear God's message? How do you know what God said? You will first hear God's message by listening to those who love God. They will tell you what God says in His Word. When you learn to read, you will know what God said from the writer's who wrote what God told them to write. There are many ways we can 'get the message'. Can you think of some other ways? Remember that the message God gives will never be confusing or hard to figure out. It will always tell how much God loves you!

How can you know what God's message is?
If the message is from God, will it be hard to figure out?

♥ Bible Love Lesson ♥

Can you ever love God enough? Loving God is what you choose to do every day.
The love you have for our wonderful Savior and God will grow and grow. Love
God with all your heart, soul and mind. God does not measure our love.
He knows and sees our heart.

Bible Story: Malachi--His Message From God

Key Points

❖ Malachi told the people that God was tired of hearing them complain.

❖ Malachi said that because they had not obeyed God's law, they were having problems.

❖ Malachi reminded them that God had promised to send a Savior--that was the most wonderful promise of all!

Malachi had bad **news** and good news to give to the people from the Lord. He told them the bad news first. He said, "The Lord is tired of all your **complaining**. He is tired of the way you **question** Him about His ways. He is tired of you always **doubting** His word.

You have broken all of God's laws. When God tells you that if you return to Him, He will return to you, you ask "How should we do that?" You have **robbed** God and not trusted Him to keep His promises.

But there is good news! God will send a Savior who will bless you if you put Him in first place in your lives. Make Him most important and let Him make you pure again. This is the most wonderful promise of all!

Word and Phrase Meanings

news:	something that is told to someone else
complaining:	to talk about unhappiness; whine
question:	to ask someone something; to find and answer
doubting:	not believing, being uncertain
robbed:	taken or stolen
deserve:	to be worthy of

Guided Prayer Thought

*Dear God, We don't **deserve** Your love. We keep doing things that hurt You. Thank You for sending Jesus to help us. We could never be good by ourselves! Amen*

Questions:
Thinking & Remembering

1. What kind of news did the prophet Malachi have for the people?
   bad news and good news

2. What was the Lord tired of?
   complaining; questioning; doubting

3. What had the people of Israel done?
   broken all of God's laws

4. What did God tell them?
   if they returned to Him, He would return to them

5. What question did they ask when God said that?
   "How should we do that?"

6. Should they have known the answer?
   Yes, they had the commandments

7. What else had they done?
   they had robbed God and not trusted Him to keep His promises

8. What was the good news?
   God would send a Savior to make them pure again

Bible Words To Remember

For I am the LORD, I do not change.   Malachi 3:6

The Lord will rejoice over you with gladness, He will quiet you with His Love,

He will rejoice over you with singing.   Zephaniah 3:17

Choosing God's Way

Complaining

The people in the Bible learned from a messenger that God was tired of them complaining. They only wanted God when they needed His help when they got into trouble. How sad that made God! They asked God "why?" and "how?" after God had told them so many times and in so many ways. Tell God how much you love Him. Thank Him for all His gifts. Don't whine and always want more things. Don't ask "How can I be happy?" God has already told us the answers in the Bible and He will help us do the right thing!

What will help us remember not to complain? When can you talk to God?